Meeting the Needs of Students and Families from Poverty

Meeting the Needs of Students and Families from Poverty

A Handbook for School and Mental Health Professionals

by

Tania N. Thomas-Presswood, Ph.D.
Gallaudet University
Washington, D.C.

and

Donald Presswood, Ph.D.
District of Columbia Public Schools

·P A U L·H·
BROOKES
PUBLISHING C?®

Baltimore • London • Sydney

·P A U L·H·
BROOKES
PUBLISHING C⁰ ®

Paul H. Brookes Publishing Co.
Post Office Box 10624
Baltimore, Maryland 21285-0624

www.brookespublishing.com

Typeset by Maryland Composition, Inc., Glen Burnie, Maryland.
Manufactured in the United States of America by
Versa Press, Inc., East Peoria, Illinois.

The case studies appearing in this book are composites based on the authors'
experiences; these case studies do not represent the lives or experiences of specific
individuals, and no implications should be inferred.

Library of Congress Cataloging-in-Publication Data

Thomas, Tania.
   Meeting the needs of students and families from poverty : a handbook
for school and mental health professionals / by Tania N. Thomas-Presswood
and Donald Presswood.
       p.   cm.
   Includes bibliographical references and index.
   ISBN-13: 978-1-55766-867-7 (pbk.)
   ISBN-10: 1-55766-867-1 (pbk.)
   1. Poor children—Education.   2. Poor families.   I. Presswood, Donald.   II. Title.

   LC4065.T56 2007
   371.826'942—dc22   2007013743

British Library Cataloguing in Publication data are available from the British Library.

Contents

About the Authors

Tania N. Thomas-Presswood, Ph.D., NCSP, Department of Psychology, Gallaudet University, 800 Florida Avenue, NE, Washington, D.C. 20002

Dr. Thomas-Presswood is Associate Professor in the School Psychology Program at Gallaudet University. She received her doctoral degree in clinical and school psychology from Hofstra University in 1989 and has had postgraduate training in school neuropsychology. Dr. Thomas-Presswood has had extensive experience working in the public schools as a school psychologist in New York and Texas. In addition to her full-time teaching position at Gallaudet, she is a practicing school psychologist with the Arlington Public Schools system in Virginia.

Dr. Thomas-Presswood was born in the Republic of Panamá and has been living in the United States since 1980. She speaks Spanish fluently and has been developing her skills in American Sign Language. She lives in Annapolis, Maryland, with her husband, Donald Presswood, and daughter, Brielle Sofía.

Donald Presswood, Ph.D., District of Columbia Public Schools, 825 North Capitol Street, NE, Washington, D.C. 20002

Dr. Presswood was born and raised on the west side of Chicago, Illinois. He earned his bachelor's degree in Spanish from DePaul University in 1980. Since August 2002, Dr. Presswood has been the principal of Ludlow-Taylor Elementary School in Northeast Washington, D.C., and he serves as an Adjunct Professor in the School of Education Educational Leadership Program at Trinity University in Washington, D.C. Before becoming a school administrator, Dr. Presswood worked as a special education teacher in Austin, Texas, from 1995 to 1998; served on active duty as a U.S. Army Infantry Officer from 1980 to 1995; and worked as a physical education teacher in Chicago, Illinois, from 1976 to 1979. Dr. Presswood earned his Ph.D. in special education administration in 1998 and his M.A. in Latin American studies in 1991 from The University of Texas at Austin.

Acknowledgments

"The world in which you were born is just one model of reality. Other cultures are not failed attempts at being you. Rather, they are unique manifestations of the human spirit."

— Wade Davis

A project of this magnitude is rarely done alone; there is always a team of family, friends, and colleagues behind the scenes facilitating the process of writing a book. There are those who provided encouragement and emotional support; those who offered to babysit so that we could write; those who entertained us and made us laugh when we were feeling stressed; those who offered suggestions, guidance, research assistance, and administrative support; and there were those who believed in us and provided unconditional love. We are thankful to them all.

This book is built upon the work of many others. Our understanding and interpretation of prior research, coupled with our practical experiences, provide the foundation for this book. We thank all the scholars and scientists cited in this book; their thorough research helped guide us and made our task much less onerous.

We thank our colleagues who helped us through their encouragement, suggestions, guidance, and support—in particular, Drs. Lynne Blennerhassett, Virginia Gutman, Robert Marion, Bryan Miller, Margery Miller, and Francisco Millet. We also greatly appreciate the administrative support and friendship we received from Ms. Carolyn Baldwin; the clerical assistance of Ms. Karen Boone; and the library and research work of our graduate assistants, Rachel Smith and Kierstin Mullin.

We express our appreciation to Paul H. Brookes Publishing Co. for seeing our vision and for the opportunity to bring this book to fruition, to our acquisitions editors Jessica Allan and Sarah Shepke for their patience and guidance, and to production editors Emily Moore and Trish Byrnes for their helpful feedback.

We are most grateful to the members of the Thomas and Presswood families, who stood by us in more ways than we can count. We thank our parents, Cecilia and Harold Thomas and Ruth and Samuel Presswood, who from the beginning made sacrifices, fought battles, and provided the emotional support that made this creative endeavor possible. They saw our potential as children, and they nurtured, encouraged, celebrated, and protected us. They taught us through their positive examples to use our gifts to benefit others. It is because of their wisdom and vision that we were able to make this contribution. We thank our siblings, Dr. Giovana Thomas-Smith, Liza Ford, Idania Thomas, Kristal Thomas, Sandra Presswood, Anthony Presswood, Samuel Presswood, and Pamela Presswood for their support and for keeping us grounded.

We have been fortunate to count on wonderful friends who have been supportive not only through this process but also through our life challenges and growth experiences. They offered a listening ear and kept us focused. They are people for whom time or distance never presented an obstacle. They all played different roles, yet each friend is an integral part of our lives. We thank José María Angulo, Xiomara Castillo, Melitza Cobham-Browne, Cecilio García, Mary Ella and Michael García, Debra Hankison, Itza Heim, Ray Henry, Odemaris Luque, Sonia Maxwell, Cecilia McKenzie, Cristela Mitchell, LaMarriol Smith, Mary Tatem, and Gloria Wilson for their enduring friendship and love.

Finally, and more important, our daughter, Brielle Sofía Presswood, was born during the writing of this book, and although she had an early arrival, we know that God sent her at the right time. We are blessed to have her, and we could not have asked for a more perfect and loving child. We have already learned so much through her, and as we watch her grow and make careful choices for her future, we know in our heads and hearts what a glorious responsibility has been entrusted to us. We can honestly say that she has made our work on this book even more meaningful because what we want for her, we want for all children.

Introduction

"There is nothing more dangerous than to build a society, with a large segment of people in that society, who feel that they have no stake in it; who feel that they have nothing to lose. People who have a stake in their society, protect that society, but when they don't have it, they unconsciously want to destroy it."

— *Martin Luther King, Jr.*

One of the greatest challenges facing educators and psychologists who work in schools located in communities characterized by poverty is understanding the unique needs of the children and families served by these schools and dispelling misconceptions and stereotypes about people who live in poverty. Addressing the educational and social-emotional needs of children increases the children's achievement, reduces their chances of dropping out of school, and improves their quality of life. Close to 13 million children in the United States live in poverty, and 5.2 million of these children are 3 years old or younger (National Center for Children in Poverty, 2006). Having an understanding of the effects of poverty on children's lives is critical to serving these communities.

It is often said that practice lags behind research (Sprague & Walker, 2005). What works to improve children's achievement is not a secret. Decades of research have identified the same factors or practices that increase children's success in school. These practices include having quality preschool programs, effective instructional strategies that focus on building good literacy and numeracy skills, a positive school climate, and strong parental involvement. In addition to these factors, children must be physically prepared to learn, and to do so, they must be well-nourished and healthy. Research has provided a road map to help children exposed to multiple risk factors become more resilient and successful in school despite their often difficult lives. The works of James Comer (1988), Robert Slavin (1991), and Henry Levin (1989) focusing on whole-school approaches offer concrete evidence of this. At present, great emphasis is being placed on accountability in the schools, so priority must be given to establishing and promoting conditions that lead to school success. First, quality health care must be available to all children. A healthy start prevents and intervenes early to halt the course of those health conditions that interfere with learning. Second, schools must be given adequate funding to address the educational needs of children at risk. Finally, federal policy should fully support and facilitate these efforts.

The purpose of *Meeting the Needs of Students and Families from Poverty: A Handbook for School and Mental Health Professionals* is twofold: to provide an understanding of poverty and its far-reaching impact on children's lives and to offer practical and research-based clinical and educational approaches to working effectively with children and families from a background of poverty. This knowledge will enable school psychologists and other professionals involved in the assessment and intervention process to gather and interpret data that leads to the development of more effective prevention and intervention strategies. This book attempts to accomplish this by organizing available scientific research on effective practices into one source. Although great efforts were made to be as comprehensive as possible, it is clear that one book cannot cover everything; there might be areas that are not dealt with as deeply as we had initially intended, and there are additional topics that could have been included. We try, however, to be comprehensive in the book's theoretical perspectives. Because poverty is a multifaceted social condition, it must be viewed and discussed from different perspectives. This book incorporates epidemiological, biological, historical, socio-political, cultural, educational, and psychological approaches to provide a broader and deeper understanding of poverty and its impact on children's lives.

Meeting the Needs of Students and Families from Poverty is organized into two sections and 10 chapters, with Section I delivering the base or rationale for understanding the material to be presented in Section II. Section I is made up of Chapters 1, 2, and 3, which frame the problem by providing the foundation knowledge critical to understanding poverty and discussing current thinking about poverty, environmental risk factors, and research findings on the effect of poverty on children's development. Chapter 1 discusses conditions that define poverty from a sociological, psychological, and educational perspective, while Chapter 2 offers information on the effect of poverty on the neurocognitive and social development of children. The reader gains knowledge of how poverty can effect the development of the brain and the cognitive and social functioning of children in school. The goal of Chapter 3 is to review environmental conditions that are common in the lives of children who live in poverty (e.g., nutrition deficiency, community disorganization, unfavorable family interactions, school instruction, homelessness). Risk factors that may lead to adjustment difficulties and protective factors that strengthen resilience are also discussed.

Section II comprises the rest of the chapters. Chapters 4 and 5 present assessment strategies for conducting psychological evaluations, with Chapter 4 focusing on comprehensive cognitive and educational assessment and Chapter 5 concentrating on social-emotional and behavioral assessment. No single method or procedure for conducting assessment is advocated, but emphasis is placed on a system that is comprehensive in order to more intentionally identify children's specific strengths and needs. Chapters 6 and 7 both address issues related to effective intervention strategies, but Chapter 6 is concentrated on educational issues and Chapter 7 is concentrated on social-emotional and behavioral issues. The interventions examined are schoolwide because these interventions have been shown to have a greater impact on improving children's achievement and positively influencing the school atmosphere. Chapter 8 discusses the effect school climate has on students and education. A positive school climate is instrumental in changing many of the problems that plague schools serving children living in poverty (e.g., high staff and teacher turnover, low achievement, minimal parental involvement, school safety). Chapter 9 extends research findings on effective ways of working with parents and creating an atmosphere conducive to parent involvement. Finally, Chapter 10 examines issues related to training school professionals and the role of educational policy.

A disproportionate percentage of children living in poverty are culturally and linguistically diverse, and although we place greater emphasis on environmental factors that have put children and families at risk for adverse conditions, such as poor school performance, we also recognize the influence of social and political structures and practices that have historically created and maintained obstacles to the progress of culturally and linguistically diverse individuals in this society.

REFERENCES

Comer, J.P. (1988). Educating poor minority children. *Scientific American, 259*(5), 2–8.

Comer, J.P., & Haynes, N.M. (1991). Parent involvement in schools: An ecological approach. *Elementary School Journal, 91*(3), 271–278.

Federal Interagency Forum on Child and Family Statistics. (2003). *America's children: Key national indicators of well-beings, 2003.* Washington, DC: U.S. Government Printing Office.

Levin, H.M. (1989). *Accelerated schools: A new strategy for at-risk students.* (Policy Bulletin No. 6, pp. 1–6) Bloomington, IN: Consortium on Educational Policy Studies.

Slavin, R. (1991). Chapter 1: A vision for the next quarter century. *Phi Delta Kappan, 72*(8), 586–589, 591–592.

Sprague, J.R., & Walker, H.M. (2005). *Safe and healthy schools.* New York: Guilford Press.

To God, from whom all blessings flow

To our parents

Harold and Cecilia Thomas

Ruth and Samuel Presswood

And to our daughter

Brielle Sofía

I

Understanding Poverty and Its Consequences

1

Current Thinking on Poverty

What should we be doing? The answer, I believe, lies not in a
proliferation of new reform programs but in some basic understanding
of who we are and how we are connected to and disconnected from one
another.

Lisa Delpit (1995, p. xv)

In this new century, amid significant technological advances, nearly 13 million
children in the United States live in poverty; of that number, 5.2 million
children are 3 years old or younger. This represents 43% of all children and
is based on the 2006 federal poverty level of $20,000 for a family of four
(National Center for Children in Poverty—NCCP, 2006). Although the
poverty rate for families with children has decreased significantly from 1993
to 2000 (from 22% to 16%) and has remained stable during that time, the
proportion of children living in low-income homes is rising again (NCCP,
2006). These statistics indicate that most practicing school and mental health
professionals educate, assess, treat, and interact with children and families
living in poverty. Poverty has a harmful effect on families and children,
especially children's physical, social-emotional, and educational development.
The effect of poverty has been investigated and documented in research
literature (see Brooks-Gunn & Duncan, 1997; Brown & Pollit, 1996; Hanson & Lynch, 2004; Huston, McLoyd, & Garcia Coll, 1994). To effectively
intervene and meet the educational, mental health, and developmental needs
of these children, psychologists, teachers, social workers, speech-language pathologists, and other professionals must develop a true understanding of the
dynamic of poverty and its deleterious effect on children and families.

WHAT IS POVERTY?

For most people, poverty refers to a lack of financial resources. Many have preconceived beliefs about people who live in poverty (e.g., they are lazy, refuse to work, are irresponsible) that often become confirmed in behaviors that are the result of the way children and their families are treated. For example, educational and psychological research demonstrates the adverse effects on children who are held to low expectations by school staff who work in urban schools where poverty rates can be high and more visible (Hallinger, Bickman, & Davis, 1996; Hauser-Cram, Sirin, & Stipek, 2003; McLoyd, 1998; Weinstein, Gregory, & Strambler, 2004). Studies have found that teachers perceive children from low-income backgrounds as behaving immaturely and having fewer regulatory skills than their peers (McLoyd, 1998). Moreover, a study conducted by Alexander, Entwisle, and Thompson (1987) found that teachers from high-income backgrounds evaluated children from low-income backgrounds and members of minority populations as immature and held lower expectations for these children's academic performances. Studies have documented that even in light of equal achievement, teachers underestimate the ability of African American children from lower income homes (Alvidrez & Weinstein, 1999; Hauser-Cram et al., 2003).

Social scientists as well as policy makers have been debating what it means to be poor or what truly constitutes poverty (Hanson & Lynch, 2004). Scholars studying development and poverty in the world initially looked at the gross national product (GNP) of many countries. The basic amount of money deemed necessary to survive was used as a measure of poverty (Graff, 2003). High rates of GNP growth were believed to be linked to low levels of poverty. It became clear, however, that in many countries the GNP was growing at an adequate rate, yet poverty was increasing (Graff, 2003). It became evident that economic growth did not protect against broadening inequality. In light of this knowledge, social scientists began studying inequalities in the population along with the GNP as measures of poverty. They also began to measure educational level, physical health, and political democracy as well as how the income of the top 10% of the population compared with that of the bottom 40% (Graff, 2003). Social scientists began to acknowledge that poverty is as much about quality of life, power, and access to resources as it is about income (Graff, 2003). In studying poverty on a global level, however, social scientists began to place great emphasis on the concept of social inequalities for moral, political, and economic reasons. From a strictly ethical and moral perspective, it seemed morally wrong for some countries to spend millions of dollars exploring the galaxy when there are starving people living in those same countries. Politically, it is a recognized fact that social and economic inequalities can lead to political instability, unrest, and civil conflicts. A country's economic growth will be severely inhibited if a great number of its citizenry are uneducated, unskilled, marginalized, and unsupported by the government in their effort to improve their condition in life (Graff, 2003).

The U.S. government (i.e., U.S. Census Bureau) uses a measurement of poverty that establishes a poverty line. The poverty line refers to the inability of families to meet the expenses of the basic necessities of living based on the budget and spending patterns of Americans with an average standard of living. Children or families living below the established poverty line based on a family's before-tax cash income are considered poor. This measurement was developed in 1965 by Mollie Orshansky, a Social Security Administration economist, when it was believed that people who were poor spent about one third of their income on food. Based on this notion, the government computes an estimated cost of a basic food budget or nutritional diet and multiplies it by three. The formula is adjusted annually for inflation and family size (Luthar, 1999), and the resulting number serves as the dividing line or threshold. This procedure constitutes the government's official measure of poverty, and it is used to make policy and conduct research. The formula used to establish the poverty line has been described at best as inadequate. Some argue that the poverty line needs to be adjusted to more accurately reflect family income requirements (Citro & Michael, 1995). A number of problems have been identified with the procedure for determining the poverty marker (Hanson & Lynch, 2004):

1. People who are poor spend approximately 20% of their income on food, which means that the government should be multiplying by five (instead of three) to determine the threshold of the poverty line. This would, however, increase the number of people classified as poor.

2. Some mothers work outside the home and pay for child care. The government formula, however, treats them the same as mothers who do not have this additional expense.

3. Even though the cost of living is different across states, the poverty line or marker is the same for everyone.

4. The calculation of the poverty threshold does not consider the cost of support programs such as food stamps and Medicaid.

5. The poverty line does not reflect the poverty gap (i.e., how far below the threshold the family falls), and pretax income is used to determine who is below the poverty line, providing an underestimation of poverty (Citro & Michael, 1995; Fisher, 1992; Hanson & Lynch, 2004; Henslin, 2006).

Nevertheless, a discussion on income level does not begin to define or describe poverty.

Hagenaars and De Vos (1988) postulated three different concepts to be considered in a definition of poverty: *absolute, relative,* and *subjective.* These concepts define poverty as having the minimum needed for basic essentials such as food, clothing, and housing (*absolute*); having less than others in terms of what is typical for most people (*relative*); and feeling one does not have enough to just survive (*subjective*) (Graff, 2003; Hanson & Lynch, 2004). Other scholars have used a number of factors to offer a broader view of poverty that does not rely primarily on a description of income level, including perception, socioeconomic status (e.g., occupation, wages, employment status), geography, education, gender, race and ethnicity, age, and timing and terms (Hanson & Lynch, 2004; McLoyd, 1998).

Perception

Relative poverty refers to a person's perception and evaluation of his or her condition (i.e., how poor a person feels). For example, a person might be able to earn enough income to meet basic needs but may feel very deprived in providing a proper education for his or her children or in paying for a needed medical procedure. A person's expectation, value, and custom in the community are relevant to defining poverty and explaining the experience of poverty (Graff, 2003). Measures of relative poverty recognize that poverty is a complex issue and more than just a physical phenomenon (Graff, 2003).

Socioeconomic Status

Socioeconomic level refers to social class, which Weber (1968) defined as a large group of people who rank close to one another in wealth, power, and prestige. According to Weber, these three dimensions divide people into a distinct way of life, provide different opportunities in life, and allow for different worldviews (see Table 1.1).

Table 1.1.   Dimensions of social class

Dimensions	Components	Examples
Wealth	Property	Real estate, automobiles, stocks and bonds, businesses, companies, animals, and bank accounts
	Income	Financial remuneration received from wages, rent, trust funds and inheritance, interest, or royalties
Power	Control, influence, access, social network, and decision makers	The ability to control and shape one's life, the lives of others, and events in one's environment, including government policies
Prestige	Respect, occupation/career, and education; differs from class to class	Jobs with higher salaries and autonomy, neighborhood, homes, clothing, schools attended, jewelry, travel/vacations, and real estate

From Henslin, J.M. (2006). *Essentials of sociology: A down-to-earth approach* (6th ed., pp. 186–191). Boston: Allyn & Bacon; adapted by permission.

Social ranking is typically dependent on how an individual measures up on these dimensions, and most people's status tends to be consistent across dimensions. In an effort to more accurately describe the class structure in the United States, Gilbert (2003) proposed a six-class model: capitalist class (represents 1% of population), upper middle class (represents 15% of the population), lower middle class (represents 34% of the population), working class (represents 30% of the population), working poor (represents 16% of the population), and underclass (represents 4% of the population). Membership in each class is measured by three major factors: education, occupation, and income (see Figure 1.1). It is believed that in the United States, social mobility is attainable primarily by hard work. The American dream of going from rags to riches is not that easy to attain. A study by the Federal Reserve Bank of Boston found that fewer families moved from one quintile, or fifth, of the income ladder to another during the 1980s than during the 1970s and that still fewer moved in the 1990s than in the 1980s (Scott & Leonhardt, 2005). Similar findings were reported in another study by the Bureau of Labor Statistics indicating that mobility declined from the 1980s to the 1990s (Scott & Leonhardt, 2005). According to Beeghley (2005), although the capitalist class is composed of 1% of the population, these individuals have accumulated 40% of U.S. assets and are worth more than the other 99% of the country. Because people tend to associate with others

Social class	Education	Occupation	Income	Percentage of population
Capitalist	Prestigious university	Investors and heirs, a few top executives	$500,000+	1%
Upper middle	College or university, often with postgraduate study	Professionals and upper managers	$100,000+	15%
Lower middle	High school or college, often apprenticeship	Semiprofessionals and lower managers, craftspeople, foremen	About $60,000	34%
Working	High school	Factory workers, clerical workers, low-paid retail salespeople, craftspeople	About $35,000	30%
Working poor	Some high school	Laborers, service workers, low-paid salespeople	About $17,000	16%
Underclass	Some high school	Unemployed and part-time workers, on welfare	Under $10,000	4%

Figure 1.1. U.S. social class ladder. (From Henslin, J.M. [2006]. *Essentials of sociology: A down-to-earth approach* [6th ed.]. Boston: Allyn & Bacon; reprinted by permission.)

of similar financial resources and social capital, each social class has very distinct worldviews and approaches to life that affect career choices, health, education, and even political views.

Race and Ethnicity

Poverty cuts across race and ethnic backgrounds. Culturally, ethnically, and linguistically diverse families, however, are overrepresented among the poor and experience persistent and extreme forms of poverty (Luthar, 1999; McLoyd, 1998). Although a greater number of Caucasian people live in poverty, in terms of their representation in the population, a larger percentage of African Americans, Latinos, and American Indians/Alaskan Natives are poor (Dalaker, 2001; see Figure 1.2). The poverty rate for African American children under age 18 is 30%, for Latino children is 29%, and for Caucasian children is 15% (National Center for Children in Poverty, 2003). Extreme and persistent poverty (i.e., continued poverty for 10–15 years) affects close to one quarter of African American youth (Duncan, 1994). Although poverty can be found across all racial and ethnic groups and geographical regions, historical events and social structure in the United States (e.g., slavery, Jim Crow laws, prejudice) have contributed signifi-

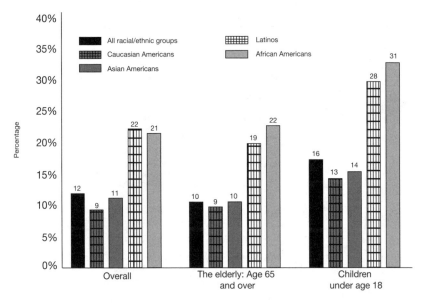

Figure 1.2. Poverty in the United States by age and race–ethnicity. Note: The poverty line on which this figure is based is $18,194 for a family of four. (From Henslin, J.M. [2006]. *Essentials of sociology: A down-to-earth approach* [6th ed.]. Boston: Allyn & Bacon; reprinted by permission.)

cantly to some groups (e.g., African American, Native Americans) experiencing higher rates of poverty than Caucasian Americans.

Education

Education is undoubtedly one of the most significant predictors of poverty. Research provides evidence that level of education is linked to poverty. Young individuals with less than a high school education and skill level are more likely to live in poverty and to receive government assistance, stay on public assistance longer than those who completed high school, show higher rates of unemployment, and become involved in crime (Boisjoly, Harris, & Duncan, 1998; Freeman, 1996; see Figure 1.3). There is also substantial research evidence that indicates that children of all ages living in poverty are more likely to show educational impairments (e.g., grade retention, special education placements, suspensions or expulsions, school dropout) than children of higher socioeconomic status (Brooks-Gunn & Duncan, 1997; Lee & Burkam, 2002). The cycle is clear: Adults with limited educational skills are more likely to live in poverty, and their children are at a higher risk of being poor and having similar educational challenges. The cycle, however, is perpetuated by an educational system that does not provide equal access to funds or to certified and experienced teachers. This leads to substandard instruction; lower expectations of students; ill-maintained and poor-quality equipment; and unsafe, unclean, and ill-functioning school buildings (Barton, 2004; Carey, 2005; Rank, 2004).

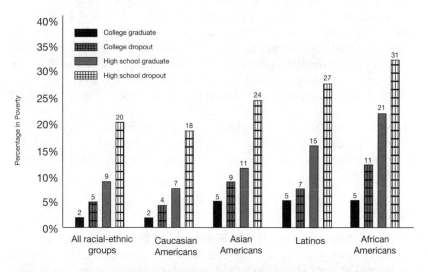

Figure 1.3. Poverty by education and race–ethnicity. (From Henslin, J.M. [2006]. *Essentials of sociology: A down-to-earth approach* [6th ed.]. Boston: Allyn & Bacon; reprinted by permission.)

The National Center for Education Statistics (NCES, 2004) has reported on high school dropout and completion rates since 1988 and indicated that in 2001, 3.8 million 16- to 24-year-olds were not enrolled in a high school program and had not completed high school. This represented 10.7% of the 32.2 million 16- to 24-year-olds in the United States in 2001. The census data demonstrated that during the 1970s and 1980s, the effort to reduce the dropout rate was successful; since then, however, these numbers have remained consistent, showing limited reduction (Kaufman, Alt, & Chapman, 2001). The data is based on the Current Population Survey conducted by the U.S. Census Bureau. High school dropout rates are higher among African American and Latino youth than Caucasians. Twelve percent of African American youth, 24% of Latino youth, 7% of Caucasian youth, and 4% of Asian American youth were not enrolled in school and had not completed high school (NCES, 2004). Fry (2003) noted that this high rate for Latino youth is partly the result of the high number of immigrants in this age group who did not attend school in the United States. Another important fact is that 27% of children younger than 9 months of age lived with mothers who had less than a high school education, and 17% lived with fathers who had less than a high school education (U.S. Census Bureau, 2004).

Limited education by itself does not cause poverty, but it causes conditions that may bring about poverty. Individuals who fail to complete high school typically do not have the minimum literacy skills, technological knowledge, or credentials to perform in today's workplace. Securing a high school diploma facilitates admission to colleges, universities, or community colleges; is the minimum requirement for most entry-level jobs; and increases the likelihood of higher salaries, promotions, and occupational status (Caspi, Wright, Moffit, & Silva, 1998; Kaufman et al., 2001; Miller, Mulvey, & Martin, 1995). McLoyd (1998) asserted that concepts of poverty such as income and socioeconomic status are ongoing and tied to unemployment and low wages. In 2003, very few countries showed stronger connections between socioeconomic background and children's performance in school than did the United States (NCES, 2004). Verstegen (1998), however, asserted that children in poverty have not historically fared well in U.S. schools. Although education provides a viable passport out of poverty, the structure of schools in the United States facilitates the class inequalities that limit the choices of children and families living in poverty and is responsible for poor educational outcomes (Bowers, 1993; Good & Prakash, 2000; Verstegen, 1998).

Gender

A great number of America's 73 million children live in poor (39% or 28.4 million) and single-parent (51% or 14.6 million) households (Kreider & Fields, 2005; NCCP, 2006). Sociologists and psychologists have pointed out that the high divorce rates, teenage pregnancies, and births to single women have brought about families headed primarily by women. Also of concern is that decades of declining wages, failing child support enforcement, and decreasing welfare benefits and welfare programs have made single mothers and their children the poorest demographic group in the United States (Thurston & Navarrete, 2003). Yet another significant contributor to women having a higher rate of poverty is that they earn less than men. Women tend to earn 70% of the income typically earned by men who head families (U.S. Census Bureau, 2004), propelling them and their families into an increased probability of being poor. Forty-five percent of children living in poverty (i.e., below the poverty line) are in households headed by mothers, whereas 12% of children living at or above the poverty line live in homes headed by a single father (NCES, 2004). Gender inequalities are evident when juxtaposed to numbers indicating that males make up 57% of high school dropouts between ages 16 and 24 (U.S. Census Bureau, 2004). In general, young, never-married mothers who are heads of families are overrepresented among families living in poverty, and teenage mothers can be at higher risk in terms of their adjustment paths and limited parenting skills (Luthar, 1999). Another factor worth mentioning is the rate of disabilities in single mothers. An Institute for Women's Policy Research analysis of disabilities among families reported that 20% of single mothers in low-income families had a disability, and 17% had a severe disability (Hanson & Lynch, 2004). Many of these women reported that they did not complete high school and experienced learning and behavioral difficulties in school (Thurston & Navarrete, 2003). They also had a higher probability of having children with special needs (Thurston & Navarrete, 2003).

Age

Children are the most likely to be poor, whereas older people are less likely to be living in poverty due to federal programs designed to help them (e.g., Medicare, Social Security, subsidized housing, federal prescription programs; Henslin, 2006). Although this is true for the general population of older people, however, individual older people who are poor have a higher chance of being from an ethnic or racial minority background.

Geography

In the United States, poverty seems to cluster in the South; historically, the South has higher poverty rates than urban areas (U.S. Department of Agriculture Economic Research Service [USDA], 2005). The poverty rate for children in rural areas (in 2000, the rate was 21%) has been most persistent and severe in Central Appalachia; the Deep South, including the Mississippi River Delta; the River Grande Border area; the Southwest; and the American Indian communities in the Northern Plains (USDA, 2005).

One fourth of all Americans live in the towns, villages, farms, and country-sides of rural America (Human & Wasem, 1991). It is estimated that 16% of people living in rural areas are poor as compared with the 12% national average poverty rate (Henslin, 2006). Unemployment is also higher in rural areas than urban because rural communities have been undergoing a dramatic shift in their economic environment (Horton & Allen, 1998; Human & Wasem, 1991). Human capital factors such as higher dropout rates, lower college completion, and less employment experience have been blamed for the discrepancy between wages in rural and metropolitan areas (Thurston & Navarrete, 2003). Morrissey (1990) reported that 1 of 10 rural families was headed by an employed worker with an income below the poverty line.

The people living in rural areas are diverse in terms of culture, occupation, wealth, lifestyle, and geographical region. Even for populations that have been geographically isolated (e.g., Appalachian Caucasians, Native Americans, southern African Americans, Latinos in the Southwest), there is great diversity (Murray & Keller, 1991). Studies revealed that people living in rural areas are three times more likely to live in substandard housing, experience poorer health status, have little or no insurance coverage, have lower educational levels, have a small propor-tion of the population in white-collar jobs, and endure great socioeconomic prob-lems (Horton & Allen, 1998; Murray & Keller, 1991; Thurston & Navarrete, 2003; Watkins & Watkins, 1984) because many of the working poor do not qualify for social services or Medicaid (National Association of Community Health Centers & National Rural Health Association, 1988). The farm crisis of the 1980s and the cyclic boom-and-bust nature of rural economies have heavily contributed to the economic hardships experienced by many rural communities. The ability of rural economies to fund services (e.g., health, mental health, medi-cal, and social services) is severely affected by the economic downswing because property taxes are the main sources of these funds.

A lot has been written about urban poverty, and it has been the focus of many sociological and political debates. During the 1960s, poverty became more concentrated in the inner-city neighborhoods throughout the United States, and most of its impact was felt by African American urban communities (Curley, 2005). Wilson (1987) reported that between 1970 and 1980, African American populations living in abject poverty in the inner cities increased by 164%, whereas the increase was 24% for Caucasians. Along with this concentration of poverty came increased rates of school dropout, unemployment, households headed by females, welfare dependency, segregation, and crime (Curley, 2005; Dearing, McCartney, & Taylor, 2006; Leventhal, Fauth, & Brooks-Gunn, 2005).

Social scientists proposed a number of theories to explain the condition of the inner cities. Two of the most influential explanations were proposed by Wilson (1987) and Massey and Denton (1993). Wilson argued that two factors best explain the rapid deterioration and present condition of the inner-city neighbor-hoods. Changes in the structure of the economy in the United States and in the social composition of inner-city dwellers were instrumental in bringing about the deterioration of urban neighborhoods. According to Wilson, suburbanization of jobs, decreased demands for low-skilled labor, removal of entry-level jobs, shift from manufacturing to the service sector, and increased demand for formal education were keys to the increased poverty in the inner cities. These changes led to elevated rates of unemployment because urban African Americans were unable to meet the job requirements for formal training. Along with this economic shift came the flight of lower-, working-, and middle-class African American families that once integrated the inner cities to suburban areas leading to socioeconomically segregated neighborhoods in the urban areas (Curley, 2005). Changes in the social condition and the overall makeup of the inner cities were inevitable. Middle- and working-class residents enhanced stability and social organization by supporting community institutions such as churches, schools, and businesses and reinforcing societal norms and values (Curley, 2005). Removal of the working- and middle-class families led to increasing isolation of disadvantaged families and with time fostered concentrated poverty and contributed to the rise in social problems (Wilson, 1987).

Another powerful thesis was advanced by Massey and Denton (1993). They emphasized the role of racism and segregation in creating and maintaining poverty in the inner-city neighborhoods. According to Massey and Denton, the downward economic shift that led to concentrated poverty of urban areas occurred as a direct consequence of residential segregation. They noted that if there had been no residential segregation, the impact of the economic changes would have been shared and its effect spread throughout the entire community—not solely absorbed by African American neighborhoods (Curley, 2005). Massey and Denton analyzed how federal housing policy played a significant role in the disinvestment in African American urban neighborhoods and the expansion of the suburbs for Caucasians. Findings led to their assertion that "the black ghetto was constructed through a series of well-defined institutional practices, private behaviors, and public policies by which whites sought to contain growing urban black populations" (1993, p. 10). Massey and Denton argued that Caucasian America systematically placed barriers to African American spatial mobility that contained and isolated them in disadvantaged neighborhoods (Curley, 2005). The emphasis on racism has received a lot of criticism. In particular, Wilson (2003) noted that one cannot ignore the role and impact of the structure of the American economy on the concentrated poverty in urban neighborhoods. Even though historic racism and contemporary discrimination aggravated the condition of poor, inner-city dwellers, a number of factors contributed to the increase of poverty in America's urban neighborhoods. Regardless of all the possible causes of poverty in particular areas of the United States, research has indicated that where one lives—one's physical environment—is important and influences one's social, educational, and economic outcome (Curley, 2005; Huston et al., 2005; Leventhal et al., 2005).

Timing and Terms

Most people living in poverty only experience this condition for short periods. Often, unplanned events or family circumstances such as illness, loss of employment, death in the family, expensive home or automobile repairs, natural disasters, and divorce may affect the flow of income and create an economic domino effect pushing a family into temporary periods of poverty (Hanson & Lynch, 2004; O'Hare, 1996). Many families living in poverty swing back and forth above and below the threshold of poverty. Gottschalk, McLanahan, and Sandefur (1994) reported that 12% of poverty periods lasted approximately 5 years or longer, whereas 59% lasted less than a year (see Figure 1.4). Henslin (2006) noted that poverty is dynamic, affecting more people than the official figure of 12%.

Living in Poverty

Poverty is a multifactored social and economic condition that affects psychological adjustment and is maintained by the interplay of many factors. According to Payne (2005), factors such as social support (e.g., family, friends, community, role models), health status, educational background (e.g., literacy skills, job skills), emotional resources (e.g., good self-control, perseverance, resilience, goal setting, problem solving, spiritual foundation), and knowledge of hidden rules have more to do with whether an individual rises above or remains in poverty, and Payne refers to them as resources. Hidden rules are beliefs that influence choices and behaviors; for example, Payne (2005) identified money as having rules associated with it. In poverty, the goal of money often is to spend it on things that help the individual not appear poor to others (e.g., jewelry, clothes); in the middle class, money is viewed as something to be managed; and those who are wealthy view money as a resource to be conserved and invested (Payne, 2005).

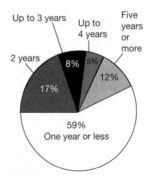

Figure 1.4.   Length of time living in poverty. (From Henslin, J.M. [2006]. *Essentials of sociology: A down-to-earth approach* [6th ed.]. Boston: Allyn & Bacon; reprinted by permission.)

These resources contribute significantly to social mobility. Having a support system capable of providing assistance is crucial to survival. For example, if the individual has an unexpected automobile repair expense, his or her ability to meet the payment of a rent or mortgage could be affected and having a support system willing and able to loan money would be important. Equally important is a support system that can assist by babysitting for little or no cost. Support systems include churches, neighbors, or people who provide social and psychological guidance (e.g., giving advice about getting a job, obtaining vocational training, gaining access to social services agencies, applying to college and for financial aid, facilitating studying). A social capital support system is composed of individuals who can offer encouragement, nurturing advice, a listening ear, opportunities, and an emotional push when it is needed. Putnam defined *social capital* as "the connections among individuals—social networks and the norms of reciprocity and trustworthiness that arise from them" (2000, p. 19). Two elements of social capital have been identified: One is related to social ties that offer social support, whereas the other is composed of ties that act as social bridges and facilitate leverage and connection to the outside world (Briggs, 1998; Curley, 2005). Research suggests that both elements are necessary to increase opportunity for social mobility (Briggs, 1998; Dominguez & Watkins, 2003; Granovetter, 1974; Wacquant & Wilson, 1989).

Emotional resources refer to the emotional energy, psychological characteristics, and spiritual beliefs a person must draw on to get through tough times. For example, perseverance, hope, and self-efficacy are what keeps an individual attending school despite inadequate conditions for studying and limited funds to purchase books and get to school. Other psychological characteristics such as problem-solving skills (making good choices) and goal setting are significant. It is the ability to stick with a situation that has the potential of improving one's condition even in the face of great adversity. Payne (2005) noted that perseverance and goal directedness are indicative of strong emotional resources.

Educational skills, such as literacy skills and the ability to obtain information from a variety of sources, are a powerful resource. Academic skills such as reading, writing, comprehending, computing, and being computer literate facilitate employability and prospect of social mobility. Health is another important resource. Being healthy and able to be self-sufficient allows a person to be independent and to gain access to other resources.

One of the most important resources is having knowledge of the hidden rules. Payne (2005) defined *hidden rules* as the salient unspoken understanding, practices, or views that cue the members of the group that this individual belongs or does not belong to that group. Every social class has hidden rules and they are many. The most salient, however, are those that pertain to possessions, language, money, personality, social emphasis, food, clothing, time, education, destiny, family structure, worldview, love, and driving force (see Payne, 2005). Each social class places a different emphasis, values distinct aspects of these social characteristics, and defines the world in which they live in specific ways. Payne (2005) charted these hidden rules as they relate to life choices and behaviors of individuals living in poverty, the middle class, and the wealthy.

Payne (2005) established a number of key points to consider when discussing poverty, including the following:

1. Poverty is relative. When everyone in the community is in similar circumstances, poverty exists only in relationship to day-to-day experiences and expectations.

2. Poverty occurs in all racial and ethnic groups, regional and geographical areas (urban, rural, and suburban), and most countries.

3. Generational poverty and situational poverty are different. *Generational poverty* is defined as poverty in two or more generations of a particular family. *Situational poverty* is generally caused by circumstances (e.g., death, divorce, unemployment).

4. Hidden social rules are determined by the social class in which an individual was raised. The income of an individual may increase. One's worldview, social interaction, belief about achievement, and cognitive strategies, however, are internalized.

5. Schools and businesses operate from middle-class norms and values. These values are not directly taught in schools, but they are associated with students' success in school. An understanding of the hidden rules, moreover, is necessary to be hired as an employee, have a career, and be successful.

6. For an individual to move up from poverty to middle-class status or wealth, he or she must embrace the hidden rules of a particular group.

7. Students who come from a background of poverty must understand these middle-class norms and values (i.e., the hidden social rules) to be successful, and school personnel must understand the hidden social rules of children to help them be successful in school.

A great number of teachers who work in schools and communities in high-poverty neighborhoods differ from the families in those communities in terms of educational background, income level, and ethnicity (Alexander et al., 1987). Social status differences between students and teachers can produce teachers' negative perceptions of students' academic skills and competencies (Alexander et al., 1987). Value differences have emerged in some studies as a core feature in teacher judgments of children's competencies (Hauser-Cram et al., 2003) and as a cause for low expectations. As such, educators must develop a better understanding of their personal values and the influence these values have on the evaluation of their experiences and on the evaluation of the children they are responsible for educating. Only then will they be equipped to help children from a background of poverty. Payne (2005) emphasized that students need to be taught the hidden rules of the middle class, not in denigration of their own hidden rules, but as an additional set of rules that can be accessed if needed. In teaching the hidden rules, Payne asserted that children are more likely to stay in school as they begin to understand and negotiate the goals and expectations of school in the United States and that this will improve their chances of social mobility. Payne's work is appealing to educators because it is simple and seems to explain frequent observations made by teachers and other school personnel who work with children and families living in poverty (e.g., parents not involved in their children's school, parents who are suspicious of school personnel, parents who spend their limited resources on expensive items of clothing, students who misbehave in class and who appear not interested in education). Some criticism leveled against Payne's (2005) framework, however, is that it failed to address the sociopolitical context for the characteristics (e.g., behaviors guided by hidden rules) that Payne associates with living in poverty. According to Rank (2004), Payne offered teachers and other school professionals an unbalanced and ungrounded understanding of the connection between poverty and education.

The argument advanced by Payne (2005) was initially discussed widely in the mid-1960s when the theory of the "culture of poverty" took root. This theory suggested that the norms and behaviors of people living in poverty can be categorized as a subculture of a larger society and characterized by a distinct way of life, including an atypical worldview and low aspirations (see Harrington, 1962, Lewis, 1966, and Moynihan, 1965) that continued from generation to generation (Curley, 2005). This theory, however, was hotly debated and criticized for being too deterministic, for blaming the victim, and for diverting attention from the structural causes of poverty (Curley, 2005). Lewis (1966) researched poverty by recording the stories of Mexican and Puerto Rican families in the 1950s and 1960s; he documented what he called a "culture of poverty" and identified patterns of behaviors that characterized this culture, including persistent unemployment, feelings of helplessness, short life expectancy, poor work habits, domestic violence, a focus on the present time, substance abuse, and different family structures. Coates and Silburn (1970) found in their research of poor families in the United Kingdom that although the above behavioral characteristics were observed, they were the *result* of poverty and not a *cause* of it. Similar findings were reported by Valentine (1968) in the United States where it was noted that poverty was the consequence of a variety of deprivations and was unrelated to individuals' attitudes and values. Others such as Rutter and Madge (1976) began to make clear connections between the poverty of parents and the effect on their children (e.g., health problems due to housing conditions, poor school attendance due to health issues, nutritional deficiencies, and inadequate clothing for the weather). More contemporary views of poverty endorse the idea that individuals who are poor form a very diverse group, without a collective identity and no indication of values that are different from mainstream society (Kane & Kirby, 2003). Contemporary views of poverty see this condition as due to global factors, changes in working practices, institutional and governmental practices, and inequalities in the labor market (Kane & Kirby, 2003).

Payne's work has been described as advancing a perspective that is classist, regressive, and stereotypical and as disregarding the sociopolitical context of poverty (Gorski, 2005). Her assertions called for teachers to instruct children living in poverty on the rules of the middle class, which was seen as consistent with a deficit or pejorative model that did not appreciate the social complexity involved and lacked a critical perspective founded in research. These scholars (Ferri & Connor, 2005; Gans, 1995; Gorski, 2005; Rank, 2004; Tozer, 2000) asserted that the work does not recognize that some of the characteristics noted may have been the result of racist and classist practices and conditions in society, does not address the historical and social roots of inequalities that maintain people in poverty (Gorski, 2005), and does not acknowledge the decades of research indicating that people living in poverty have hopes and values similar to people from the middle and upper economic strata (Brantlinger, 2003).

Poverty is caused and maintained by multiple interrelated factors that act together to hinder social mobility. It is a complex phenomenon with historical, economic, social, political, and psychological dimensions (Graff, 2003). Poverty can be described as a whole pattern of interlocking factors where removing one of them may have little effect on the solution of the problem (Webster, 1990). The effect of poverty is observed on a number of contexts (e.g., health, development, school, neighborhood) as evidenced by current research. Systematic changes on all levels of society are required.

2

Cognitive and Social-Emotional Development

A Neuropsychological Perspective

The honor of one is the honor of all.
The hurt of one is the hurt of all.

Creek Indian Creed

Research in various fields of study and practice such as pediatric medicine, infant and early childhood neuropsychology, sociology, and developmental psychology have offered evidence of the effect of environmental factors on the cognitive, emotional, behavioral, and physical development of children (see Aylward, 1997; Brooks-Gunn & Duncan, 1997; Kolb & Whishaw, 2003; McLoyd, 1998; Schwean & Saklofske, 1999). Biological and environmental factors can potentially operate together to influence either a positive or negative outcome. Consider that one in five young children live in poverty and are exposed to many environmental risks. Children at environmental risk are overrepresented in special education classes, and 75% of children with mild mental retardation come from lower-income homes (Aylward, 1997; Zill & Schenborn, 1990). This chapter discusses the affect of environmental factors on brain development and the subsequent effects of these on cognitive development and behavioral adjustment.

The concept of risk is often used to understand the effect of environmental and biological factors on the development of children. This concept of developmental risk refers to the likelihood that individuals with particular characteristics or life experiences may be vulnerable to psychological, physical, or adaptive difficulties during their developmental years and beyond (Sattler & Hoge, 2006). Tjossem (1976) highlighted three types of risk: established, environmental, and biological. *Established risks* refer to medical disorders of an identified etiology whose developmental outcome are well known (e.g., Down syndrome). *Environmental risks* include the lack of opportunity for cognitive stimulation or health care and mothers' behaviors during and after pregnancy (e.g., the mother–child interaction). *Biological risks* refer to the exposure to potentially noxious prenatal, perinatal, or postnatal development events such as asphyxia and intraventricular hemorrhage (Aylward, 1997). Although all three types of risk must be considered in any discussion on childhood development, environmental risks and their effect on a child's functioning has been receiving much attention (Aylward, 1996; Bradley, Whiteside, Mundfrom, & Blevins-Kwabe, 1995; Brooks-Gunn & Duncan, 1997; McLoyd, 1998). Children and families living in poverty tend to be overly exposed to environmental risk factors such as inadequate prenatal care, low birth weight (LBW), environmental toxins, poor nutrition, drugs and alcohol, and limited access to quality medical care (Aylward, 1997). Risk factors may be influential during infancy and childhood when their effects might be seen. Others may appear in adolescence or may become evident in later years (Sattler & Hoge, 2006).

The combination of environmental and biological risks is referred to as double jeopardy or double hazard (Escalona, 1982; Parker, Greer, & Zuckerman, 1988). One recognized model of environmental influence is the transactional approach, which postulates that biological risk factors and environmental stressors act synergistically to shape outcomes (Sameroff & Chandler, 1975). The transactional model holds that a degree of plasticity is considered inherent in both the child and the environment in such a way that the child is continually reorganizing, correcting, and "self-righting." According to this model, an impoverished environment hinders this "self-righting," whereas a positive environment improves the child's resiliency (Sameroff & Chandler, 1975). The likelihood of a dysfunctional child–environment transaction increases when the child's environment offers limited stimulation (Aylward, 1997). The transactional model is supported by breakthroughs in neuroscience, specifically brain-imaging techniques that further acknowledge the enduring influence of environmental conditions such as nutrition, care, surroundings, and stimulation on the developing structure and chemistry of an infant's brain (Shore, 1997).

What kinds of environmental factors affect development? Many factors associated with poverty can negatively influence children's development. These include inadequate prenatal care, poor diet and malnutrition, LBW, limited cognitive stimulation, learning difficulties, stress, lead poisoning, and drug and alcohol abuse, among others. Many of the factors that place children at risk are also outcome factors. For example, poor prenatal care (a risk) can lead to LBW in an infant (an outcome). LBW (a risk) can lead to illness (an outcome), and illness (a risk) can lead to problems in school (an outcome). Problems in school (a risk)

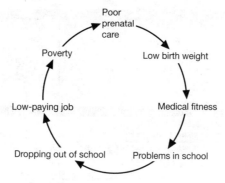

Figure 2.1. Cycle of risk and outcome factors. The diagram illustrates how factors associated with poverty can be pervasive and how these factors can be risk or outcome factors. (From Sattler, J.M., & Hoge, R.D. [2006]. *Assessment of children: Behavioral, social, and clinical foundations* [5th ed., p. 21]. La Mesa, CA: Author; reprinted by permission.)

can lead to dropping out of school (an outcome), and dropping out of school (a risk) can limit a person to a low-paying job (an outcome). A low-paying job (a risk) can lead to poverty (an outcome), and poverty (a risk) can lead to poor prenatal care (an outcome) (Sattler & Hoge, 2006; see Figure 2.1). The National Collaborative Perinatal Project, a seminal study conducted in the 1970s, emphasized the effect of family and income on outcomes. The study followed 26,700 infants and found that the two factors most likely to predict cognitive performance at 4 years of age were income level as indicated by socioeconomic status and maternal education (Werner & Smith, 1980). The study also identified other crucial variables: the effect of high-risk pregnancies, the function of social class in perinatal mortality, and unfavorable environmental factors on long-term child development (Kopp & Krakow, 1983).

BRAIN DEVELOPMENT

Development must be understood in the context of brain function. Moreover, any discussion of the influence of environment on development must consider function and dysfunction of the brain structures. As noted earlier, there has been a significant breakthrough in brain research attributed to advanced brain imaging techniques that have been crucial to confirming earlier theories about how the brain functions (Fogarty, 1997; Teeter Ellison & Semrud-Clikeman, 2007). Numerous changes occur in the central nervous system during prenatal development, and they continue throughout life (Hale & Fiorello, 2004). The changes that take place during the periods of development are so specific and predictable that geneticists can identify when certain congenital (birth) defects occurred (Gra-

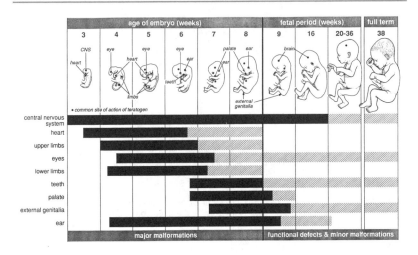

Figure 2.2.   Embryogenesis and fetal development. Teratogens can potentially alter the development of specific organs or systems of organs by acting during the time these structures are being developed. Damage to an organ during the time represented by a solid bar will lead to a major malformation. Damage during the time represented by the hatched bar will lead to functional defects or minor morphological abnormalities. (From Moore, K.L., & Persaud, T.V.N. [1998]. *Before we are born: Essentials of embryology and birth defects* [5th ed., inside cover]. Philadelphia: Elsevier; reprinted by permission.)

ham & Morgan, 1997; see Figure 2.2). To understand the effect of the environment on the development of brain structure and subsequent cognitive and social abilities, it is important to first appreciate the typical process of the development of the human brain. Kolb & Whishaw (2003) provided an account of the development of the brain summarized as follows:

1. At the point of egg fertilization, a human embryo consists of a single cell that soon divides.

2. By the 14th day, the embryo consists of several sheets of cells with raised areas in the middle that becomes the primitive body.

3. By the third week after conception, a primitive brain emerges that is basically a sheet of cells at one end of the embryo. This sheet forms the neural tube that begins to turn over to form the spinal cord.

4. By the seventh week, the embryo begins to look like a miniature person.

5. By 100 days after conception, the brain looks human but does not begin to form gyri and sulci until about 7 months. The spinal cord, brainstem, and a significant part of the forebrain are developed at 40 weeks gestation (Jacobson, 1991).

6. By the end of the ninth month, the brain has the gross appearance of the adult human brain, even though its cellular structure is different.

Fetal development is a prolonged process, and the brain is the most vulnerable of all embryonic organs to teratologic influences (Aylward, 1997). During the third trimester, the brain begins a major prenatal growth spurt that continues postnatally until age 2 years (Gardner, 1975). Research has identified a series of changes that occur in the early development of a child's brain. These changes occur in a relatively fixed sequence:

1. Cell birth (neurogenesis, gliogenesis; 3–4 weeks gestation): This is the first phase of central nervous system development. The neural tube is where cells are born that make up the brain. The cells lining the neural tube are referred to as neural stem cells, and one of their functions is to produce progenitor cells that divide and produce nondividing cells called neuroblast and glioblast that mature into neurons and glia (Kolb & Whishaw, 2003).

2. Cell migration (3–5 months of gestation): This process begins after the first neurons are produced and continues for weeks after neurogenesis has been completed. Cells travel or migrate from the site where they were generated to their predetermined regions or final positions in the cortex (Kolb & Whishaw, 2003). Once in their final position, they aggregate into layers, clusters, and tracts, making the many structures that make up the brain (Wolfe, 2001). Several cortical layers are apparent during the fifth month of fetal development (Kolb & Fantie, 1989). If the migration process is disturbed, it could produce conditions that may appear later in a child's development such as epilepsy, dyslexia, and even schizophrenia (Scheibel, 2000). Abnormality in genetic programming may disrupt cell migration; environmental toxins such as alcohol or drugs present a threat to the migration process, and based on the time and stage of fetal development, different brain areas can be impaired resulting in cognitive and behavioral deficits later in life (Teeter Ellison & Semrud-Clikeman, 2007).

3. Cell differentiation (dendrite and axon growth): This is the process in which neuroblasts become specific types of neurons. It is initiated when cell generation has been completed and typically ends at birth (Kolb & Whishaw, 2003).

4. Synaptogenesis (formation of synapses): This phase is characterized by cell maturation or the growth of dendrites, axons, and synapses and is ongoing for years (Kolb & Whishaw, 2003). Cells begin to grow dendrites to provide the surface area for synapses with other cells. Cells form random synaptic connections (more than are needed), and they are guided into place by a number of cues and signals (Kolb & Whishaw, 2003; Wolfe, 2001). The formation of the right neural pathways can be disrupted in many ways. Scarring from head trauma in the early months of life, anoxia, the ingestion of toxic substances, and malnutrition may interfere with the growth of axons, affecting the behavior supported by that area of the brain (Kolb & Whishaw, 2003).

5. Cell death, synaptic pruning, and myelogenesis (formation of myelin) take place during this phase. When neurons fail to form enough synaptic contact points or migrate to the wrong region, they are pruned away in a programmed cell death (Wolfe, 2001). The process of pruning is affected by many variables, specifically sensory and gonadal hormones (Kolb & Whishaw, 2003). The brain creates and eliminates connections to reach an equilibrium that optimizes beneficial pathways and minimizes dysfunctional ones (Hale & Fiorello, 2004).

The central nervous system is comprised of the brain and the spinal cord, which are made up of neurons and glial cells (Wolfe, 2001). Neurons differ from other cells in the body in three ways: They do not regenerate on a regular basis, they are able to transmit information, and they are shaped in ways that facilitate communication with other neurons through electrical and chemical signals (Wolfe, 2001). Glial cells form part of a blood barrier that protects the brain from toxic molecules that might be in the bloodstream. They also form a layer of insulation (myelin) around nerve fibers, which is instrumental in strengthening and increasing the neural messages or speed of transmission of the nerve impulse (Fogarty, 1997). Myelination happens over an extended period of time. It starts in the sixth month of gestation and continues into adulthood. Myelination increases brain weight from 400 grams at birth to 850 grams at 11 months, to 1,100 grams at 36 months, to 1,350 to 1,410 grams at age 15, and the process continues through adulthood (Kolb & Whishaw, 2003). Changes in visual, motor, social, and cognitive development appear to be correlated with myelination (Teeter Ellison & Semrud-Clikeman, 2007). Malnutrition is among a number of events that can interfere with the process of myelination. Disruption in the process of myelination can be the cause of some degenerative diseases, cerebral white matter hypoplasia (a clinical syndrome characterized by spastic quadriplegia, seizures, and cognitive impairment), and amino acid deficits (e.g., phenylketonuria) among others (Aylward, 1997).

Neurons receive messages from the senses, muscles, and other neurons as electrical impulses that are processed inside the cell and sent out to other neurons via the axons (Fogarty, 1997). Electrical impulses travel to the end of the axon where chemical neurotransmitters are released into the synapse and are received by the dendrites (Sylwester, 1995). It is the synapse that facilitates communication between the neurons. Synaptic networks grow more elaborate in the postnatal period (Brodal, 1992). Neurotransmitters are chemical messengers that work between neurons at the synapse and are released as the electrical neural impulse are passed from one neuron to another (Fogarty, 1997). They are stored in bulb-like terminals of the axon branches (Wolfe, 2001). Neurotransmitters are grouped into three broad categories: amino acids, monoamines, and peptides (Fogarty, 1997). These neurotransmitters underpin all behaviors (Wolfe, 2001).

Scientists have identified between 50 and 100 neurotransmitters. Amino acids are the main neurotransmitters that hold excitatory or inhibitory messages (Fogarty, 1997), and they are derived from protein foods. They are involved in quick point-to-point communication between neurons (Wolfe, 2001). Amines (e.g., epinephrine, norepinephrine, dopamine, acetylcholine, serotonin) are the second group of neurotransmitters. They are slow acting and modulate the action of the amino acid neurotransmitters (Pliszka, 2003; Wolfe, 2001). These neurotransmitters have a powerful role in the daily functioning of the human body. They are involved in maintaining waking patterns, emotional tone, and motor behavior. A decrease or loss of these neurotransmitters in the brain is associated with disorders such as depression, mania, Alzheimer's disease, Parkinson's disease, schizophrenia, and obsessive compulsive disorders (Kolb & Whishaw, 2003). Peptides (e.g., endorphins [reduces pain or enhances euphoria], vasopressin [involved in water retention, blood pressure, and memory]) are a third group of neurotransmitters. They affect complex behavior patterns such as pain and pleasure (Fogarty, 1997; Pliszka, 2003). They act in the body or in the brain, and they have the ability to alter mood (Fogarty, 1997; Pliszka, 2003). For more in-depth information on neurons and the neurotransmitter systems, please see Pliszka, 2003.

Kolb and Whishaw (2003) pointed to three ways to study the relationship between brain and behavioral development. One way entails looking at the nervous system maturation and correlating it with the development of specific behaviors. For example, linking development of particular brain structures to the development of speech or crawling. The point being illustrated is that as brain structures develop, their function emerges and shows up as observable behaviors (Kolb & Whishaw, 2003). The second method involves looking at a developing child's behavior and making inference regarding neural maturation. For example, when language emerges in a young child, corresponding changes are expected in the neural structures that are involved in language (Kolb & Whishaw, 2003). The third approach calls for identifying and studying factors that influence brain and behavioral development. From this view, knowing the experiences (e.g., effects of hormone, injuries, and abnormal genes) that shape how brain structures function and how they lead to the production of particular behaviors is important (Kolb & Whishaw, 2003).

ENVIRONMENTAL FACTORS AND BRAIN DEVELOPMENT

The environment in which fetal development occurs can significantly influence growth, behavior, and learning. For example, problems in the genetic program and intrauterine trauma and the effect of toxic agents may lead to peculiarities in development and may contribute to significant deformities of the infant (e.g., anpncephaly, microencephaly) or mild impairments such as learning disabilities in the child (Graham & Morgan, 1997; Kolb & Whishaw, 2003). Moreover, although heredity plays a significant role in determining the potential for brain growth and cognitive abilities, there is ample evidence that an enriched environment stimulates brain activity and the development of higher cognitive functioning (Diamond, 1988; Fogarty, 1997; Teeter Ellison & Semrud-Clikeman, 2007). *Brain plasticity* refers to the ability of the brain to adapt to its environment by making vital neural connections and changes in the brain. These changes in brain structure are influenced by experience.

The power of the environment in the form of experience can be appreciated at the level of neurons. Greenough and Juraska (1986) identified two types of synapses (i.e., experience-expectant, experience-dependent) during periods of synapse proliferations. *Experience-expectant* synapses are genetically programmed to receive sensory experiences that are adaptive, likely to happen, and necessary for the organization of cortical circuit (Aylward, 1997). *Experience-dependent* synapses are those that are specific to an individual organism and are produced in response to experiences that are unique and personal (Kolb & Whishaw, 2003). They are not genetically programmed, they are formed from unique environmental experiences, and they are produced in the brain as a child encounters novel experiences in his or her surroundings. Experiences in the environment cause the neurons to activate, and the continued activation stabilizes and makes permanent connections. Pruning occurs in unused synapses, and the stabilization of synapses allows an infant brain to store experiences from the environment and build neural structures that are part of a functioning brain (Aylward, 1997).

In the same manner that positive and expected experiences mold brain development, abnormal experiences alter brain structure and behavior as well. The brain's sensitivity to experiences or injury varies with time because there are periods in the process of development when various brain regions are more sensitive to different events. Two concepts relevant to understanding brain development are critical periods and sensitive periods. *Critical periods* refers to the time when the action of a specific internal or external influence is necessary for normal developmental progress. In contrast, a *sensitive period* refers to the time when damage to the central nervous system can produce variation, reorganization, and possible abnormality of the system (Aylward, 1997).

A rich environment has a diversity of sensory and language experiences that stimulates a profusion of dendritic growth (Fogarty, 1997). Exposure to a highly stimulating versus impoverished environment increases brain size, density of glial cells, the length of dendrites, the number of excitatory synapses, and the size of synapses (see Figure 2.3). Even prenatal experiences can alter brain structures as demonstrated in studies noting that newborns can identify their mother's voice heard in utero (Kolb & Whishaw, 2003). Other studies have documented the influence of experience on the brain. One seminal study conducted by Hubel and Wiesel (1963) investigated the effect of restricting visual experience to one eye on ocular dominance and brain structure in kittens. They found that when vision in one eye is restricted early in life, the restricted eye became functionally

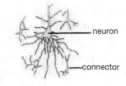

A newborn baby

A child about one year old

A 2-year-old child

Figure 2.3.   Brain wiring and experience. These diagrams show how nerve cells in an infant's brain form connections at a rapid rate as it is shaped by early life experiences. At the beginning, nerve cells are unconnected. By the time the child reaches his or her first birthday, cells have made many more connections. By the time the child is 2 years old, there are more dense and complex connections, and synaptic pruning begins. (From Sunderland, M. [2006]. *The science of parenting* [p. 21]. New York: DK Publishing; reprinted by permission.)

blind for a period of weeks after opening. Later, stimulation in the deprived eye often failed to activate cells in the cortex and transmit to other brain areas. Moreover, when these cells worked, they were abnormal due to weakened connection to the eye (Kolb & Whishaw, 2003). Hubel and Wiesel (1963) found that environmental deprivation has the ability to retard development and that early deprivation is the most damaging. Elbert, Heim, and Rockstroh (2001) conducted another study documenting the effect of experience on brain development. Elbert et al. (2001) studied stringed-instrument players to investigate how experience can affect the organization of the sensorimotor maps of the hand in the brain. Through neuroimaging, they found that representation of the fingers of the left hand (the ones used in fingering the strings) occupied more space than the thumb or the fingers of the right hand and that the amount of change was proportional to the age when musical training started (Elbert et al., 2001).

Brain research reveals that rich early experiences have a positive effect on brain development, and deprivation has a damaging effect on brain growth. Also relevant is the timing of the experiences. Rich stimulation that occurs early produces positive changes in brain structure and subsequent functioning, whereas experiences occurring later in life or past critical periods may not have the same degree of effect as those that happen early. Deprivation that occurs early in development and continues for a prolonged period of time tends to have a more severe effect on brain development than those that are of short duration.

BRAIN MATURITY AND COGNITIVE DEVELOPMENT

There is a parallel between brain maturity and development of a child's ability to act, think, and feel (Dawson & Guare, 2001; Teeter Ellison & Semrud-Clikeman, 2007). The emergence of particular behaviors is dependent on the maturation of specific regions of the brain and of the supporting neural circuitry that is involved in those behaviors.

Children's ability to reason and to explore the world is constantly evolving. These alterations are accompanied by changes in brain structure. Three changes that are both qualitative and quantitative include change in the billions of neurons that make up the brain, change in some structures in the brain, and change in the brain as a whole.

One of the changes in the brain occurs at the level of the neurons. Nerve cells in the embryonic brain divide to generate new neurons (Wolfe, 2001). Billions of neurons are generated, which is more than is needed. After the process of migration, in which neurons travel to their designated location to form different structures, the cells begin to form synapses. The excess cells are pruned away in order to eliminate neurons that have not made the right connections and to strengthen the connections that remain (Wolfe, 2001). Over the course of early development, the density of synaptic connections increases tenfold between birth and 12 months. By age 2, the density is about twice as much as in adults. After age 2, however, the number of synaptic connections begins to decrease so that by age 7, it is similar to adult levels (Siegler, 1998). Experience is a significant determinant of which synaptic connections will be maintained. Basically, if experiences promote synapses firing so that neurotransmitters are released, then the synapses are maintained. If not, then they are pruned away (Greenough, Black, & Wallace, 1987).

Changes in the relative size and level of activity of the two major regions of the brain (subcortical structures and cortex) are modified in the process of development (Siegler, 1998). Subcortical structures include the thalamus, medulla, and pons; the cortex includes the cerebral cortex. This region facilitates high-level cognitive skills, such as language and problem solving, that characterize human beings (Siegler, 1998). It is the area that is least developed at birth, and it is responsible for various types of cognition not apparent at early stages of development (Siegler, 1998).

The cerebral cortex is divided into four lobes: the frontal lobe, the parietal lobe, the occipital lobe, and the temporal lobe. Although they are connected by fiber pathways and communicate through these pathways, these regions are each responsible for producing certain types of cognitive activity. The occipital lobe is involved in processing visual information. The frontal lobe is involved in motor consciousness, planning, and the regulation of cognitive activity. The temporal lobe is involved in processing auditory stimuli and the perception of speech. The parietal lobe is involved in analyzing and integrating information, maintaining focus or spatial attention, and processing perception of touch, pain, and spatial awareness (Siegler, 1998; Wolfe, 2001). The frontal lobe is the least developed part of the cerebral cortex at birth, and it matures as the child develops. The increasing maturity of the frontal lobe brings about advances in cognitive capabilities that unfold throughout the process of cognitive development. The frontal lobe plays a major role in problem solving, attending, analyzing, organizing and planning, and self-monitoring. These cognitive skills are generally referred to as executive functions, and they are associated with frontal brain systems (the frontal/prefrontal cortex and connections to adjacent areas; Dawson & Guare, 2004).

Brain size represents another one of the changes that happen in the brain as a whole. Brain growth occurs uniformly after birth. These periods of growth are referred to as growth spurts, which are believed to be the result of the growth of glia cells, synapses, and increased metabolic demands (Kolb & Whishaw, 2003; Teeter Ellison & Semrud-Clikeman, 2007). The first four growth spurts that occur during childhood concur with the four main stages described by Piaget (1971) as part of the process of cognitive development. This suggests that changes in neural functioning are associated with the onset of each of the four stages of cognitive development (see Table 2.1; Kolb & Whishaw, 2003).

It is clear that brain development involves a complex interplay of genetics and experience (Siegler, 1998; Teeter Ellison & Semrud-Clikeman, 2007). One example of this interplay is the development of problem-solving and reasoning skills. Piaget (1971) depicted four stages of cognitive development: sensorimotor period (birth to about 2 years), preoperational period (2 years to about 6 or 7 years), concrete operational period (6 or 7 years to about 11 or 12 years), and formal operational period (11 or 12 years and onward). These developmental stages are marked by continuing qualitative and organizational changes in the child's ability to reason on an increasingly more abstract level and to interact with the environment in a more sophisticated manner. As described by Piaget (Piaget & Inhelder, 1969), the sensorimotor period is characterized by motor reflexes that are used to develop more sophisticated behaviors by repeating and systematically linking behaviors and generalizing these activities to other situations (Siegler, 1998). The preoperational stage is identified by the acquisition of ways of representing the world symbolically—mental imagery and language. Specifically, language skills grow more complex, but children in this stage view the world from their perspective, which is referred to as egocentric communication (Siegler,

Table 2.1. Cognitive development and brain changes

Piaget's stages of cognitive development	Relevant age ranges	Developmental milestone	Brain changes
Stage 1: Sensorimotor Begin to experience the world through the senses and actions change. At the end, toddlers interact with objects and people in their immediate environment.	Birth to 18–24 months	Coordination of action into routines; varying behaviors to change outcomes; object permanence	Brain growth 3–10 months; a 30% increase in brain weight by 18 months
Stage 2: Preoperational Characterized by representational ability. Represents things with images and words, but unable to solve problems with critical logical reasoning.	2 years to 6 or 7 years	Language development, egocentrism, communications, and pretend play	Growth spurt between ages 1 and 4; a 5%–10% increase in brain weight
Stage 3: Concrete operations Reasons logically about concrete events as well as dynamic aspects of the environment. Understands concrete analogies and performs arithmetic operations.	6 or 7 years to 11 or 12 years	Understanding of conservation: liquid quantity, solid quantity, and number; mathematical transformations	Growth spurt between ages 6 and 8; an increase of 5%–10% in brain weight
Stage 4: Formal operation Adolescents become aware of particular reality in which they live as only one of a number of imaginable realities. They think about justice, truth, and morality and develop a more systematic approach to reasoning.	11 or 12 years and onward	Logical and scientific reasoning; applying abstract and systematic complex thinking to problem solving	Growth spurt between ages 10 and 12 and again between ages 14 and 16 and older; an increase in brain size of 5%–10%

From Siegler, R.S. (1998). *Children's thinking* (3rd ed.; pp. 32–41). Upper Saddle River, NJ: Prentice Hall; adapted by permission.
From Kolb, B., & Whishaw, Q. (2003). *Fundamentals of human neuropsychology* (5th ed.; pp. 619–621). New York: Worth Publishers; adapted by permission.

1998). Concrete operations is the third period and is characterized by children demonstrating a better ability to understand other perspectives and representing transformations and static situations. But they solve problems from a more concrete manner rather than utilizing abstract reasoning (Siegler, 1998). The last stage is the formal operations period in which children reason from a more logical and sophisticated base of theories and abstractions (Siegler, 1998). Upon maturation of brain structures, associated behaviors emerge, develop rapidly, and are further enhanced by experience or interaction with the environment.

There is a reciprocal interaction between biology and the environment. From birth, children interact actively with their environment through their parents, siblings, grandparents, and other children. The interaction includes objects (e.g., books, computers, television sets), culturally related tasks (e.g., reading, writing, playing video games, computer programming, performing mathematic operations) as well as social values that guide strategies and problem solving (e.g., accuracy, speed, efficiency, work ethics; Siegler, 1998). These social manifestations have a defined effect on the way children reason and solve problems (Gauvain, 1995). Vygotsky (1962) emphasized the influence of children's social worlds on the way that children think. His sociocultural theories shed light on the role of other individuals in the child's environment. These roles involve assisting children in acquiring the skills necessary to meet the expectations and demands of their culture. According to Vygotsky (1978), one way that parents or caregivers assist children is in providing social scaffolding. Vygotsky defined *social scaffolding* as activities such as modeling, hinting, and guiding problem-solving skills. This allows children to learn how to reason in more advanced ways. Upon acquiring some basic structure and understanding, this support is gradually withdrawn and the child operates independently at higher levels. Vygotsky's theory actively involves the child's social surrounding as an important force in the child's cognitive development. Diversity of experiences or circumstances, social milieu, and time bring about individual differences. Piaget (1971), however, advocated the universal aspect of cognitive development as well as the child being internally motivated to construct reality from his or her mental and physical actions. The theories proposed by both Vygotsky and Piaget are complementary in that they explain the two important forces in development—the universal and the individual aspects of cognitive development (Siegler, 1998). They each recognize the role of nature and nurture (biology and experience) in the development of children's abilities to think and organize the world around them.

BRAIN MATURITY AND SOCIAL AND EMOTIONAL DEVELOPMENT

Brain maturity influences cognitive development and, in turn, shapes emotions and behavior. An infant brain continues its development after birth as it is being sculpted by both negative and positive experiences (Perry, 1997; Sunderland, 2006). Different parts of the brain, specifically the frontal lobe, are involved in the expression and abilities associated with social, emotional, or behavioral functioning. For example, the orbitofrontal region of the brain is implicated in the management of strong feelings, to respond sensitively to others, and to effectively read social cues (Sunderland, 2006). The dorsolateral prefrontal region plays a role in the ability to reason, organize, and make choices. The ventromedial area is involved in the ability to reason and analyze emotional experiences (Perry, 1997; Sunderland, 2006). The anterior cingulated is the region that allows the brain to focus attention and self-monitor (Sunderland, 2006). Children's early experiences affect those brain structures responsible for social, emotional, and behavioral functioning (see Figure 2.4).

As noted earlier, infants are born with billions of neurons that proceed to make connections based on the experiences they receive. These connections are largely responsible for the emotional and social intelligence of the developing child (Perry, 1997; Sunderland, 2006). Negative experiences can change brain structure and functioning mainly through stress hormones such as cortisol and adrenaline. These neurotransmitters respond to psychological or physical danger and prepare the body for fight or flight. When the danger is over, the body returns to its normal state (Kotulak, 1997; Perry, 1997). Persistent stress experienced during prenatal development or early childhood, however, affects genetic regulation and creates an abnormal network of connections between brain cells, marking and reinforcing mislearned patterns or strategies (Kotulak, 1997; McEwen, 1995). Negative experiences, such as stress, can affect genes by switching

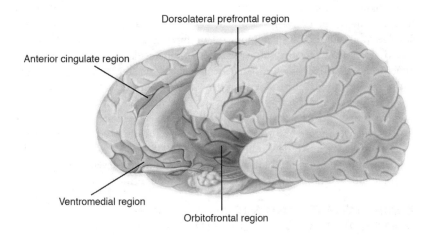

Figure 2.4. Parts of the frontal lobe. Different parts of the frontal lobe can develop in children exposed to caring and responsive parenting practices and experiences. They may, however, remain underdeveloped or might be altered in the presence of minimal protective factors or recurring negative experiences. (From Sunderland, M. [2006]. *The science of parenting* [p. 22]. New York: DK Publishing; reprinted by permission.)

them on or off at incorrect times and by driving them to create abnormal networks of brain cell connections (Kotulak, 1997; McEwen, 1995; Schore, 2003). Consequently, a child may express unreasonable rage in a situation in which compromise would be a typical response for an average child or a depressive episode under circumstances in which pleasure and delight would be expected (Kotulak, 1997; Perry, 1997; Schore, 2003). Intense maternal stress can increase levels of stress in the developing fetus, and this stress has been associated with low birth weight infants as well as irritable, restless, colicky babies (Teeter Ellison & Semrud-Clikeman, 2007). Other researchers (e.g., Reinis & Goldman, 1980) indicated that maternal stress creates vasoconstriction that decreases circulation and produces fetal asphyxia causing brain damage in the fetus.

Experience helps build connections between the cells in the higher brain. The brain is designed to adapt to the positive as well as to the negative experiences that might be encountered (Sunderland, 2006). This adaptability can work in favor or against a developing child. For example, if a child is raised in an environment where her parents play with her, listen to her, validate her experiences, comfort her, and establish proper boundaries and discipline, then she would be more successful coping with disappointment, dealing with stress, managing anger, showing compassion, developing a sense of self-efficacy and motivation, and building healthy and fulfilling relationships. Yet, if a child is raised in an environment where he experiences physical abuse and/or bullying by a sibling or parent and his feelings are ignored and suppressed, then he can become accustomed to living in an environment where he cannot trust others, share his thoughts confidently, or express his feelings safely (Schore, 2003; Sunderland, 2006; Teeter Ellison & Semrud-Clikeman, 2007). In such an environment, changes in brain structure and chemical systems reinforce an abnormal learning strategy and may result in hypervigilance, a heightened aggression or fear response, or heightened attack/defense impulses (Perry, 1994). Emotionally responsive parenting helps forge vital connections in the brain that enable a child to cope better with day-to-day stress and develop healthy relationships (Sunderland, 2006). The brain systems are designed to produce both fear and pleasure, and a child must be able to recognize danger and be motivated to flee it (Pliszka, 2003). Disturbances in the brain systems may be related to a wide range of emotional disorders (Kotulak, 1997; Pliszka, 2003).

Most children who have encountered extreme experiences, such as living in abject poverty, succeed in spite of these threats to their development. Scientists believe that this occurs because the brain is resilient (Gunnar, 2001; Kotulak, 1997). The average child is exposed to circumstances that operate as protective factors (e.g., having parents or adults who care, being exposed to effective instructional strategies and early childhood education or intervention, having a good quality home life and parent–child relationship, experiencing a sense of security and safety; Goldstein & Brooks, 2006b; Gunnar, 2001; Kotulak, 1997). Protective factors serve as neutralizing agents that increase positive adaptation and a successful outcome despite risk factors.

3

Poverty and Its Effect on Children's Development

Life consists not in holding good cards but in playing those you hold well.

Josh Billing

Living in poverty increases the exposure to environmental risk factors, which can begin even before conception and can interfere with brain development, negatively influencing cognitive and behavioral development. Some social scientists have argued that racism and classism play a pivotal role in creating the conditions in society that support the continuance of poverty and its effects. For example, Giscombé and Lobel (2005) asserted that the disproportionately high rates of adverse birth outcomes among African Americans can be attributed to the stress due to racism. Ferri and Connor (2005), Hooks (2000) and Kozol (1992) noted the role of the schools in perpetuating a system that leads to school failure, special education placement and labeling, school drop out, and the cycle of poverty. Poverty has a chronic and pervasive effect that raises the probability that the negative effect of early environmental and biological risk factors will accumulate and persist over time (Aylward, 1997). Limited access to timely health care services also interferes with early intervention services and follow-up medical programs. Many working families with low incomes do not qualify for public health benefits (Cauthen & Lu, 2003), and many employers of parents with low incomes do not offer health coverage or sufficient coverage. A number of risk factors associated with poverty and their ongoing influences on school performance are reviewed in this chapter, and the chapter concludes with a discussion on protective factors and resilience.

35

There is a proven relationship between poverty and developmental outcomes (Fujiura & Yamaki, 2000). Scholars have been studying the effect of many variables, both biological and environmental, on the development of children. Poverty is associated with a negative influence on children's health and development. It is related to increased neonatal and postnatal mortality rates; greater risk of injuries resulting from accidents, physical abuse, or neglect; higher risk for asthma; exposure to teratogens; and lower developmental scores in a range of tests at different ages (Aber, Bennett, Conley, & Li, 1997). The effects of many environmental risk factors are well documented. Consuming alcohol during pregnancy is linked to neurodevelopmental impairments, and young children's exposure to lead is associated with learning disabilities. Environmental influences that alter the normal development of the embryo or fetus are called teratogens, which can be divided into four categories: drugs (e.g., alcohol, thalidomide), physical agents (e.g., hyperthermia, radiation), congenital infections (e.g., HIV, rubella, cytomegalovirus, syphilis), and metabolic conditions that affect the mother (e.g., maternal PKU-phenylketonuria; Saddler, 1995; Scott, 1994). Studies have revealed the role of several factors in determining the effect of teratogens: dose, duration, genetic makeup of the fetus, and the mother's condition (Saddler, 1995; Scott, 1994).

Having a working knowledge of the possible effects of environmental variables on child development is fundamental to the effective provision of services to children and families living in impoverished conditions because many of these are preventable and the effects can be ameliorated by early intervention. The following is a review of some critical and preventable environmental risks that may help educators and mental health professionals better understand the challenges faced by children and families living in poverty.

NUTRITION

Good nutrition is the basis for typical growth and development (Farber, Yanni, & Batshaw, 1997) during prenatal and childhood periods. During pregnancy, proper nutrition or a balanced diet that includes the daily requirement of essential vitamins is critical to meet the needs of the fetus and the changes in maternal tissue that supports the fetus (Chomitz, Cheung, & Lieberman, 1995). Maternal malnutrition early in a pregnancy (specifically deficiency in fatty acids, vitamin E, and trace elements) can decrease the number of cells and synapse formation and may disrupt neuronal migration in the developing fetus (Aylward, 1997). Folic acid is another necessary vitamin in the diet of pregnant women at the time of conception and in the first 3 months of prenatal development (Liptak, 2002). Women of child-bearing age and/or those considering pregnancy are strongly advised to take folic acid because research has shown that it prevents brain and spine defects such as neural tube defects (e.g., spinal bifida, encephalocele, anencephaly; Liptak, 1997) and other birth defects (e.g., cleft palate; Shaw, Schaffer, Velie, Morland, &

Harris, 1995). Folic acid or folate is a water-soluble vitamin in the B-complex that is essential to tissue growth and cell function and is needed for the production of red cells and for the synthesis of DNA (Shils, Olson, Shike, & Ross, 1999). It is associated with tissue growth and cell function, maintains new cells, and is particularly critical during periods of rapid cell division and growth that occur during pregnancy and infancy (Shils et al., 1999). Deficiency of folic acid may be responsible for poor growth, certain types of anemia, and birth defects, which include congenital malformations of the spine, skull, and brain (Milunsky et al., 1989; Mulinare, Cordero, Erickson, & Berry, 1988; Shaw et al., 1995). Folic acid can be found in dark green leafy vegetables, citrus fruits and juices, beans and legumes, liver, pork, shellfish, wheat bran, and fortified cereals. These dietary sources of folic acid, however, may not be found in the typical diet of pregnant women and children living in disadvantaged conditions due to limited income and poor knowledge of proper nutrition.

Generally, concerns regarding nutrition during pregnancy fall into two categories: maternal weight gain and intake of nutrients (Chomitz et al., 1995). A number of variables are associated with maternal weight gain during pregnancy: dietary intake, prepregnancy weight and height, length of gestation, and size of the fetus (Chomitz et al., 1995). Research has documented that maternal weight gain during pregnancy is highly correlated with the birth weight of the infant because a great deal of the weight gain is from the fetus (Chomitz et al., 1995). The last 3 months of pregnancy are associated with weight and height gain for the fetus. During this period, the fetus grows from 2 pounds to about 7 pounds and increases in length from 14 to 19 inches (Graham & Morgan, 1997). It is in the last trimester that intrauterine growth retardation (i.e., inadequate growth of the fetus) typically occurs, and it is often the result of maternal undernutrition during pregnancy, maternal illness, or uteroplacental insufficiency (Farber et al., 1997). Therefore, adequate nutrition is essential throughout a woman's pregnancy for the development and delivery of a healthy infant. The average weight gain for mothers during pregnancy is 30 pounds. Teenage mothers, unmarried mothers, older mothers, and mothers with limited education, however, tend to have low or insufficient weight gain (less than 22 pounds) during pregnancy (Chomitz et al., 1995). Higher maternal weight gain is associated with healthier fetal weight gain (Chomitz et al., 1995).

LBW is one of the consequences of inadequate nutrition during pregnancy, and LBW infants are at a higher risk than infants of typical weight for health problems as newborns, developmental delays, and possible learning difficulties later in childhood (Blanc & Wardlaw, 1995; Shiono & Behrman, 1995). After an infant is born, good or balanced nutrition continues to be imperative to physical, cognitive, and social development. Early in an infant's life, malnutrition can interfere with brain development by causing decreased synthesis of myelin. Myelination occurs postnatally up to adulthood (Teeter Ellison & Semrud-Clikeman, 2007) and facilitates the rapid communication between neurons. The risks for developmental problems, such as cognitive deficiencies and difficulties with attentional and social responsiveness, exist (Teeter Ellison & Semrud-Clikeman, 2007).

Breast milk is the best and most complete source of nourishment for babies; it is rich in nutrients including the proper ratio of carbohydrates, proteins, fats, minerals, and vitamins (Farber et al., 1997), and breast milk changes in accordance with the infant's growing nutritional needs (Renfrew et al., 2005). Mothers are highly encouraged to breastfeed their infants except when there is a chance of passing infections or toxic substances from mother to infant. For example, mothers who are HIV positive, are actively using street drugs and/or alcohol, have actively untreated tuberculosis and varicella, or who are being treated for breast cancer with certain medications may not breastfeed their babies (Pugh, Milligan, Frick, Spatz, & Bronner, 2002). Breastfeeding has been associated with many positive benefits to the young child including protection from postneonatal death, chronic and acute childhood diseases, and obesity (Davis, 2001). Studies of the benefit of breastfeeding note that it protects young children against common diseases such as juvenile onset insulin-dependent diabetes mellitus (Sadauskaite-Kuehne et al., 2004), urinary track infections (Marild, Hansson, Jodal, Oden, & Svedberg, 2004), gastroenteritis and respiratory diseases (Kramer et al., 2001), and obesity in childhood (Fewtrell, 2004). Studies have also found positive outcomes and benefits for the mother such as lowered ovarian and endometrial cancers and premenopausal breast cancer (American Academy of Pediatrics, 1997; American College of Obstetricians and Gynecologists [ACOG], 2000). Breastfeeding plays a major role in public health because it helps prevent diseases in the child and mother (Renfrew et al., 2005). Breastfeeding is not only cost effective (e.g., less financial resources spent on baby formula and medical visits) but also, some studies have found a positive correlation between breastfeeding and cognitive development in children who are breastfed for extended periods of time (Renfrew et al., 2005). Although breastfeeding has been shown to ameliorate health risks typically faced by families of low income, breastfeeding rates are lower in these families (Pugh et al., 2002). The influence of societal norms, cultural norms, health problems, and lack of preparation and health services promotion and support of effective breastfeeding practices are some of the reasons cited as responsible for the lower breastfeeding rates in women of low income.

Nutritional deficiencies are not only of concern during prenatal development and infancy, but also can have significantly negative effects during childhood. It is important to understand two concepts relevant to nutrition and development: undernutrition and malnutrition. *Undernutrition* refers to the under consumption of energy (calories) or nutrients, and *malnutrition* is defined as severe undernutrition that can manifest itself as severe failure to thrive (Farber et al., 1997). The earlier the experience of undernutrition or malnutrition, the greater the effect on the child's neurological development (Farber et al., 1997). Signs of undernutrition include poor weight, reduced rate of growth and head circumference, and low muscle and fatty tissue. This condition is called failure to thrive and it applies to children who do not meet the standard for age in growth and development (Farber et al., 1997). Infantile malnutrition severely affects brain development by reducing brain cell count by as much as 20% (Brown & Pollit, 1996; Crosby, 1991). Although malnutrition and failure to thrive are more commonly seen in children living in poverty and children living in extreme conditions in developing countries, it can occur on many socioeconomic levels. For example, children who are offered a diet lacking in proper nutrients; children who have restricted food choices; children who are not given a diet that is developmentally appropriate; and children with severe disabilities whose intake of food might be erratic or low due to difficulty with ingestion, digestion, or side effects of medications (Farber et al., 1997) can become malnourished.

Malnutrition can lead to learning problems; may interfere with the full expression of genetic potential for cognitive development; and can affect motivation, concentration, social interaction, and time required for learning (Sattler, 2001). Research suggests, however, that if malnutrition is corrected early in infancy or childhood and if affected children are placed in educationally enriched environments, then the negative effects of malnutrition (e.g., low cognitive abilities) can be mitigated or reversed (Colombo, de la Parra, & Lopez, 1992). Adding or supplementing the diet of children who are malnourished or undernourished with vitamins and minerals has been found to raise affected children's nonverbal IQ scores by an average of 9 points, and supplementing the diet has a greater effect on younger children than on teenagers (Brody, 1992; Sattler, 2001).

LOW BIRTH WEIGHT

Low birth weight (LBW) is the term used to describe infants born too small, whereas *preterm* is the term used to described infants born too soon (Shiono & Behrman, 1995). LBW infants may be premature or small for gestational age (SGA). Premature infants are those born at or before the 36th week of gestation. Infants whose weight as newborns is below the 10th percentile for gestational age are referred to as SGA or as having intrauterine growth retardation (Bernbaum & Batshaw, 1997; Farber et al., 1997). Infants born SGA can be full term or premature. The SGA infant typically looks malnourished and wasted at birth and can experience growth retardation due to maternal illness or malnutrition (Bernbaum & Batshaw, 1997). Half the SGA infants are described as having normal length and growth potential, and the other half are described as short and small and as having a tendency toward poorer outcome (Bernbaum & Batshaw, 1997). Sixty percent have proportional growth impairment (i.e., the head and brain growth have been affected), and 40% have disproportionate growth impairment in which the brain has not been significantly affected (Farber et al., 1997). These infants have a higher incidence of developmental disabilities, learning disabilities, behavioral difficulties, and attention-deficit/hyperactivity disorder (ADHD; Bernbaum & Batshaw, 1997).

LBW infants are born weighing less than 5 pounds, 8 ounces (2,500 grams), and 1 out of every 13 infants born in the United States every year is LBW (Linden, Paroli, & Doron, 2000; Martin et al., 2002). The factors that increase the chances of having an infant with LBW are genetic and environmental, including mother's health and lifestyle (e.g., hypertension, abnormal uterus that may lead to premature birth, deficient nutrition, substance use, cigarette smoking) and socioeconomic factors (e.g., poverty, limited education; Linden et al., 2000). An infant's birth weight is a measure of the mother's health and the infant's probability for adequate growth, long-term health, and cognitive and social development (Blanc & Wardlaw, 2005). A high percentage of these children have problems in school and often receive special education services (Hack, Klein, & Taylor, 1995). Children who were born as LBW infants tend to score lower on intelligence tests and have lower language, academic, and visual-motor skills than their peers (Bernbaum & Batshaw, 1997). More significantly, the lower the birth weight, the higher the rates of neurodevelopmental disorders such as cerebral palsy, hydrocephalus, microcephaly, blindness, deafness, and seizures (Hack et al., 1995). Despite these risks, the great majority of LBW children have normal outcomes (Hack et al., 1995), especially when they receive regular medical care and early educational services. Bernbaum and Batshaw (1997) emphasized that the best treatment for LBW is prevention—identifying women at high risk for premature delivery, implementing measures to detect early preterm labor, offering education regarding risk factors, and providing comprehensive health care.

TEENAGE PREGNANCY

Teenage pregnancy rates steadily declined between 1991 and 2004. One million children, however, are born to teenage mothers each year in the United States (Hamilton, Ventura, Martin, & Sutton, 2005; National Center for Health Statistics [NCHS], 2003). Teenage pregnancy is associated with health risks for the child as well as for the mother. Teenage mothers may experience health problems that include premature labor, anemia, toxemia, pregnancy-induced hypertension, and placenta previa. Infants born to teenage mothers are at a higher risk for medical complications such as preterm birth, infant death, chronic respiratory difficulties, cerebral palsy, and mental retardation. These complications are often the result of LBW (Maynard, 1996). Statistics documenting all births in the United States indicate that the proportion of LBW infants born to teenagers is 21% higher than the proportion for mothers ages 20–24 (Martin et al., 2002). Being born LBW doubles the chances that a child will later be diagnosed as having dyslexia, hyperactivity, or another disability (Maynard, 1996). These infants frequently face health, social, and psychological difficulties (Luthar, 1999).

Other important facts that contribute to the increased chances of infants born to teenagers experiencing medical complications and health problems are that teenagers often eat an unbalanced diet and do not gain sufficient weight; may smoke, drink, or take drugs during their pregnancy; and are less likely to take prenatal vitamins and get early and regular prenatal care (Maynard, 1996; NCHS, 2003). All these behaviors increase the chances of premature birth and thereby its negative consequences on children's cognitive and social development.

LEAD POISONING

Lead poisoning has been of great concern in the United States for decades (Ellis & Kane, 2000) because it is one of the most common environmental health problems in this country (Kinder, 1993). Lead is a very toxic metal that is absorbed by the body mainly through the lungs and stomach and was used over the years in American homes (U.S. Environmental Protection Agency [EPA], 2006). Lead poisoning occurs as the consequence of persistent exposure to lead sources and the slow accumulation of the toxin in bone and tissue. Lead poisoning has been associated with blood levels of lead equal to or greater than $10\mu g$ per dL ($0.50\mu mol$ per L; Rosen, 1995). Four percent or greater of preschool-age children have blood lead levels above $10\mu g$ per dL (0.50 μmol per L; Ellis & Kane, 2000). Gradual and persistent exposure to lead can accumulate to toxic levels and potentially damage brain structures and internal organs. It is also associated with renal defects in vitamin D metabolism and microcytic anemia (Trachtenbarg, 1996; Wright, Shannon, Wright, & Hu, 1999).

High levels of lead are found more often in African American children, children from limited income families, and children who live in urban areas (Pirkle et al., 1994). Before 1978, lead was used to make many consumer products, including paint, gasoline, bathtubs, and plumbing. Lead-based paint and residential soil are the greatest sources of high-dose lead exposure for young children (Kinder, 1993). Houses and apartment buildings built before 1978 have lead-based paints on the walls; deteriorating old paint commonly peels, flakes, and leaves dust in the air. These paint chips are the source of lead exposure for preschoolers who touch, suck, and swallow paint chips and ingest and breathe leaded house dust. Lead can also be found on old furniture, glazed bathtubs, window sills, railings and banisters, porches and fences, doors, and in water due to pipes and corroded lead-based plumbing. Although lead is no longer used in gasoline, paint, and other consumer products in the United States, old buildings and houses may still have lead-based paints or plumbing, exposing children to this toxin. It is believed that lead in drinking water composes between 10% and 20% of total lead exposure in preschoolers (EPA, 2006). Moreover, infants whose diet is made up primarily of formula that is made with drinking water show a larger proportion of lead exposure—40%–60% (Ellis & Kane, 2000; Kinder, 1993). Lead can be found in food stored in foreign-made cans, ceramic containers, and even some foreign-made cold medicines (Farber et al., 1997), placing foreign-born immigrant children living in the United States at risk. Children living in inner-city neighborhoods or large cities are at significantly higher risks of being exposed to lead, but children living in the suburbs are at risk as well due to exposure to dust from renovating projects on old houses and lead-contaminated soil surrounding these homes (Kinder, 1993; Pirkle et al., 1994).

In 1995, 14 million children under the age of 8 lived in housing contaminated with high concentrations of lead from paint (Rosen, 1995). Unborn children, infants, and preschoolers are the most vulnerable to lead poisoning because their young brains are developing. They explore their environment by placing things in their mouths, and their bodies absorb lead more rapidly than adult bodies (National Institute of Environmental Health Sciences [NIEHS], 2005). The effects of lead poisoning can range from subtle biochemical changes to death. Children's mental and physical development can be stunted by high exposure to lead. Research evidence supports a modest link between lead poisoning and lower IQ scores (Bellinger & Dietrich, 1994). Other harmful effects include learning disabilities, ADHD, speech and language disabilities, kidney disease, heart disease, and death (Ellis & Kane, 2000). Blood levels below 70μg per dL (3.40 μmol per L) may lead to damage to the central nervous system, kidneys, and alteration in red blood cell metabolism as well as neurodevelopmental abnormalities that include memory impairments (e.g., spatial memory span, spatial working memory), behavioral disturbances, and impairments in fine and gross motor skills (Ellis & Kane, 2000; Rosen, 1995). School-related skills are greatly affected, specifically cognitive abilities essential to learning (e.g., executive functioning; reaction time; vocabulary; visual-motor integration; attention, social behavior, and motor skills; Chiodo, Jacobson, & Jacobson, 2004; Coscia, Douglas, Succop, & Dietrich, 2003). For women who are expecting, elevated lead blood levels may lead to premature birth, LBW, increases in blood pressure, physical weakness, poor coordination, and death (Kinder, 1993).

Lead poisoning is a pediatric health hazard that is highly preventable. Preventative measures have been implemented only since the early 1980s (Ellis & Kane, 2000), including mandated removal of lead from gasoline and paint by the EPA, family education about lead poisoning, interior dust abatement, high-efficiency particulate air vacuums, soil abatement and residential paint hazard remediation, and dust-control strategies (Ellis & Kane, 2000; Farber et al., 1997; Kinder, 1993). Once a child has been found to have elevated blood lead levels, measures such as chelation therapy (i.e., the use of chemical compounds to remove metals from the blood), pharmacologic treatments, and diet are considered as treatments to reduce the levels of lead in the blood (American Academy of Pediatrics, Committee on Drugs, 1995; Farber et al., 1997). A balanced diet that is high in calcium, zinc, and iron and low in fat has been found to prevent or minimize vulnerability to lead toxicity by decreasing absorption of lead in children (Farber et al., 1997). An empty stomach has been found to increase lead absorption (NIEHS, 2005). Other levels of intervention include parent education regarding sources of lead exposure and prevention strategies and yearly screening of lead blood levels in children between the ages of 6 months and 6 years because young children's blood lead levels tend to increase rapidly from 6 months to 12 months of age and to peak at 18 months to 24 months of age (EPA, 2006). As a direct consequence of research and various interventions and prevention measures taken by many governmental agencies, lead poisoning has decreased by approximately 86% since the late 1970s (NIEHS, 2005). There are alarming demographic trends, however, indicating that lead poisoning continues to occur primarily among children from low-income and urban households who reside in older housing (Centers for Disease Control [CDC], 2000; Ripple & Zigler, 2003). Given these facts, the CDC (1997) has recommended universal screening for all children living in high-risk areas (Ripple & Zigler, 2003).

ASTHMA

Asthma is one of the most significant and common chronic diseases in children. It is the primary cause for school absenteeism and is responsible for more than 10 million days lost from school annually (Lurie, Bauer, & Brady, 2001; Smith, Hatcher-Ross, Wertheimer, & Kahn, 2005; Taylor & Newacheck, 1992). Urban settings have a disproportionately higher prevalence of asthma, as well as hospitalization rates and morbidity, due to asthma than nonurban settings (Lurie et al., 2001; Warman, Silver, & Stein, 2001). Asthma is a chronic disease that affects the airways or tubes that carry air in and out of the lungs. In some people, the insides of the airways are very sensitive and react to allergens. When this happens, the airways become narrower, causing less air to flow through them (National Institutes of Health [NIH], 2006). This brings about symptoms such as wheezing, coughing, chest tightness, and difficulty breathing. A severe attack includes symptoms such as muscles tightening around airways, increased irritation and inflammation of the airways, and cells in airways producing extra mucus (NIH, 2006). These symptoms can lead to the reduction of oxygen reaching vital organs, producing death (NIH, 2006). Asthma cannot be cured but it can be controlled with medication and managed through education about environmental triggers and the proper use of medications (Lurie et al., 2001).

Asthma affects more than 3 million children and their families in the United States, and a disproportionately high number of African American and Hispanic children are vulnerable (Malveaux & Fletcher-Vincent, 1995). Asthma mortality for African American and Hispanic children is five to seven times higher than that of Caucasian children. Studies suggest that the differences in mortality and morbidity are closely linked to socioeconomic levels and that poverty, not race/ethnicity, is a more significant risk factor (Malveaux & Fletcher-Vincent, 1995). Many factors have been identified as contributors to this problem: inadequate preventive medical care for asthma management, limited awareness of asthma management skills among children and families, psychosocial factors, and persistent environmental exposure to allergens (Lurie et al., 2001; Malveaux & Fletcher-Vincent, 1995; Tartasky, 1999). Regarding the development of asthma, however, there is mounting evidence that inner-city children may be exposed to a greater number and concentration of allergens and irritants that create increased sensitivity. A great number of children in urban areas live in substandard housing where they are exposed to allergens and pollutants such as tobacco smoke, molds or indoor fungi, dust mites, and vermin and cockroach waste. Studies have shown that exposure to elevated levels of dust mites during infancy or in the first year of life led to an increased likelihood of sensitization to these allergens and the development of asthma (Malveaux & Fletcher-Vincent, 1995). Moreover, allergens associated with dust mites and cockroaches are believed to be relevant in the onset and worsening of asthma symptoms (Malveaux & Fletcher-Vincent, 1995). Studies have yielded results suggesting that cockroach allergy in asthmatic children of limited income is common, ranging from 52% to 78% (Fletcher-Vincent, Reece, & Malveaux, 1994). Sixty percent of children ages 2–10 living in the metropolitan Washington, D.C., area were found to be sensitive to cockroach allergens, and 72% were allergic to dust mites (Malveaux & Fletcher-Vincent, 1995; Ramsey, Celedon, Sredl, Weiss, & Cloutier, 2005). In addition to these environmental variables, intrinsic factors such as underdeveloped or abnormal lungs due to premature birth and family history of asthma also contribute to the development of asthma. A study of African Americans living in urban areas revealed that maternal history of asthma, lack of prenatal care, smoking during pregnancy, history of bronchiolitis, positive pressure ventilation at birth, and low maternal weight gain were strong predictors of asthma (Oliveti, Keresmar, & Redline, 1996).

The proper management of asthma in families with low incomes can be challenging for a number of reasons: limited access to health care and inadequate treatment of the condition, chronic exposure to allergens and irritants, limited education regarding ways of reducing exposure to allergens, underuse of prescribed medication due to limited income, and reliance on an emergency room as opposed to preventive measures (Malveaux & Fletcher-Vincent, 1995; Tartasky, 1999). Psychosocial as well as socioeconomic factors are critical to controlling asthma (Tartasky, 1999). Successful asthma management rests on avoiding triggers, adjusting management of symptoms, adhering to treatment, obtaining regular medical follow up, and being educated and aware of preventive care (Tartasky, 1999; Warman et al., 2001). Moreover, research findings suggest that home-based environmental intervention programs are successful and cost-effective measures for improving the health of inner-city children who have moderate to severe asthma (Kattan et al., 2005). These measures included allergen-impermeable covers for children's mattresses, box springs, and pillows; air purifiers with high-efficiency particulate air (HEPA) filters; vacuum cleaners equipped with HEPA filters; and professional pest control (Kattan et al., 2005).

DRUGS AND ALCOHOL

Another set of powerful environmental risks to children's cognitive and emotional development is exposure to drugs and alcohol while in the womb. Wheeler (1993) reported that each year approximately 11% of newborns are born to mothers who use illicit drugs, and another 25%–30% are born to mothers who use alcohol and nicotine. Alcohol and drug abuse can be found in all races and socioeconomic brackets, and the prevalence is not decreasing (Batshaw & Conlon, 1997). Maternal drug abuse is among the highest in 18–25-year-olds, African Americans, and inner-city residents (Batshaw & Conlon, 1997).

A number of drugs can alter the development and function of the central nervous system in fetuses and infants (Aylward, 1997). There have been many studies that have investigated the impact of different drugs on infants' and children's development. Three quarters of individuals involved in substance abuse use more than one drug (e.g., alcohol, cocaine, nicotine), however, and this contaminates or confounds the results of these studies (Aylward, 1997; Batshaw & Conlon, 1997; Center on Addiction and Substance Abuse, 1996). Other methodological concerns include limited control of confounding variables (e.g., maternal nutrition, poor prenatal care, sexually transmitted disease), small numbers of subjects, and weak outcome measures. Nevertheless, some general knowledge has emerged from these studies (Aylward, 1997).

The CDC (1995) reported that 20% of women consumed alcohol after knowing they were pregnant. Maternal ingestion of alcohol during pregnancy has been found to be linked to an array of physical and neurodevelopmental effects on the fetus (Astley & Clarren, 1996). These physical and neurological impairments have been termed *fetal alcohol syndrome* (FAS), and a diagnosis is made when an identified pattern of malformation is recognized (i.e., facial abnormalities, somatic growth failure, organic brain dysfunction; Aylward, 1997). This pattern of malformation also includes craniofacial malformations (e.g., unusually wide spacing between eyes, flat midface, small jaw, short eye slit), cardiac anomalies, hemangiomas, genitor-urinary malformations, middle ear malformation, minor joint and limb deformities, and brain abnormalities (e.g., small brains, abnormal gyri or abnormal cluster of cells, misaligned cells in cortex; Batshaw & Conlon, 1997; Kolb & Whishaw, 2003). Alcohol has a significant effect on the development of nerve cells on multiple levels such as cell proliferation, migration, synaptogenesis, myelination, and neurotransmitter function (Aylward, 1997). There are also cognitive impairments, behavioral disorders (e.g., poor judgment and social skills, difficulty with impulse control, oppositional defiant behaviors, social withdrawal, ADHD, anxiety, mood liability), and learning disabilities (Aylward, 1997; Batshaw & Conlon, 1997). These children typically have significant learning and social problems in school.

The CDC studies (2006) reported prevalence rates of FAS ranging from 0.2 to 1.5 per 1,000 live births in different areas of the United States based on patterns of alcohol consumption (Kolb & Whishaw, 2003). FAS is manifested in degrees. Children with FAS range from those with hardly any obvious physical and psychological symptoms, to typical appearance and mild cognitive dysfunctions and behavioral disorders, to full-blown FAS (Kolb & Whishaw, 2003). The degree of severity depends on when during pregnancy alcohol was consumed, how much alcohol was ingested, and how frequently alcohol was consumed during the pregnancy. Drinking during the first trimester of a pregnancy is associated with the worst outcome. Other factors that affect outcome and magnify the teratogenic effect of alcohol are maternal nutrition status, polydrug use, and binge drinking (Batshaw & Conlon, 1997; Kolb & Whishaw, 2003). Women that are most at risk of giving birth to infants with FAS are those living in poverty with limited education and those with drinking problems before the pregnancy, poor prenatal care, and lack of awareness regarding the effect of alcohol on the developing fetus (Kolb & Whishaw, 2003). Children may also be diagnosed with *fetal alcohol effects* (FAE); these children are born with less overt and noticeable physical defects, but they tend to exhibit significant behavioral and social characteristics such as those identified with FAS.

The consequence of using illicit drugs during pregnancy can be detrimental to the growing fetus and later to the developing child. Substance abuse can be found in different socioeconomic strata, but some substances such as cocaine, nicotine, and heroin are more often used by women with low incomes, whereas marijuana use is more prevalent in middle-class women (Batshaw & Conlon, 1997). Cigarette smoking during pregnancy is observed in one third of women living in poverty, whereas drugs such as crystal methamphetamine are more prevalent in Caucasian individuals living in urban and rural areas, even though "crystal meth" use is becoming more popular in diverse populations (National Institute on Drug Abuse [NIDA], 2002).

Women who smoke during pregnancy exhibit adverse effects such as elevated risk of miscarriage and of having LBW infants. According to Wheeler (1993), intrauterine growth retardation occurs from the accumulation of carbon monoxide from the tar in cigarettes and decreased placental blood flow of nutrients as a consequence of the vasoconstrictor action of nicotine. At birth, infants may show subtle neurobehavioral abnormalities as a direct result of recent maternal nicotine intake and may represent a mild withdrawal (Batshaw & Conlon, 1997). Research focusing on the behavior patterns of toddlers prenatally exposed to cigarettes found that these toddlers had higher levels of behavior problems and exhibited negative and disruptive social behaviors (e.g., aggression, refusal to follow directions; Brooks, Brooks, & Whiteman, 2000; Cornelius, Leech, Goldschmidt, & Day, 2000; Wakschlag, Pickett, Kasza, & Loeber, 2006).

In 1992, NIDA conducted a national survey of drug use in pregnant women in the United States. Data collected from 4 million women who delivered infants in 1992 were published in 1995 (see Table 3.1). The information from most studies examining women's use of drugs and alcohol relies heavily on self-reported

Table 3.1.   Drug use during pregnancy

Substance	Percentage of pregnant women	Number of pregnant women
Marijuana	2.9	118,700
Cocaine	1.1	45,100
Crack	0.9	34,800
Methamphetamine	0.1	4,500
Heroin	0.1	3,600
Alcohol	18.8	756,900
Cigarettes	20.4	819,700
Any illicit drug	5.5	220,900

Source: National Institute on Drug Abuse. (1995, January/February). *Drug use during pregnancy. NIDA Notes, Vol. 10*(1).

data, subjecting this data to reporting and recall bias (Office of Special Education Programs, 2000); the information gained from these studies, however, has provided researchers and practitioners with a wealth of knowledge about alcohol and drug use during pregnancy (OSEP, 2000).

It has been challenging for researchers to discriminate the long-term effects of specific drugs on fetal development because substance abusers typically use more than one substance. Moreover, there are also confounding effects from prenatal, genetic, and environmental factors (Aylward, 1997; Batshaw & Conlon, 1997). The use of illicit drugs such as cocaine, heroin, and crystal meth during pregnancy, however, are associated with fetal injury such as decreased blood and oxygen reaching the fetus, premature births, LBW, abnormal sensorineural activity, and increased central nervous system structural lesion (Aylward, 1997). Infants who were exposed to drugs while in the womb may exhibit neonatal withdrawal symptoms and display behaviors such as increased irritability, altered sleep patterns, poor state modulation, reduced self-quieting, attention and behavior difficulties (Aylward, 1997; Batshaw & Conlon, 1997). In school-age children, behaviors such as attentional difficulties, learning disabilities, social and behavioral problems, and language delays may be observed (Wheeler, 1993).

HIV/AIDS

Women who use illicit drugs and share needles are at an increased risk of becoming infected with HIV and viral hepatitis (Rutstein, Conlon, & Batshaw, 1997). Although HIV infection occurs in all socioeconomic levels in the United States, there is an increased rate of infection in minority women with low incomes in which the primary mode of transmission is sharing infected syringes or being with infected sexual partners (CDC, 2006). What places these women at higher risk is their lack of awareness of their male partner's possible risks for HIV infection—unprotected sex with multiple partners, bisexuality, or injection drug use (CDC, 2006). HIV/AIDS is increasingly becoming a disease of poor inner-city dwellers due to the rate of infection in large urban centers (Rutstein et al., 1997). Seventy-five percent or more cases are reported by African American and Hispanic women, and 50% or greater of intravenous drug users are infected (Rogers, Caldwell, Gwinn, & Simonds (1994; Simonds & Rogers, 1992). Approximately 50% of new HIV/AIDS cases are African Americans (CDC, 2006).

The CDC (2006) reported that 73% of infants perinatally infected with HIV were born to African American women. More than 90% of children diagnosed with HIV infection in 1997 had acquired the virus vertically (i.e., infection passed perinatally from mother to child), during gestation (virus crossing the placenta), birth (exposure to infected genital fluids), or postnatally (breastfeeding; Rutstein et al., 1997). Not all infants born to infected mothers are infected, however. There are several factors that play a role in why some infants are born infected and others are not. Women with symptomatic HIV infection, an AIDS diagnosis, low CD4 count, untreated sexually transmitted disease, and illicit drug use during pregnancy have a greater risk of transmitting HIV to their infants (Rodriguez et al., 1996; Rutstein et al., 1997). Thus far, the treatment that has been shown to prevent or reduce the risk of HIV infection in unborn children is administering AZT (zidovudine) during pregnancy to the mother and to the newborn for 6 weeks after birth (Aylward, 1997; Rodriguez et al., 1996; Rutstein et al., 1997).

Today, many children who acquired the infection from their mothers are now living into their teens and longer. The disease seems to take one of two pathways, however. One quarter of these children will exhibit severe symptoms associated with the infection by their first birthday (developmental delays, slowed growth, or opportunistic infections) and they may die by their third or fifth birthday (Abrams et al., 1995). Another group typically remains asymptomatic in the first 5 years of life but continues to be sensitive to opportunistic infections, and if they become ill, infections have the potential to reduce their median life span of more than 9 years (Barnhart et al., 1996) to less than 12–18 months (Sanders-Laufer, DeBruin, & Edelson, 1991). Research has shown that there are neurodevelopmental effects of HIV infection. In the first 2 years of life, the development of children who are infected can be slower than children who are not infected (this includes subtle cognitive impairments), even when controlling for poverty, maternal drug use, and illness (Fowler, 1994). In addition, there appears to be a higher incidence of ADHD and learning disabilities in children who are of school age (Grubman et al., 1995). Social-emotional factors are prominent and further complicate the social and emotional adjustment of children and families living with HIV. For example, repeated or long-term hospitalizations, parental illness or death, substandard housing, limited income, substance abuse, neglect, foster care placements, and social stigma of the illness present stressful life situations that add to the effect of HIV infection (Rutstein et al., 1997). Children and families challenged by HIV infection must receive frequent medical care and monitoring. Young children also need regular comprehensive psycho-educational or neurodevelopmental evaluations to monitor their development (Butler et al., 1991). Families require extensive guidance and support from social agencies that provide education, connections to resources, service coordination, employment resources, counseling, and crisis intervention (Rutstein et al., 1997).

SOCIAL AND PSYCHOLOGICAL FACTORS

The home environment has long been identified as playing a critical role in the psychosocial development of children. Sattler (2001) pointed out that studies focusing on the effect of psychosocial factors on family background and home environmental variables significantly correlated with children's IQ scores, with many of the correlations hovering above $r = .50$. Psychosocial factors such as intellectual environment of the home, educational stimulation in the home, type of disciplinary strategies employed, and the presence of family risk factors (e.g., limited maternal education, parental unemployment, father's absence from home, rigid maternal behavior) affect the development of children's cognitive and emotional intelligence (Sattler, 2001).

Environmental stressors have a decided effect on the cognitive, emotional, and societal aspects of children's lives (Oberg, Bertrand, & Muret-Wagstaff, 1999). The source of these stressors is in the daily struggle to meet basic needs. The consequence of economic hardship and limited education is typically substandard housing, socially decaying neighborhoods, poor health and mental care, unemployment, inadequate schools and deficient instruction, and exposure to violence in the community.

Luthar (1999) noted that the well-being of every child is intricately tied in with the functioning of his or her parents, and when socioeconomic resources are unremittingly scant, the challenges of daily living can substantially erode a parent's mental health. The stress of trying to make a living on limited resources affects the psychological adjustment of parents and their children. Family stress that occurs from exposure to these stressors and the accumulation of multiple risk factors in disadvantaged environments may be harmful to children's social-emotional functioning (Dearing et al., 2006). A number of stressors directly link to limited economic resources that specifically affect the psychological adjustment of children and families living in impoverished conditions.

Parents' Mental Health Status

There is evidence that rates of psychopathology and different types of mental disorders, including substance abuse, are greater among individuals with lower incomes than among individuals with higher incomes (Wadsworth & Achenbach, 2005). Moreover, parental psychopathology has been associated with children's behavioral problems. Maternal depression is a risk factor for disruptive behavior in children (Goodman & Gotlib, 1999) because it adversely affects a number of parenting behaviors (Luthar, 1999). Literature reviews on maternal depression documented higher levels of depressive symptoms during pregnancy among mothers who were poor and as their children grew (Alpern & Lyons-Ruth, 1993; Hay, Angold, Pawlby, Harold, & Sharp, 2003). Other findings indicated that depressed mothers are inclined to be less attentive to their children, vacillate between disengagement and intrusiveness, and demonstrate lower reciprocity and synchronicity; are likely to show more negative effects and make more negative attributions regarding their children; and are at a higher risk for hostile, coercive parenting strategies and child maltreatment (Dearing et al., 2006; Dumas & Wekerle, 1995; Fantuzzo, McWayne, & Bulotsky, 2003; Hay et al., 2003; Luthar, 1997). Negative parent–child interaction can have long-term implications for children's ability to regulate their emotions (Hay et al., 2003). Infants of mothers who were depressed postpartum tend to have attentional problems, cognitive difficulties, and uncommon brain function (Dawson, Frey, Pangiotides, Osterling, & Hessl, 1997; Galler, Harrison, Ramsey, Forde, & Butler, 2000; Hay et al., 2003). Moreover, the problems exhibited by these children of depressed mothers continue as they grow (Hay et al., 2001). Developmental outcomes linked to persistently higher social-emotional difficulties during childhood may extend into adulthood, increasing the chances of educational failure, unemployment, psychiatric disorder, suicide attempts, and criminality issues (Cohen, 1998; Dearing et al., 2006; Kazdin, 1997).

Alcohol and substance abuse are other sources of parental psychopathology that can exert a negative effect on children beyond that associated with poverty. Parents who abuse substances, whether it is alcohol or illicit substances, have a significantly higher tendency to utilize ineffective parenting strategies and physically abuse and neglect their children and are less responsive and supportive of their children (Luthar, 1997). Mothers who are substance abusers respond less to their infant's cues and make fewer attempts to encourage communications from their infants. In addition, they tend to employ authoritarian disciplinary strategies that reinforce negative attention-seeking behaviors in their older children (de Cubas & Field, 1993; Luthar, 1997; Mayes & Bornstein, 1997).

Fathers who are substance abusers tend to be less able or motivated to provide supervision and establish the structure children require, especially adolescents (Tarter et al., 2002). Children who grow up in an environment where parents are dependent on illegal substances are more likely to have difficult temperaments, externalizing disorders, and oppositional defiant disorder and to show more aggressivity (Tarter et al., 2002). Developmental contexts that interfere with children's self-regulatory efforts, that negatively prejudice children's social information processing, or that consist of role models of antisocial behavior may increase the chances of children's developing externalizing difficulties (Dodge & Pettit, 2004; Evans, 2004).

Teenage Mothers

Teenage mothers are overrepresented in families living in poverty, and their youth and limited education can present a significant risk factor in raising children. Specifically, teenage mothers' immature parenting attitudes and behaviors pose the greatest risk because they are more likely to be insensitive and impatient with their infants' needs; do not understand the reality of being a parent; and provide less responsive, stimulating affective environments for their children (Brooks-Gunn & Chase-Lansdale, 1995; Kelley, Power, & Wimbush, 1992; Luthar, 1997). Research findings consistently report that children born to teenage mothers demonstrate negative outcomes and are more susceptible to developing problems in their middle-school years such as behavioral problems in school, truancy, delinquency, hyperactivity, anger and hostility, and substance abuse (Apfel & Seitz, 1997; Brooks-Gunn & Furstenberg, 1987; Hetherington, 1997; Luthar, 1997).

Neighborhood Context

Neighborhood context is beginning to receive attention as a factor in mental health. Where people live influences many facets of their lives, including daily stress level, personal safety (Cutrona et al., 2005), municipal agency involvement, quality of schools, maintenance of housing structures, community recreational programs, and availability of shops and stores. Neighborhoods with concentrated poverty are indexed by variables such as high rates of dwellers living below the poverty line, percentage of single-parent households, and unemployment (Cutrona et al., 2005). These neighborhoods often offer ineffective instruction in school and few high-quality child care centers, inadequate housing, few opportunities for employment and healthy recreational activities, few role models in the community, limited involvement from municipal agencies (e.g., police, street cleaning, public works) and high refusal services such as taxi services, credit applications, and food delivery (Cutrona et al., 2005; Sooman & Macintyre, 1995). Yet, they have more liquor stores, fast-food establishments, and predatory money lending companies.

Neighborhood economic disadvantage and social disorder are two significant dimensions that affect the well-being of residents (Massey & Shibuya, 1995). Cutrona et al. (2005) defined *social disorder* as the breakdown of processes and structures that maintain order, civility, and safety. Signs of social disorder include unsupervised and delinquent youth, public intoxication, drug use and sales, and poorly maintained and vacant buildings. Social disorder signals to the residents in these neighborhoods that public officials and decision makers are not interested in their well-being, which promotes feelings of helplessness, alienation, and abandonment in residents (Cutrona et al., 2005; Taylor & Hale, 1986). Studies investigating the effects of living in neighborhoods with a high concentration of poverty yielded results suggesting that neighborhood-level economic disadvantage was significantly associated with depressive symptoms in a representative community sample of Illinois residents (Ross, 2000). Women who live in neighborhoods marked by poverty and crime are more likely to react to negative life experiences by becoming depressed than women living in more affluent neighborhoods (Cutrona et al., 2005).

Living in poor neighborhoods also has a negative influence on children on a social, emotional, and educational level. Unfortunately, in this country, parent income level and neighborhood determine the quality of education of their children. Schools that predominantly serve students from families with low incomes, in urban and suburban areas, tend to spend less per capita for materials, supplies, and books (Hanson & Lynch, 2004). Teachers working in schools with high populations of children living in poverty tend to have low academic expectations of their pupils, employ strategies that undermine pupils' self-confidence and motivation to learn (e.g., indiscriminate praise and sympathy for failure; Comer, 1988), are poorly paid and have limited training in working with poor children (Luthar, 1997), and are frustrated by the lack of resources in the schools and often burdened by the academic and social-emotional needs of the children. The disparity in the quality of instruction, school materials available, and condition of the school building can exercise a negative influence on children's achievement. Bouchard and Segal (1985) reported that between 2% and 10% of the variance in cognitive functioning may be associated with school quality.

Parental involvement in school also plays a role in children's education. Often, parents living in poverty may not be able to attend meetings and participate in their children's education due to job schedules, inadequate education and academic skills to help children at home, and limited English proficiency. In addition, as a consequence of inadequate housing and low income, parents move frequently, causing children to fall behind academically. Not surprisingly, these children's academic achievement tends to be lower than their middle-class counterparts, and their high school completion rate is also low, negatively affecting life outcomes (Brooks-Gunn & Duncan, 1997; Hanson & Lynch, 2004).

Children living in inner-city neighborhoods are exposed to alarmingly high rates of violence as witnesses and victims (Luthar, 1997, 1999); for example, an estimated 3 to 10 million children witness domestic violence each year (Straus, 1992), and in 2001, Child Protective Services agencies reported that 1.1 million children were victims of confirmed abuse or neglect (National Center for Children Exposed to Violence, 2003). When exposed to community violence, especially when personally victimized, these children exhibit symptoms of trauma in various ways across the developmental spectrum (Fitzpatrick, 1993; Garbarino, 1995). Children exhibit symptoms from sleep disturbances and depression to full post-traumatic stress disorder (Garbarino, 1995). Another consequence of frequent exposure to violence is that children begin to develop a predilection for aggression and to identify with aggressive adults in their communities (e.g., family members, gang members; Coie & Jacobs, 1993; Garbarino, 1995; Luthar, 1997).

Homelessness

Research since the mid-1990s has documented the effect of homelessness as an environmental risk that engulfs, increases, and intensifies other risk factors, even when compared with children who are housed and live in abject poverty (Oberg et al., 1999). The fastest growing segments of the homeless population are families. Close to 40% of the homeless in the United States are families, and this percentage is higher in some cities (77% in Trenton, New Jersey, and 68% in Philadelphia; Stearn & Nuñez, 1999). Families more susceptible to homelessness are those headed by single mothers who are poor and unskilled, young, with young children, and at low-income levels (Masten, 1992). The ethnic makeup of these families tends to reflect poor families in that region (Masten, 1992). The reasons for homelessness are varied but all are income related. Families fall into crisis because of loss of employment and not enough money saved to weather the loss of income. Others experience relationship conflicts resulting in their leaving the residence. Or they were evicted due to rent delinquency or the building being condemned, and they had no money for the up-front cost of another apartment. Or they could move from one place to another seeking employment (Masten, 1992).

The effect of homelessness on children is great and far-reaching. Most children are homeless for an average of 10 months at a time or even an entire year, and many children have been homeless more than once (Stearn & Nuñez, 1999). Homeless families move three or more times a year, and this high mobility coupled with frequent school transfers and excessive absences affects children's educational growth and social relations. Children with multiple relocations are not in one place long enough to truly master what is taught, become part of a class, or form social relationships with peers. A large percentage of homeless children receive special education services. Preschool children are three times more likely to be identified with developmental delays, and school-age children have a higher chance of showing below grade-level skills in reading, dropping out of school, developing a negative self-image, and repeating a grade (Oberg et al., 1999; Stearn & Nuñez, 1999). Homeless children tend to have more health problems and to be underinsured, underimmunized, and undernourished. Health problems in homeless children include asthma (20%), LBW (17%), and mental health issues (47%; e.g., depression, anxiety, stress, aggression; Stearn & Nuñez, 1999). A body of research documents an increased prevalence of acute illness (e.g., asthma) and chronic disease (e.g., respiratory and stomach problems, skin conditions) that are precipitated by unmet health care needs (Knyder-Coe, 1991). Homeless status is a powerful marker of high cumulative vulnerability and risk for child development (Masten, 1992). It has a deleterious effect on children's physical, cognitive, emotional, and behavioral developments.

Support Network

A support network can promote positive outcomes and mitigate the adverse effects of poverty. Support from extended family members, meaningful friendships, or affiliation with an organization (e.g., church, community agencies) can decrease the stress level of parents and children. Social support can envelop an individual in relationships that offer love, care, and assistance such as financial support, babysitting, and emotional support (Aponte & Barnes, 1995; Gopaul-McNicol & Thomas-Presswood, 1998). Having a meaningful support system buffers individuals against the alienating effects of poverty and psychopathology. McLoyd and Wilson (1994) reported that inner-city mothers with high levels of perceived support were more likely to exhibit relatively few depressive symptoms, experienced less negativity regarding their parental role, and used less punishment. Being affiliated with a church and believing in a higher being can promote positive adjustment by offering a support network of others in the church community, by exposing children to healthy role models, by emphasizing positive self-worth and a divine purpose despite life circumstances, and by encouraging the use of prayer as a coping strategy as opposed to maladaptive coping strategies such as alcohol and drug use to deal with life stressors (Brody, Stoneman, & Flor, 1996; Luthar, 1997).

Immigration

According to Greenberg and Rahmanou (2004), approximately 20% of children living in the United States (17 million) have at least one foreign-born parent. These children have a greater chance of living in low-income homes than children born to parents who were born in the United States (Greenberg & Rahmanou, 2004). Children born to immigrant parents make up more than 26% of all children living in low-income homes in the United States and are less likely than other children to receive the benefit of governmental programs designed to help families living in poverty, often due to their immigration status (Greenberg & Rahmanou, 2004).

Given the history of immigration in the United States, many studies have focused on investigating the link between migration and mental health. The stress involved in migration is associated with the multiple levels of adjustment necessary to be integrated into mainstream America, and socioeconomic level also plays an important role (Foster, 2001; Gopaul-McNicol & Thomas-Presswood, 1998). Migration typically brings about disruption in families. In the Caribbean as well as in Central and South America, mothers from low-income backgrounds usually migrate first to seek work as nannies, housekeepers, and nurses' aides (Pottinger,

2005). These mothers go overseas to earn income to help support their families in their native countries; some work for short periods to improve the financial condition of their families (6 months at a time), or they may stay for several years, leaving their children with relatives in their native country (Gopaul-McNicol & Thomas-Presswood, 1998; Pottinger, 2005). The goal of those who migrate for several years is to reunite the family in the United States, but the financial cost of such plans and the immigration laws in the United States slow this process and extend family separations for more than 5 years (Pottinger, 2005). Although leaving children in the care of extended family members is a common and acceptable practice in these countries, when relatives fail to provide proper supervision and protection of these children, the children can become victims of sexual abuse, drug use, and even prostitution (Crawford-Brown & Rattray, 2001; Leo-Rhynie, 1993; Pottinger, 2005). Moreover, the protracted separation from parents creates its own problems including feelings of grief and loss, anger and resentment, and abandonment in the children (Crawford-Brown & Rattray, 2001). Upon reunification with their parents in the United States, these feelings and experiences compromise their ability to adjust to their new lives, and the families often report children as exhibiting "acting out" and rebellious behaviors (Gopaul-McNicol & Thomas-Presswood, 1998). Foster (2001) identified four migration states in which there is potential for traumatogenic experiences that are associated with psychological distress:

1. Premigration trauma: Events experienced immediately prior to migration that precipitated the relocation

2. Traumatic events experienced during the journey to the new country

3. Continuing traumatogenic experiences during asylum-seeking and resettlement (encountering hostility in the host country)

4. Substandard living conditions in the host country due to unemployment, inadequate support, and prejudice and discrimination

Consistent with research findings investigating low income and mental health, research concentrating on migration and psychopathology have yielded results suggesting that individual immigrants of low socioeconomic status are more heavily burdened by stressors, mostly associated with being poor, added to all the necessary adjustments to meet the expectations of the new culture (Aponte & Barnes, 1995; Foster, 2001). These adjustments include learning a new language and understanding values and beliefs of the majority culture, finding employment, and forming new social networks. Major barriers exist for immigrants, especially for those who are of low economic means. For example, prejudice and discriminatory practices, limited educational background and job skills, immigration status (documented or undocumented), low-paying employment opportunities, and limited personal resources and social networks are typical barriers encountered by poor immigrants entering the United States (Gopaul-McNicol & Thomas-Presswood, 1998). Although there is great diversity in socioeconomic status among immigrant groups, high percentages of Hispanic and recent immigrants from Vietnam, Thailand, and Cambodia live in poverty (Aponte & Barnes, 1995) due to limited English proficiency, poor literacy and occupational skills, and low-paying jobs. These conditions limit choices in areas such as housing, job prospects, and educational opportunities for their children. Most schools are ill-equipped to address the educational needs of immigrant children (e.g., bilingual education, trained staff, remedial services, early intervention strategies, parent education), which leads to increased school dropout rates (Gopaul-McNicol & Thomas-Presswood, 1998).

EDUCATIONAL IMPLICATIONS

The educational implications of living in persistent and abject poverty are unquestioned. There is strong evidence that there is a relationship between poverty and achievement (Fujiura & Yamaki, 2000). Poverty creates an accumulation of risk factors that complicates its hardship (Hanson & Lynch, 2004). The effect of living in poverty begins in the womb and has the potential of reaching out and affecting later life functioning. Its effect on educational performance takes many forms: 1) negative environmental influences can change brain structure at the prenatal level, 2) inadequate nutrition can affect cognitive development, 3) parent education can influence children's school performance, 4) parent mental health can affect children's social adjustment, 5) inconsistent health care monitoring and inadequate access to mental health services can affect overall health conditions and school performance, and 6) inability to sustain involvement in services can affect overall quality of life. School-related factors that affect school achievement include 1) low-quality educational instruction, 2) limited teacher experience, 3) inadequate teacher preparation, 4) large class size, 5) limited access to technology, and 6) school safety (Barton, 2004). Community factors that affect students' achievement are 1) negative social and community influences (e.g., crime, peer pressure, inadequate role models) and 2) concerns about safety. Poor academic achievement and high dropout rates characterize many schools predominantly populated by children from low-income households (Cartledge & Lo, 2006; Tucker & Herman, 2002). Equally high rates of children from low-income households are represented in special education programs (Cartledge & Lo, 2006) and are at greater risk of dropping out of school. Research findings consistently show that children of all ages living in poverty tend to exhibit more educational impairments (e.g., grade retention, learning disabilities, school dropout, suspension or expulsion) than children who have more economic advantages (Brooks-Gunn & Duncan, 1997).

Long-term exposure to stressors during early childhood threatens children's psychological adjustment and achievement (Fantuzzo et al., 2003). Weiss and Fantuzzo (2001) conducted a population-based study to investigate the effect of multiple health and caregiving risk factors on the school adjustment of first-grade students. The investigators integrated relevant databases in a large urban center that included linking records of major municipal agencies for an entire cohort of first graders (19,000 students) from the city's public school district (Weiss &

Fantuzzo, 2001). The purpose of the study was to understand the effect of early childhood risk factors, including child maltreatment, on children's first-grade academic performance, school behavior, grade retention, and attendance. Results of the study indicated that poverty, households headed by a single mother, and child maltreatment were among the major risk factors for academic and behavioral difficulties in the first grade, as well as for attendance issues and retention. LBW was a risk factor for academic difficulties and retention, teen pregnancy was a risk factor for attendance issues, and lead poisoning was a risk factor for behavioral difficulties in school in the first grade (please see Weiss & Fantuzzo, 2001, for more details). There is mounting evidence that in the absence of effective early interventions, children who exhibit learning difficulties early are likely to have those problems later. Studies of reading difficulties have revealed that if a child was a poor reader at the end of the first grade, then the probability that a child would remain a poor reader at the end of the fourth grade was .88 (Juel, 1988; Torgesen, 2004). Therefore, providing high-quality instruction early and throughout children's school experiences is key to curtailing the effect of poverty on achievement.

Systemic Bias in the Schools

Educators have long been highlighting the need to reduce the overrepresentation and underrepresentation of African American children in special education categories (Artiles & Trent, 1994; Gopaul-McNicol & Thomas-Presswood, 1998; Losen & Orfield, 2002). Studies assert that African American children are over-identified in 9 out of 13 disability categories and are placed at a higher rate in restrictive settings than their Caucasian peers (Losen & Orfield, 2002). Although many agree that poverty presents great risk factors that affect children's school performance, some researchers insist that poverty alone cannot account for the overrepresentation of culturally and linguistically diverse children in special education classes (Losen & Orfield, 2002; Oswald, Coutinho, & Best, 2002). Racial and ethnic disparities in the identification of Hispanic and African American children in special education classes and classes for the gifted and talented are believed to be rooted in systemic bias that occurs within the schools. Ferri and Connor (2005) argued that race and disability are social constructs and that overt racial segregation of schools has evolved into covert forms of racial segregation by means of some special education practices. Ferri and Connor stated:

> White privilege and racialized conceptions of ability allowed some parents and educators to use certain special education categories as a tool for continued racial segregation. Children of different races have been classified into different categories, with Black and Latino students most likely to be overrepresented in the majority of categories, and placed in more restrictive settings. (2005, p. 456)

Three critical factors have been discussed as contributing to the problem of over- and underrepresentation of culturally and linguistically diverse children in special education services and gifted programs: instructional factors, referral procedures, and assessment practices (Gopaul-McNicol & Thomas-Presswood, 1998; Rhodes, Ochoa, & Ortiz, 2005). Instructional factors include ineffective instruction, lack of certified and experienced teachers, limited knowledge of second language acquisition processes and their effect on learning, failure of schools to implement known effective programs for English language learners with strong empirical support (e.g., maintenance programs, dual bilingual programs; Thomas & Collier, 2002), and limited understanding of cultural and socioeconomic factors in learning. Bias in the referral process is evident in the lack of real prereferral intervention (e.g., some schools insist that participation in English as a Second Language programs is an intervention when these programs do not provide instruction in the child's native language) and inappropriate reasons for referral (second language acquisition issues and cultural and class disconnect between teachers and students). Assessment factors include test bias; poorly trained assessment staff in terms of issues of diversity and assessment; inadequately trained interpreters who work with bilingual students, examiners, and parents; inadequate assessment practices; and noncompliance with federal law regarding the assessment of culturally and linguistically diverse children (i.e., nondiscriminatory assessment and assessment in the child's native language). These factors need to be addressed via systematic social and political changes that include 1) addressing diversity issues in all its forms through staff development programs and teacher- and psychologist-training programs; 2) observing equity in funding across schools; and 3) scrutinizing school practices (tracking, referral process, testing and labeling, special education exit and mainstream criteria).

RESILIENCE AND PROTECTIVE FACTORS

Poverty is a risk factor associated with teenage pregnancy, school failure, and violent crime (Schorr, 1988). Despite these odds, many children living in poverty manage to stay in school, obtain employment, and live productive lives. Researchers have found that resilience is the difference between the children that rise above negative circumstances and those who do not. Amidst the negative circumstances, these children have enough positive experiences in their lives to protect them from harmful outcomes. Experiences such as a healthy parent–child relationship, an effective and encouraging teacher, a nurturing relative, a neighbor who helps with homework, adequate housing, and an academically strong friend can all serve as protective factors that shield a child from the detrimental effects of living in poverty on developmental processes. Resiliency is defined by those factors that enhance the speed and degree of potential recovery after exposure to stress (Goldstein & Brooks, 2006a). Protective factors are those experiences that ameliorate or minimize the effects of negative events in a child's life by enhancing his or her coping strategies and feelings of self-efficacy.

Rutter (1990, 2000) studied different types of supportive factors that foster resilient outcomes to potentially stressful situations.

1. Distancing oneself from the source of stress or parents who protect their children from the exposure to continued negative influences

2. Preventing or reducing a negative string of reactions such as teaching and modeling coping strategies that diffuse anger and hostility

3. Promoting self-esteem and self-efficacy in children such as supporting caring relationships, achieving and doing well, and using effective coping strategies when faced with stressful situations

4. Evaluating and cognitively processing a situation in a positive light (e.g., reframing negative experiences around positive concepts)

5. Being provided with positive opportunities (e.g., starting over in a new school, moving to a new community away from negative peer influences, being offered new academic and career opportunities, changing home environment)

Other studies examined risk and protective factors and found that poor developmental outcomes were connected to perinatal trauma coupled with poor environmental conditions, whereas favorable outcomes were more likely when environmental conditions were good despite biological risks in the beginning (see Cicchetti & Rogosch, 1997; Werner & Smith, 1992; Wright & Masten, 2006). Thus, it appears that a child who had a poor start (e.g., born LBW) can strive physically and cognitively if his or her parents feed him or her properly, obtain good medical follow-up care, secure early intervention services, and provide him or her with an enriched and stimulating environment. Children have different vulnerabilities based on their developmental status (e.g., infants are more vulnerable to certain risk factors because they are more dependent on their parents), but at the same time, their young age protects them from the effect of experiences (e.g., a natural disaster) because they lack understanding (Wright & Masten, 2006). Thus, older children are more vulnerable to conditions in the community and school setting.

Early studies on resilience focused on recognizing the predictors of positive adaptations at all levels of risk and on individual differences, which allowed a number of correlates or protective factors to be identified. Masten (2001) discussed four general areas: 1) child characteristics (e.g., pleasant temperament in infancy, good cognitive and problem-solving abilities, faith or spirituality, self-efficacy), 2) family characteristics (e.g., stable and supportive home environment, parental involvement in school, socioeconomic resources, college-educated parent, religious affiliations), 3) community characteristics (e.g., good quality neighborhood, effective schools, responsive public services), and 4) cultural and societal characteristics (e.g., protective child policies, emphasis on effective educational practices and provision of resources to support it). Research findings, however, pointed to a more complex model to explain positive adaptation despite exposure to significant stressors (Wright & Masten, 2006); simply identifying protective factors is not enough.

Literature in this area now describes resilience as a process and not solely as a group of factors that can lead to positive adaptation. Wyman (2003) defined *resilience* as reflecting a diverse set of processes that alter children's transactions with adverse life conditions to reduce negative effects and promote mastery of normative developmental tasks. More research efforts emphasized the interrelatedness of a number of problems and the necessity to intervene largely and comprehensively in the lives of children exposed to ongoing risk factors (Wright & Masten, 2006). It has become clear that a view of resilience as a framework encompassing practice and policy is necessary. Therefore, intervening to change the lives of children at risk for psychopathology or other difficulties by increasing resources, decreasing exposure to risk factors, or mobilizing protective systems is itself a protective process (Wright & Masten, 2006). An understanding of the process of resilience is key to developing intervention and prevention strategies that would offset the negative impact of multiple risk factors and positively affect the future of children and their families.

II

Working with Children and Families

4

Comprehensive Individualized Assessment of Children from Poverty

We did not weave the web of life, we are merely a strand in it.
Whatever we do to the web, we do to ourselves.

Chief Seattle, 1852

Children living in an environment characterized by poverty are more likely to be identified with educational needs that require special education services than children from more economically advantageous backgrounds. This is further supported by research that suggests that pervasive poverty has harmful effects on children's test scores and school performance (McLoyd, 1998). When children are from culturally and linguistically diverse backgrounds and are also poor, the effect of poverty is even greater (Farley, 1997). Moreover, children with these backgrounds have been consistently overrepresented in special education programs (see Artiles & Trent, 1994; Gopaul-McNicol & Thomas-Presswood, 1998; Losen & Orfield, 2002; Ortiz & Dynda, 2005; Rhodes, Ochoa, & Ortiz, 2005; Zhang & Katsiyannis, 2002). When children are identified as having a disability when they do not, they are more likely to be provided with educational programs that do not match their educational needs. Inclusion in special education programs excludes misidentified children from the full-range of academic activities of a general education curriculum and limits their educational opportunities in the future. Since the special education assessment process is key to identification of children who may have an educationally disabling condition, an assessment process that is nondiscriminatory and that is comprehensive in its approach is paramount.

Thus, assessment poses a formidable challenge. As an essential component of the special-education process, children are psychologically and educationally evaluated to determine their instructional needs and strengths and their eligibility to receive special education services. McAfee and Leong (2002) asserted that whenever human judgment is involved, the potential for human bias increases. For the assessment process to be successful in helping children with diverse background experiences, the assessor must have an understanding of the effect of poverty on children's cognitive and social development and be able to incorporate this knowledge into the assessment process. This knowledge provides the groundwork for the development of interventions and implementation of strategies that have a realistic chance of helping children succeed in school. Moreover, it minimizes many of the concerns that have plagued the assessment process in schools: the overrepresentation of economically disadvantaged and culturally and linguistically diverse children in special education categories and underrepresentation of these same populations in programs for the gifted and talented (McAfee & Leong, 2002).

The first three chapters of this book provided the groundwork for conceptualizing the critical issues in terms of demographics, developmental processes, and risk factors that have an undeniable effect on the cognitive, emotional, social, and behavioral development of children living in poverty. This chapter provides information on how psychologists and others who evaluate children can incorporate this knowledge base into their assessment strategies to effectively identify children's needs and strengths, work with their families, and design interventions that respect these children's diversity and their unique experiences. It is not intended that these children's difficulties are solely due to their background of poverty and not to legitimate disabilities. The goal is to make assessors and other school staff sensitive to the fact that these differences do have an effect on children's performance in school.

A conceptual framework for assessing children living in poverty is presented, and the cognitive and educational assessment process is discussed in this chapter. Several assessment strategies are reviewed, and an assessment model that takes into account the unique needs of children living in poverty is outlined.

CONCEPTUAL FRAMEWORK FOR THE PSYCHOLOGICAL ASSESSMENT OF CHILDREN LIVING IN POVERTY

Poverty is a multifaceted and dynamic condition. Thus, the assessment procedure for a child whose experiences have been colored by poverty must be multidimensional and capable of providing information on the whole child. Gibbs and Huang

(1998) discussed three overlapping conceptual perspectives in the assessment of culturally diverse children: developmental perspective, ecological perspective, and a cross-cultural mental health perspective. The authors believe that this model, with some adaptations, is applicable to the unique experiences of children living in poverty.

In Gibbs and Huang's (1998) model, the developmental perspective considers cognitive, physical, and linguistic developments. It includes not only maturational processes that are universal but also variations in behavioral manifestations that occur across racial/ethnic and cultural lines. For example, psychologists and other practitioners who work with children who speak other languages at home must be aware of second language acquisition issues as they can affect English language development and achievement.

The ecological perspective, based on the work of Bronfenbrenner (1979), offers a model for understanding the relations between the developing child and the environment and emphasizes the effect of forces exerted by a series of interconnected social systems. These systems include the *microsystem*—the interpersonal relationships, experiences, and activities that a developing child encounters (e.g., family, school); the *mesosystem*—the connections between the microsystems where the child interacts (e.g., child care, early intervention programs, hospital); the *exosystem*—systems in which the child is not actively involved but which have a direct influence on the child and his or her family (e.g., neighborhood, parents' social network, parents' employment); and the *macrosystem*—a broader level that affects what occurs at a lower system (e.g., cultural beliefs, societal expectations, governmental and educational policies; Bronfenbrenner, 1979, 1986). The ecological perspective facilitates the analysis of the influence of family functioning, school life, and poverty on the child in the assessment process (Gibbs & Huang, 1998).

The cross-cultural perspective considers a comparative context for viewing social-emotional, cognitive, and behavioral issues among diverse ethnic groups (Atkinson, Morten, & Sue, 1989). This perspective assumes that all behaviors have meaning, rules govern behaviors, and behaviors are influenced by cultural beliefs and practices. This cross-cultural perspective focuses on many aspects of functioning including mental illness, belief system regarding the origin of emotional and behavioral difficulties, coping strategies, help-seeking behaviors, utilization of services, and responsiveness to intervention (Gibbs & Huang, 1998).

Another level of analysis that was not included in the Gibbs and Huang (1998) model is one that focuses on learning strengths and needs that would serve as a guide to identify interventions on an educational and behavioral level. A perspective that emphasizes the brain–behavior relationship recognizes the contribution of the environment in the development of the brain and hence learning, and it presents an approach useful in understanding the overall functioning of a child. A brain–behavior perspective with its multifactorial, integrative, and flexible approach considers developmental issues and genetic, medical, environmental, behavioral, and sociocultural influences that determine how a child matures

(Baron, 2004). It provides a unique perspective that links diverse human behavior or neurocognitive functions to brain substrate (Baron, 2004). A brain–behavior approach to assessment typically is organized to provide a systematic evaluation of the integrity of the brain functions associated with learning and everyday activities. Research has demonstrated a clear link between environmental experiences and brain development and their effect on learning and psychopathology (Aylward, 1997; Baron, 2004; Kolb & Whishaw, 2003; Pliszka, 2003; Shaywitz, 2003). De Fina (2004) noted that the concept of learning consists of the integration of multiple neurobehavioral factors that rely on critical processes that include sensory perceptual, attention, executive functions, memory, language, social-emotional, and motor output. The emphasis is on a need for a more comprehensive, diagnostic, and inclusive approach to assessment with less reliance on a standard battery that is out of step with current research on learning and strict score interpretations. Crespi and Cooke (2003) noted that one of the most important trends in school psychology has been the increasing recognition of the significant contributions of a brain–behavior framework as it applies to children and learning. Crespi and Cooke (2003) further asserted that many of the instruments administered by school psychologists have evolved as part of neuropsychological assessment, and many of the newer test batteries include the contribution of a brain–behavior or neuropsychological framework (e.g., Kaufman & Kaufman, 2004; Naglieri & Das, 1997). With the growing recognition of the contribution of biological factors in children's psychopathology and learning difficulties (e.g., ADHD, Tourette syndrome, autism, dyslexia, traumatic brain injury [TBI]), many school psychologists are using instruments that assess memory, executive functions, and attention. They are seeing the benefit of adding such instruments to the assessment battery to obtain a richer view of children's functioning. A neuropsychological approach, however, is not only about the instruments; it is about the interpretation as well, and to conduct these types of evaluations and interpretations, additional training and experience is required.

This book advocates a comprehensive and integrative paradigm that allows practitioners in school and clinical settings to understand and accurately interpret the behavior of children with a background of poverty. This paradigm organizes these diverse perspectives to create a conceptual framework that provides a critical analysis on how issues of poverty affect children's performance in school and facilitates the interpretation of psychological evaluation performance in a manner that assists in the development of interventions. This conceptual framework provides the theoretical foundation of the Comprehensive Individualized Assessment System (CIAS; see Figure 4.1). This conceptual framework is an assessment blueprint for working with children raised in an environment of poverty and takes into account the wide spectrum of experiences and risk factors that may have influenced the child's life functioning. The blueprint also recognizes protective factors that are preventive in many instances or that facilitate the implementation

- Developmental perspective: Cognitive, motor, and language development
  - Protective factors (e.g., prenatal care, proper nutrition, current immunization, breastfed, met all developmental milestones)
  - Risk factors (e.g., substance use during pregnancy, witness abuse or victim of abuse, delayed developmental milestones)
- Ecological perspective: Home, school, community, workplace, social structures
  - Protective factors (employment, support network, extended family, good grades)
  - Risk factors (e.g., unemployment, school dropout, limited social resources)
- Cross-cultural perspective: Ethnic and cultural membership, religious beliefs and practices
  - Belief about success and education
  - Belief about family relationships, parenting, development, gender roles, coping strategies
  - Belief about mental illness, learning and behavioral difficulties
  - Belief about help-seeking behaviors and utilization of services
- Assessment perspective: Information is gathered from different sources, using different methods, and integrating cultural, developmental, and ecological information. Data are analyzed from multiple levels to provide a comprehensive picture of the child.

Figure 4.1. Conceptual framework of the comprehensive individualized assessment system.

and success of interventions. The overarching goal of this model is to establish an assessment template for understanding and interpreting children's functioning on various levels and linking these results to interventions.

COMPREHENSIVE INDIVIDUALIZED ASSESSMENT SYSTEM FOR CHILDREN LIVING IN POVERTY

The assessment model being proposed in this book represents an amalgamation of perspectives that emphasizes and respects individual differences or diversity in all its forms. Information is gathered from multiple sources, using multiple methods, and analyzed and interpreted on multiple levels from various perspectives; thus providing a comprehensive study of the child as a whole. The purpose of assessment is to obtain deeper understanding of the child in order to make informed decisions, as well as to develop interventions that effectively address the needs of the child (Sattler, 2001). Best practice in the assessment of children demands a multistage process that involves planning, collecting data based on referral concerns, evaluating results, interpreting based on the child's unique experiences and characteristics, formulating hypotheses, developing interventions that are linked to assessment results, communicating results and recommendations to key stakeholders, and monitoring the child's performance as needed (Sattler, 2001). Ecological validity is of the utmost importance to any assessment model. This term refers to the match between behaviors and observations in a natural setting with those obtained and seen in a standardized test environment. An increase in ecological validity occurs when consideration of how the child's environment affects the child is incorporated into the assessment process. Family life, cultural beliefs, linguistic variables, neighborhood context, school culture, migration experiences, and community resources are used to develop a plan for the assessment process and to interpret test results (Sattler, 2001). According to Sattler, a skilled assessor evaluates what effects seem to have been caused by an impoverished environment and tries to separate these effects from other factors such as genetic disposition or family interaction.

Emphasis on an assessment process that is culturally competent and sensitive is also critical. Padilla defined *culturally sensitive* as a continuing and open-ended series of substantive and methodological insertions and adaptations designed to mesh the process of assessment and evaluation with the cultural characteristics of the group being studied (2001, p. 6). By insertion and adaptations, Padilla referred to developing or adapting instruments, selecting tests, determining assessment procedures, administering tests, and analyzing and interpreting test performance. Present throughout the process is a concern with the effect of culture, language, and socioeconomic differences on test performance and with interpreting results in light of the child's background history.

Outline of the Comprehensive Individualized Assessment System

To properly work with and serve children from low-income backgrounds, the mental health and school professionals must have a complete understanding of not only how poverty affects the lives of children (home, school, and community) but also how to address learning needs through a proper assessment model. Assessment in schools typically focuses on identifying children for services (e.g., gifted programs, special education services, remedial services). Children whose achievement surpasses that of their typical peers are referred to gifted programs, and children who are not making expected progress in learning are targeted for remedial programs or for assessment to identify the presence of a disability. The traditional approach to the assessment of children who are suspected of having a disability in the educational and clinical settings has typically focused on a fixed battery of tests (i.e., most children are administered the same tests) consisting of a few tests in various domains (e.g., cognitive, achievement, behavioral checklist, visual motor tests), and the results are interpreted strictly from a quantitative approach. This approach not only lacks depth but also ignores the information from other settings that may contribute positively or negatively to the child's learning. D'Amato, Crepeau-Hobson, Huang, & Geil (2005) noted that educational and medical settings typically embrace an assessment process that is deficit based and that conceptualizes problems as within the child. As a consequence, much effort is placed on finding the problem with the student, and little time is devoted to analyzing the learning environment or other systems that might affect the child's ability to be successful in an academic setting (D'Amato et al., 2005). Due to this emphasis, efforts to intervene or remediate the identified problems have had limited success. An approach that is strength-based and that considers the child as well as the systems within which the child interacts when assessing, diagnosing, and intervening would better serve the educational and learning needs of the child (D'Amato et al., 2005). The experiences that children from low-income homes and children from culturally and linguistically diverse backgrounds bring to the learning settings are often unrecognized in school environments (e.g., culturally relevant strength and dual language; García, 2000). Often what teachers perceive as a lack of achievement are just different forms of diverse learners' preliterate experiences (Donovan & Cross, 2002; Neuman & Celano, 2001). The CIAS assessment procedure is global in its approach and incorporates the child, as well as the environments and settings where the child interacts, to obtain a comprehensive understanding of the child's learning strengths and needs. The assessment procedure is outlined below.

Phase 1: Information Gathering

1. Social history/background information: Family history and current functioning, prenatal information, developmental and medical history, school history, neighborhood and community resources
2. Interview parents and teachers: Behavioral observation in classroom and other settings
3. Review of educational records: Data gathered through systematic problem-solving activities, review of cumulative files, performance on districtwide standardized tests, report cards and teachers' comments, and disciplinary records

Phase 2: Assessment Method

Determine an assessment procedure that best addresses the needs of the referred student and is based on referral concerns. For children with a history of living in poverty, an assessment method that is comprehensive and rooted in a strong theoretical base with empirical support can better integrate the diverse and unique experiences of this population.

Phase 3: Present Level of Performance

Evaluating cognitive/learning, academic, and social/behavioral strengths and needs.

Phase 4: Data Interpretation and Educational Implications

All data gathered throughout the assessment are integrated and analyzed, focusing on their effect on school performance. A problem-solving approach is adopted to test hypotheses and arrive at valid decisions.

Phase 5: Develop Interventions and Strategies for Implementation

Interventions are developed based on assessment results and background experiences. Plans are made to properly implement interventions. Staff that would be involved should be trained on the interventions so that they are applied with integrity.

Phase 6: Monitoring Students' Progress

A procedure for monitoring students' progress is designed and checked on a regular basis.

PSYCHOEDUCATIONAL ASSESSMENT PROCESS

The concern regarding the overrepresentation of African American, Native American, and Hispanic children as well as children from low-income homes in high-incidence disability categories has been studied by the Office of Civil Rights (an office that tracks and monitors schools' overidentification of children from diverse linguistic and ethnic backgrounds in special education programs) and educational researchers. For example, placement of African American children in special education programs for children with learning disabilities, mental retardation, and emotional disturbance shows disproportionate ratios that are statistically significant; specifically, Parrish (2002) reported that African American children are 2.8 times as likely as Caucasian children to be identified and placed in special education programs for children with mental retardation; they are 1.92 times as likely to be identified and placed in special education programs for children with emotional disturbance; and they are 1.32 times as likely to be identified and placed in special education programs for children with learning disabilities. The identification of children for special education services begins with a referral for assessment, and the result or outcome of the assessment helps determine eligibility for special education services. The appropriateness of a referral is important, but the integrity of the assessment process is even more significant because it has the power to identify a child as having a disability and to assist in placing that child in special education programs.

The assessment process in school follows a course that has been outlined by special education law. This process begins with a referral for a comprehensive assessment and ends with the provision of special education services if the child is found eligible. The referral concerns guide the assessment process. The referral concerns pose questions to the assessor, and the assessment procedure is then designed to answer the questions. The referral questions help determine the focus of the assessment (e.g., more academic due to suspected learning disability, more social-emotional due to behavioral and emotional concerns) and the procedure that would be used to assess the child.

As a direct consequence of the 2004 reauthorization of the Individuals with

Disabilities Education Act (IDEA), now renamed the Individuals with Disabilities Education Improvement Act (IDEIA), a strong focus has been placed on scientifically based intervention strategies that should be implemented prior to formal psychological assessment. In the case of children suspected of having learning disabilities, the data obtained from these strategies can be used to determine eligibility for special education services. It has long been considered best practice in education to provide sound instruction before referring a child for special education assessment. Unfortunately, this practice was not the case in many schools nationwide.

Hale and Fiorello (2004) emphasized *intervening to assess,* which means that systematic intervention strategies should be in place to help struggling students prior to a formal referral for a comprehensive assessment. An assessment should be given only after those evidenced-based interventions are determined unsuccessful. There are a number of advantages to interventions being implemented prior to an assessment, including benefiting the child by avoiding unnecessary labeling and pitfalls of special education (e.g., low teacher expectation, stigmatization, low self-esteem), reducing the number of inappropriate referrals because it guides instruction, targeting individual needs and decreasing the chance of children slipping through the system, and providing rich baseline data that can effectively guide the assessment process by helping the assessor formulate diagnostic hypotheses (Hale & Fiorello, 2004).

IDEA strongly embraces a best practice model called Response to Intervention (RTI) that utilizes research-based intervention strategies before formal referrals are made, and decisions regarding comprehensive assessment, specifically for special education eligibility, are reached based on the children's RTIs. The focus of RTI is on all children experiencing academic and/or behavioral difficulties. Failure to make expected progress results in a formal referral for a comprehensive psychoeducational assessment, and in the case of children who are suspected of having a learning disability, it may constitute the assessment to determine eligibility for special education services. Because RTI occurs prior to any formal special education process, it is a general education initiative in which all children participate. Prevention of academic difficulties is central to the RTI philosophy. Research strongly shows that children who receive early intervention or children who learn to read, write, and compute during their elementary school years are more likely to experience personal wellness across the lifespan (Brown-Chidsey, 2005).

RESPONSE TO INTERVENTION

RTI is basically a set of procedures for imparting school- or districtwide scientifically based instruction and assessment activities to every student (Brown-Chidsey, 2005). RTI was included in the reauthorization of IDEA as a response to widespread dissatisfaction with the IQ-achievement discrepancy formula used to identify children with learning disabilities. Some of the limitations associated with the discrepancy formula are the following:

1. It failed to inform instruction (Elliot & Fuchs, 1997)

2. It prevented some children from low socioeconomic status from obtaining special education services, even when these children demonstrated similar learning problems as students from high socioeconomic status, because the discrepancy between achievement and ability was not met (Siegel, 1999)

3. The discrepancy formula lacked validity on theoretical and empirical grounds (Aaron, 1997)

4. The discrepancy model interfered with young children receiving intervention services early (Lyon et al., 2001)

Although the 2004 reauthorization does not prohibit the use of the discrepancy formula for identifying learning disabilities, it gives the states the option to adopt the RTI model to identify and address the educational needs of children with learning disabilities.

RTI is conceived as a problem-solving paradigm and as such it considers children's strengths and needs by identifying research-based instructional interventions, collecting data to monitor children's progress, and evaluating the effectiveness of interventions implemented (Canter, 2004). Moreover, many researchers assert that no student characteristics (e.g., race, ethnicity, socioeconomic status, disability category, neighborhood) determine a priori what intervention will be implemented (Fuchs, Mock, Morgan, & Young, 2003). In the same manner, no given intervention is effective for all children regardless of the perceived homogeneity of the group (Fuchs et al., 2003). The RTI process that originates in the general education setting allows for the nonreliance on test scores to determine children's education needs and eligibility for more intensive special education services (Marston, 2002; Reschly & Tilly, 1999).

RTI is frequently articulated as a three-tier model of instruction and assessment that tenders preventive and prescriptive instruction to children on the basis of what each child needs (Brown-Chidsey, 2005). This three-tier model systematically determines which children are at risk of school failure and provides instructional services accordingly.

Response to Intervention: Three-Tier Model

1. Universal instruction and assessment

2. Supplementary instruction and assessment

3. Specialized instruction and assessment

Tier 1: Universal Instruction and Assessment

The first tier of the RTI model emphasizes interventions that are delivered to all students. It is referred to as universal instruction and assessment because the primary goal of the strategies is to prevent academic difficulties or to promote academic competence (Brown-Chidsey & Steege, 2005). Two essential components of this tier were reviewed by Brown-Chidsey (2005):

1. Scientifically based instructional activities: These are methods validated by sound research design and have yielded evidence that the methods are effective in producing positive results.

2. Reliable and valid universal assessment methods: These methods are used to measure children's progress toward the instructional goals, to gather baseline data, and to monitor children's progress.

Curriculum-based measurement (CBM) is central to RTI assessment activities. These CBM activities are standardized assessment measures designed to be sensitive to instructional gains (Shapiro, 2004). CBM is a well-known and researched general outcome measurement of curriculum-based assessment (CBA). CBA is a criterion-referenced test that is teacher constructed and designed to reflect curriculum content (Idol, Nevin, & Paolucci-Whitcomb, 1999). This model has been researched with a wide range of diverse learners, including children with disabilities (e.g., learning disabilities, mental retardation, ADHD), children at risk for school failure, bilingual students, gifted and talented students, various age groups (preschool children to high school students), and various academic areas (e.g., reading, math, writing; see Idol et al., 1999, and Shapiro 2004, for a review). There is substantial research documenting the reliability and validity of CBM (see Shinn, 1989, 1998 for a review).

Children first receive whole-class or small-group instruction using evidenced-based strategies. The effectiveness of these interventions is initially assessed with CBM, as data are used as a baseline to monitor children's progress and to identify children at risk for school failure. CBM probes can be quickly administered and graphed to show if the intervention is effective at the classroom and individual levels. Children who are not making desired progress can be identified for Tier 2 activities.

Some caution is warranted in the implementation of CBM with students who are culturally and linguistically diverse. Rhodes et al. (2005) documented some issues of concern that may affect outcomes on CBM procedures:

1. Children's educational experiences (e.g., amount, type, location—in United States or in home country) or history of formal education

2. Quality of bilingual programs (e.g., English as a second language, dual bilingual, maintenance programs)

3. Children's level of language proficiency and level of acculturation

4. Children's mobility and school attendance patterns and their effect on academic progress

5. Home, school, and neighborhood experiences that support or detract from academic progress

Tier 2: Supplementary Instruction and Assessment

At this level, children who are identified as not making expected progress at Tier 1 are provided with supplemental instruction. Instructional activities at this level can include small-group remediation, before- and after-school programs, title programs such as remedial reading and math, peer tutoring, and computer-based programs. Again, all instructional programs must be scientifically based and implemented with integrity. CBM activities are essential to assessing student's progress. Under Tier 2, two options are available for determining which students need more individually tailored and targeted instruction: using specific skill criterion (e.g., number of simple additions solved in a minute) and identifying those students who performed in the lowest 20th percentile on the Tier 1 universal assessment activities (Brown-Chidsey, 2005). Children receiving Tier 2 instruction should be provided with ongoing monitoring at least once per week so that changes in instructional strategies can be made readily available to accommodate the needs of the children. In this way, the data gathered can document if the level of response to intervention was effective. Brown-Chidsey (2005) recommended a single-subject design that includes graphing each child's progress and reviewing the data to identify academic needs and trends. Basically, if a child performs above the baseline data on Tier 2 activities on the chosen outcome measures, then the intervention is deemed effective. If the student obtains scores that are below the baseline data, then the interventions are considered ineffective and would need to be replaced or modified. Brown-Chidsey (2005) recommended that three data points are identified before any analysis of scores can be carried out. In the case of mixed results, more data should be gathered before instructional changes are implemented.

Tier 3: Specialized Instruction and Assessment

This tier is designated for children who do not make adequate progress in Tier 2 and require more intensive instruction, possibly on a more permanent basis. At this level, children are referred for a deeper assessment that includes standardized cognitive, academic, and behavioral measures. Although a more formal assessment procedure is being implemented, the child should continue receiving more targeted, individualized, and intensive instruction. This level of intervention should include longer sessions and should bring together all the data collected during the child's journey throughout the RTI process. Best practice would be to consider as one's goal to provide the child with a thorough psychoeducational evaluation to determine learning strengths and needs in order to develop an individualized education program (IEP) that would be effective in guiding instruction and improving learning. Data gathered from Tiers 1 and 2 are used as baseline data to assist in determining eligibility for special education services and to guide educational programming.

The benefits of the RTI model have been documented by Fuchs and Vaughn (2005): 1) facilitating early intervention and identification, 2) reducing screening bias or inappropriate referrals, and 3) linking identification assessment with instructional planning. Yet, potential disadvantages noted by Fuchs and Vaughn include 1) the limited availability of validated intervention models and measures to assure instructional validity, 2) the failure of RTI can be the result of different disabilities and not solely a learning disability, 3) the degree of intensity required of an intervention within a general education setting (e.g., can a general education setting sustain a long-term intensive intervention program if it is effective in eliciting response from a student), and 4) the limited availability of trained staff to implement an RTI model and CBM with integrity.

BACKGROUND INFORMATION AND SOCIAL HISTORY

Every comprehensive psychological assessment should begin with a thorough social history that includes family history, prenatal and medical history, developmental history, and school history. Test interpretations should be made in light of the data gathered during this phase of the assessment. Although most assessors are trained to understand the relevance of good history taking, it is not always done in the schools, and it is common to find many reports written with little consideration for the child's social history. The reason for this is related in part to assignments of duties and responsibilities in the schools. For example, many school systems task a social worker or a special education coordinator with gathering background information on all students referred for a comprehensive assessment. These individuals interview the parents. The social history is then shared at the multidisciplinary team meeting, at which point the school psychologist has already completed his or her report with little consideration of the child's history. Such practices do not work in favor of students because the psychological or psychoeducational report failed to take into account the child's unique experiences that undeniably influence the child's response to test items. When assessors do not obtain such information before conducting the assessment, the resulting data does not consider the type of information that is important to planning the assessment procedure (e.g., information regarding family history of learning disorders or mental illness, traumatic experiences, acquired brain injuries [ABIs], neighborhood and community resources).

When working with children from a background of poverty, it is critical to have access to relevant background information. Parents, teachers, and other important individuals in the child's environment should be interviewed. Most schools have established forms that are used to obtain a thorough social history from caregivers. In some schools, parents are interviewed in person, and in other schools, these forms are sent home to be completed and returned by parents. Assessors are encouraged to interview parents in person because parents often are not aware of what type of information is important. Some do not have the time to be thorough in completing the forms, whereas others have literacy challenges or speak a language other than English. Although an in-person interview is preferred, an interview by telephone can be used when parents cannot visit the school building. Many places of employment are not sensitive to employees' needs and desires to attend school meetings on behalf of their children. An interview (in person or by telephone) can elicit critical information from parents. Some parents neglect to report information regarding the child witnessing community violence, being sexually molested, or experiencing an ABI because they did not realize that such experiences could have an effect on school performance and adjustment. Assessors must directly assess the presence of risk factors through parent and teacher interviews, record review, and standardized measures. Please see Figures 4.2 and 4.3 for checklists of risk factors and protective factors.

RISK FACTORS CHECKLIST

Child's name: _____   Examiner's name: _____

Age: _____   Grade: _____

School: _____   Date: _____

	Check one				Check one	
I. Individual	Yes	No			Yes	No
1. Genetic vulnerabilities	☐	☐	6. Parents with mental illness		☐	☐
2. Birth deficiencies	☐	☐	7. Parents with physical problems		☐	☐
3. Failure to bond with primary caregiver	☐	☐	8. Parents who are antisocial		☐	☐
4. Exposure to toxins	☐	☐	9. Parents who are poorly educated		☐	☐
5. Medical problems	☐	☐	10. Parents who are substance abusers		☐	☐
6. Chronic underarousal	☐	☐	11. Parents under considerable stress		☐	☐
7. Mental illness	☐	☐	12. Parents who maltreat their children		☐	☐
8. Exposure to violence	☐	☐	13. Parents who reject or neglect their children		☐	☐
9. Aggressive and hostile behavior	☐	☐	14. Parents who are noninvolved with their			
10. Antisocial attitudes or beliefs	☐	☐	children		☐	☐
11. Antisocial behavior	☐	☐	15. Lax and ineffective parental discipline		☐	☐
12. Cognitive delays or disorders	☐	☐	16. Parents who use inconsistent, harsh, or			
13. Poor problem-solving skills	☐	☐	permissive methods of parenting		☐	☐
14. Anxiety	☐	☐	17. Parents who provide poor supervision		☐	☐
15. Hyperactivity	☐	☐	18. Parents with inappropriate expectations for			
16. Restlessness	☐	☐	their children		☐	☐
17. Impulsivity	☐	☐	19. Disruptive family relationships		☐	☐
18. Attention difficulties	☐	☐	20. Delinquent siblings		☐	☐
19. Concentration difficulties	☐	☐	21. Domestic violence		☐	☐
20. Shallow affect	☐	☐	22. Residential mobility		☐	☐
21. Risk-taking	☐	☐	23. Homelessness		☐	☐
22. Victim of violence	☐	☐	24. Large family size		☐	☐
23. Under considerable stress	☐	☐	25. Single parent		☐	☐
24. Depression	☐	☐				
25. Substance abuse	☐	☐	**III. School/Community/Environment**			
26. Academic failure	☐	☐	1. Inferior schools		☐	☐
27. Learning difficulties	☐	☐	2. Inferior teachers		☐	☐
28. Language deficits	☐	☐	3. Community disorganization and violence		☐	☐
29. High truancy rates	☐	☐	4. Access to firearms and drugs in community		☐	☐
30. Failure to understand consequences of			5. No access to health care and social			
actions	☐	☐	services		☐	☐
31. Maladaptive methods of handling stress	☐	☐	6. No mentors in community		☐	☐
32. Poor coping ability	☐	☐	7. Rejection by peers		☐	☐
			8. Antisocial peers		☐	☐
II. Family			9. No supportive church community		☐	☐
1. Maternal substance use during			10. No leisure or sport facilities in community		☐	☐
pregnancy	☐	☐	11. Racism		☐	☐
2. Obstetrical complications	☐	☐	12. Residential segregation		☐	☐
3. Low socioeconomic status	☐	☐	13. Presence of environmental toxins		☐	☐
4. Unemployed parents	☐	☐	14. Recent natural disaster		☐	☐
5. Poverty	☐	☐	15. Economic recession		☐	☐

Figure 4.2. Rick factors checklist. (From Sattler, J.M., & Hoge, R.D. [2006]. *Assessment of Children: Behavioral, social, and clinical foundations* [5th ed.]. La Mesa, CA: Author; reprinted by permission.)

PROTECTIVE FACTORS CHECKLIST

Child's name: _____   Examiner's name: _____

Age: _____   Grade: _____

School: _____   Date: _____

	Check one				Check one	
I. Individual	Yes	No			Yes	No
1. Close bond with primary caregiver	☐	☐	3. Competent parents		☐	☐
2. Physical health	☐	☐	4. Stable, cohesive, and well-adjusted family		☐	☐
3. Emotional maturity	☐	☐	5. Warm, nurturant, or supportive relationship			
4. Mental health	☐	☐	with at least one parent		☐	☐
5. Positive, prosocial attitudes	☐	☐	6. Supportive and caring other family members		☐	☐
6. High self-esteem	☐	☐	7. Parents provide competent supervision and			
7. Good problem-solving skills	☐	☐	direction		☐	☐
8. Good social skills	☐	☐	8. Small family size		☐	☐
9. Good school performance	☐	☐	9. Financially stable family		☐	☐
10. Participates in positive leisure or sport			10. Stable and attractive home environment		☐	☐
activities	☐	☐	11. Assigned chores		☐	☐
11. Highly motivated to address problems	☐	☐				
12. Nonexposure to violence	☐	☐	**III. School/Community/Environment**			
13. Good coping ability	☐	☐	1. Good schools		☐	☐
14. Self-discipline	☐	☐	2. Good teachers		☐	☐
15. Adaptable	☐	☐	3. Good neighborhood		☐	☐
16. Compassionate	☐	☐	4. Limited accessibility to firearms and drugs			
17. "Easy," engaging temperament	☐	☐	in community		☐	☐
18. Special talent	☐	☐	5. Access to health care and social services		☐	☐
19. Impulse control	☐	☐	6. Mentors in community		☐	☐
20. Achievement motivation	☐	☐	7. Peer acceptance		☐	☐
21. Persistence	☐	☐	8. Supportive peers		☐	☐
22. Faith	☐	☐	9. Supportive church community		☐	☐
23. Internal locus of control	☐	☐	10. Leisure or sport facilities in community		☐	☐
24. Intolerant attitude toward deviance	☐	☐	11. Tolerance of ethnic groups		☐	☐
25. Understands consequences of actions	☐	☐	12. Integrated neighborhood		☐	☐
			13. Nonpolluted environment		☐	☐
II. Family			14. No major natural disasters		☐	☐
1. Good prenatal care	☐	☐	15. Economic prosperity		☐	☐
2. Educated parents	☐	☐				

Figure 4.3. Protective factors checklist. (From Sattler, J.M., & Hoge, R.D. [2006]. *Assessment of Children: Behavioral, social, and clinical foundations* [5th ed.]. La Mesa, CA: Author; reprinted by permission.)

Assessors should obtain information regarding

1. Parent health status before pregnancy
2. Parent health status during pregnancy
   a. Nutrition
   b. Exposure to substances (e.g., lead, drugs, and alcohol)
   c. Chronic stress
   d. Parents' age of first pregnancy
   e. Complications during pregnancy or delivery
3. Student birth history
   a. Weight
   b. Condition at birth, complications, and so forth
   c. Developmental history
   d. Milestones (e.g., walk, talk, toilet trained)
   e. Delays (e.g., motor, language)

4. Medical history
    a. Asthma, allergies, ABIs, significant illnesses
    b. Hearing and vision status
    c. Medications
    d. Nutritional status (current dietary practices)
    e. Sleep issues (give parents examples)
    f. Family history of mental health, learning disorders, medical problems (give parents examples)

5. Family history/functioning
    a. Parent employment and educational status
    b. Status of parents' relationship
    c. Discipline practices
    d. Child's relationship with siblings and caregivers
    e. Recreation activities and affiliation with religious organizations
    f. Extended family and support networks
    g. Language spoken in the home and migration history
    h. Expectations, concerns, and goals for children

6. Neighborhood and community
    a. Resources available (e.g., recreation activities, municipal responsiveness)
    b. Neighborhood violence and parental concerns
    c. Role models/gang influence
    d. Perception of achievement in the community or by neighborhood peers

7. Child adjustment
    a. Description of child's personality from caregiver's perspective (e.g., strengths and weaknesses)
    b. Child's response to frustration and disappointment
    c. Child's response to discipline strategies
    d. Child's relationship with friends in neighborhood
    e. Child's preferred recreational activities and hobbies
    f. Child's academic strengths and needs as perceived by the caregivers
    g. Source of the problem as perceived by caregivers

8. Traumatic experiences
    a. Vehicular accidents, man-made disasters, natural disasters, wars
    b. Home and/or community violence
    c. Threats to life or fear for life
    d. Migration experiences

9. Protective factors

   a. Functional family life/relationship with parents

   b. Support network

   c. Access to social services

   d. Affiliation with religious organizations

   e. Parents educational and employment status

   f. Role models

   g. Before- and after-school adult supervision

   h. Community resources

   i. Opportunities to be involved in ongoing enriching and stimulating educational experiences

OBTAINING MULTIPLE SOURCES OF INFORMATION

An assessment procedure should be built on multiple sources of information that help generate logical and viable hypotheses about the child's educational needs. Interviews with parent, teachers, and the child help clarify the areas of concern. Behavioral observation provides a vital link to the child's performance in a natural setting. Review of educational records assists in establishing and documenting the child's educational and behavioral strengths and needs over a long period of time as well as interventions attempted. Assessment of academic ecology is also important to the overall assessment process because it provides information regarding classroom behaviors that reinforce or inhibit learning.

Interview

Parents as well as school personnel (e.g., teachers, educational assistants, bus driver) who are involved on a daily basis with the child should be interviewed. Often when the interview involves the parents, the assessor establishes rapport with the parent by encouraging an atmosphere of acceptance, respect, and empathy (Sattler, 2002). Parents must feel comfortable sharing private and sensitive information. Assessors should come to the interview prepared with questions that relate to the referral concerns; facilitate the gathering of relevant background information; and allow the parent to express his or her concerns, perception of the situation, hopes, and expectations for his or her child. Good listening skills are essential. Frequently, parents have experienced learning difficulties similar to their children's, and they find it difficult or painful to discuss them. In some cases they harbor resentment regarding the way they were treated in school, and this resentment is exhibited when discussing their children's school problems. Interviewers must accept or validate the parent's frustration by listening and showing empathy with appropriate body language.

Cultural competence is paramount when interacting with parents from diverse linguistic and cultural backgrounds. Knowledge of the typical influence of poverty on parents' ability to gain access to resources in their community and in school should be considered by the interviewers. These sensitivities should extend to making recommendations to parents. For example, recommending to a parent of limited income that he or she should consider hiring a tutor can be insensitive. A better recommendation would be to match the parent with a community agency that offers free tutoring or educational services on a sliding scale. In the same way, recommending that a parent with known reading difficulties help his or her child by reading with the child may show a lack of understanding on the part of the psychologist or educator. Connecting the parent to community resources or to after-school programs is a much more considerate and helpful solution.

The assessor should explain the assessment and special education process to the parents. For example, explaining the reason for the interview and for the type of questions asked, confidentiality, description of the assessment procedure, review of the problem or concern, and description of the typical multidisciplinary meeting serve to further improve the rapport with the parents and it facilitates parents' participation in the process. Parents should be prepared for the multidisciplinary meeting (who attends, what would be discussed, and their role in the meeting). The assessor should make every attempt to meet with the parents to discuss the results of the assessment before going to the multidisciplinary meeting because this allow parents to prepare themselves emotionally, to feel more comfortable asking questions, and to participate in the process. Assessors prepare and empower parents for the special education process by discussing results of the assessment, encouraging questions and expression of concerns, describing the process (pro and con), explaining procedural safeguards, listening and accepting preoccupations about labeling, acknowledging disappointment with the system, giving suggestions of things that parents can do to help the child that are within the parents' abilities, being empathetic (verbally and nonverbally) when giving less than optimal results, and discussing positive characteristics of the child and not only the areas of needs.

Interviewing the child's teachers is also crucial. Information that should be obtained includes all areas of basic academic skills, instructional procedures, specific material used, the curriculum, and the child's performance (current level of functioning in the curriculum, expected levels of skills of the average student in the class, type of instructional setting [small- or large-group setting], cooperative learning, and learning centers; Shapiro, 2004). Bergan and Kratochwill (1990) described a behavioral consultation process that consists of a series of interview questions developed to identify the problem, analyze the critical variables contributing to the problem, develop and implement intervention plans, and assess the effectiveness of the intervention. This format has shown good reliability (see Erchul, Covington, Hughes, & Meyers, 1995; Kratochwill, Elliot, & Busse, 1995) and has been validated (see Noll, Kamps, & Seaborn, 1993; Witt, 1990). Teachers should be asked how the instructional time is allotted and divided, how changes are made in the instructional program, and what student skills were targeted (Shapiro, 2004). The Appendix in the back of the book contains a form that illustrates the interview process. Other variables that affect children's performance (e.g., motivation, study skills, behavioral concerns, lack of practice) should also be explored with the teacher.

Observation

Observing a child in a natural setting is an assessment's greatest source of ecological validity. Behavioral observation contributes to the assessment process in the following ways: offers a picture of the child's spontaneous behavior, gives information about the child's interpersonal behaviors and learning style, provides a systematic record of the child's behaviors, allows for validation of the accuracy of teachers' and parents' reports, facilitates comparisons between behavior during tests and behavior in a natural setting, offers comparisons between the child and classmates, and permits functional assessment of behavior (Sattler, 2002).

When planning a behavioral observation, the child should be observed not only in the environment where he or she is experiencing difficulties, but also in environments where he or she is meeting success. This allows the assessor to identify factors within the environments that encourage or reinforce success and those that may influence the child's performance negatively. When observing a child in the classroom, it is important to document not only what the child is doing, but also the behavior of the teacher and class peers. Depending on the goal of the assessment, a systematic observation system or a more descriptive or narrative approach can be used. A narrative approach is more useful in situations where one is seeking to develop a hypothesis about the child's behavior. An observation that seeks to record the frequency, duration, and intensity of a behavior would necessitate a more systematic and quantitative approach. Interval (i.e., document behaviors as they occur within a specified period of time), rating (i.e., rating behavior on a scale), and event (i.e., document each instance of a targeted behavior during the observation period) recordings allow the assessor to better quantify and evaluate specific behavior as well as compare the child's behavior to that of others (Sattler, 2002). The approach used depends on the questions that need to be answered by the assessment.

Review of Educational Records

Schools keep records of children's advancement or school performance. These records provide valuable information to diagnosticians or assessors because they may help validate referral concerns. The child's cumulative records hold a history of grades, report cards, performance on districtwide assessments, teachers' concerns, and communications with parents regarding the child's school progress. It may also contain disciplinary notes and slips describing behavioral incidences and outcomes. Report cards and districtwide assessments provide a history of the child's academic progress or lack of progress and also document teachers' concerns over an extended period of time. When compared with the reason the child was referred, it helps assessors or diagnosticians determine if the problem has been ongoing or if it is a new concern. Review of the child's educational records helps the assessor gain insight into the child's learning problems in order to develop a hypothesis that would contribute to decisions about the assessment process.

Classroom Ecology

A complete examination of the academic or classroom ecology is a crucial component of the evaluation of a child's academic skills (Shapiro, 2004). A number of factors are relevant to this process: academic engaged time, classroom contingencies, teacher expectation, progress monitoring, and goal setting. These factors have been shown in research to influence student performance. Academic engaged time refers to the time the student is actively involved in academic tasks, and research has yielded a positive association between time engaged in academics and learning (Gettinger, 1986). This type of information can be obtained through classroom observation. Shapiro (2004) emphasized the assessment of engaged time or active learning and not simply time on-task. Linked to the concept of engaged time is opportunity to respond, which clearly reflects active involvement in learning. Behaviors that happen before and after the child responds influence a child's performance. Instructional factors such as instructional style (e.g., instructional pacing and presentation), teacher feedback, competing contingencies, and teacher–student monitoring procedures and expectations have been shown to influence a student's performance and can be assessed by observing the classroom ecology (for more details, see Shapiro, 2004).

In a classroom setting, there are other stimuli that affect the child's behavior. One of these is teacher expectation, and there have been many studies to substantiate the notion that teacher expectation has an effect on children's performance in school. Teachers who instruct in schools where children are from a background of poverty expect less and provide less rigorous academic instruction and a lower standard of achievement (Hauser-Cram, Sirin, & Stipek, 2003; McLoyd, 1998). Studies have shown that children's self-perceptions of ability and effort affect achievement behavior (Pintrich & Blumenfeld, 1985), and attributional studies note that teacher feedback, feedback obtained from comparison with peers, and performance influence self-perception (Pintrich & Blumenfeld, 1985). In a study that explored the relationship among teachers' appraisal of intelligence, concurrent child characteristics, and future high school performance, researchers found that the judgments teachers made about the children's cognitive abilities before the students began kindergarten had a predictive relationship with school achievement 14 years later, before any early differences were apparent in IQ scores, socioeconomic status, and perceived behavioral attributes (Alvidrez & Weinstein, 1999). These predictions were stronger for children for whom teacher perceptions were negative and weaker for children from more advantageous backgrounds (Alvidrez & Weinstein, 1999). Teachers' appraisals and expectations for their students have an influential effect and implications for curricular and instructional opportunities as well as educational programming. Psychologists and other diagnostic school practitioners must be cognizant of the critical effect teacher expectation can have on children's performance and referral for special education services.

ASSESSMENT PROCEDURE

Students who are culturally and linguistically diverse and children from low socioeconomic backgrounds have traditionally been overrepresented in special education categories, specifically learning disability, mental retardation, and seriously emotionally disturbed (Rhodes et al., 2005). Several researchers have asserted that bias plays a significant role in the overrepresentation and/or underrepresentation of some culturally and linguistically diverse populations in special education (Losen & Orfield, 2002). This bias and discrimination is believed to be inherent in school practices in terms of instructional issues, referral procedures, and assessment practices (Rhodes et al., 2005). Other reasons that have been provided for this overrepresentation include lack of prereferral interventions—increasing the likelihood of a referral; inadequately trained practitioners; inappropriate assessment practices; and failure to comply with federal or state guidelines by administering tests in a language other than the child's native language (Rhodes et al., 2005). Regarding common test instruments used to assess children from nonmajority backgrounds, Padilla (2001) identified three major ways these tests may be biased: 1) the very content or construction of test items may reflect bias in that they provide unfair advantage to one group over another; 2) features of the tests such as formatting, mode of administration, vocabulary and sentence structure, or even examiner personality may offer advantage to one group over another; and 3) inappropriate application of tests that may result in identifying one group of students over another. Assessment procedures of these children's strengths and needs calls for more comprehensive and flexible assessment practices that include children's functioning in everyday life (Alper, 2001).

Another relevant factor in the assessment of these children is the experience of the individual who is conducting the assessment. Many assessors are not trained to test children who are linguistically and culturally diverse. They administer tests solely in English to children who are bilingual, overestimate the child's proficiency in English, rely on poorly trained interpreters, or select inappropriate instruments and interpret the resulting data without consideration for linguistic and cultural differences (Ochoa, Rivera, & Ford, 1997; Rhodes et al., 2005). In the same manner, many assessors do not understand the ethnocultural and socioecological context that shape the lives of children who come from low-income families and are culturally and linguistically diverse (Rosado, 1986). Although they may recognize that poverty plays a role in these children's plight, they do not know how to incorporate such knowledge into their assessment practices (Rhodes et al., 2005; Rosado, 1986).

Guided by the background information and the referral questions, the assessment procedure is planned. The assessment procedure consists of the selection of psychological instruments that are appropriate for the child, answers the referral questions, and accommodates the child's unique background and diverse experiences.

Test Selections

The assessor's decision regarding tests is based on a number of factors beginning with the reason for the referral, the unique characteristics of the individual being assessed, and important aspects of the tests. Test selection should be made based on the following considerations.

1. *Select tests that answer the referral questions.* The referral question is the guiding force behind test selection because it provides the goals for the assessment and determines the scope and focus of the assessment (i.e., how broad or narrow). If a child is referred because he or she is not making expected progress in most areas of achievement in school, then the scope would be broad in the beginning to identify possible reasons for the lack of progress in learning. Once these areas of concern in learning have been identified, a keener focus is placed on further examining the areas of need to obtain information that would be instrumental in developing strategies for effective intervention. If a child is referred because he or she is not making expected progress in reading, then the scope of the assessment is narrower, with the focus placed more tightly on determining aspects of reading that are deficient.

2. *Select tests that are valid and reliable.* Narrowing the selection of tests to those that meet reasonable criteria for validity and reliability and that have appropriate norms is essential (Lezak, Howieson, & Loring, 2004). *Validity* is defined as the extent to which a test measures what it intends to measure and the appropriateness with which one can make inferences based on the results of the test (Sattler, 2001). *Reliability* refers to the consistency or regularity of test results (e.g., dependable, reproducible, stable results under similar conditions; Sattler, 2001).

3. *Select tests that are less affected by the child's background (ethnicity/race, culture, language, and literacy level).* The examiner must be aware of cultural, linguistic, and socioeconomic influences and bias when working with children from diverse backgrounds. There has been greater availability of tests standardized and normed on major cultural and linguistic groups in the United States (e.g., Spanish WISC–IV, Wechsler, 2004; Bateria III, Muñoz-Sandoval, Woodcock,

McGrew, & Mather, 2005; KABC–II, Kaufman & Kaufman, 2004). It is, however, impossible to develop tests that are appropriate for all cultural, linguistic, and socioeconomic groups; moreover, there are differences within these groups. Therefore, it is best to use instruments that demonstrate the least cross-cultural differences (Lezak et al., 2004). Examiners must be aware of the influence of diverse background experiences on test behaviors and scores. For example, educational experience plays a significant role in affecting test scores in unwanted ways because a low score may not be indicative of cognitive deficiency but lack of experience. Tests that have teaching items, however, allow the examiner to account for the lack of, and possibly minimize the effect of, experience.

4. *Build an assessment battery that is comprehensive and has a theoretical foundation.* Batteries that assess multiple skills critical to learning provide a more valid and rounded picture of children's functioning. They also facilitate ascertaining the influence of children's diverse background experiences. Test selection should also represent a strong theoretical and research foundation such as the Cattel-Horn-Carrol (CHC) Gf-Gc theory, which has significant support from factor analytic studies (for more information on the CHC theory, please see Carroll, 1993). Other approaches include the brain–behavior perspective that has significant research support based on neuroimaging techniques (see Baron, 2004, and Lezak et al., 2004, for a more detailed review), and the Planning, Attention, Simultaneous, Successive (PASS) model (see Naglieri & Das, 2005). These approaches allow examiners to identify intervention strategies that are based on the results of the assessment.

5. *Include nonstandardized or informal tests in the battery.* These instruments can include examiner-made tests or materials used in different ways (e.g., grade-level reading books can be used informally to assess reading difficulties). Informal tests allow examiners to test-teach-retest children to see the benefit of different kinds of interventions and to ascertain the child's level of learning need. As part of a battery, informal tests make up for the typical pitfalls of standardized tests: inflexible, nonreflective of real-life school demands (McAfee & Leong, 2002), unsuitable for diverse populations (Padilla, 2001; Thomas, 1992), highly contextualized, and reflective of middle-class values and practices (Gopaul-McNicol & Thomas-Presswood, 1998; Sattler, 2001). Standardized tests, however, do have their place in the assessment process, but assessors must be aware of their limitations and supplement assessment procedures with informal or nonstandardized materials that afford a better understanding of a child's functioning in a real-life situation with authentic school materials. Children, particularly young children, who are not able to respond to structured tasks of standardized tests may demonstrate their skills and knowledge in informal real-life situations (McAfee & Leong, 2002).

Gathering and analyzing children's work is another effective way of assessing their learning strengths and needs. Using a portfolio presents such a method of examining and assessing the child's work over a period of time. A portfolio is an organized collection of material documenting a child's development of a skill and learning over a period of time. Portfolios can fulfill the needs of an assessment because they can be used to establish children's status and progress, guide instruction, give information for reporting and communicating, and provide initial identification of children who might need special services (McAfee & Leong, 2002). Other informal assessment strategies include teacher and/or parent anecdotal records, frequency counts, descriptive narratives, checklists, participation charts, and the child's notebook. (For more detailed information on alternative assessment, see McAfee & Leong, 2002.)

The referral question, the child's characteristics, and the examiner's experience are primary in determining the test instruments that would be employed. During the assessment, however, skilled examiners may drop some tests or add others as they obtain a fuller picture of the child's skills (Lezak et al., 2004).

Verbal and Nonverbal Testing Procedures

Many assessors use nonverbal tests when assessing children of diverse backgrounds because language is often considered the factor most influenced by cultural and linguistic differences and low socioeconomic backgrounds. Nonverbal tests differ, however, in the extent to which they depend on receptive and expressive language in the administration and in eliciting response from the examinee. Tests are considered nonverbal when they include tasks designed to assess cognitive or other abilities in a manner that oral or verbal communication are not necessary from the assessor to administer the test or from the child to complete the task (McCallum, 2003). Other modes of administering and responding are used (e.g., gesturing, pointing). One must note, though, that a small number of nonverbal tests exist that successfully employ both an administration and a response style that is completely nonverbal.

Assessors need to consider the characteristics of the particular nonverbal test because a number of these tests require that the child respond nonverbally, whereas the administration relies on a verbal presentation. Being aware of the linguistic demand of a test is critical to the selection of tests because a nonverbal test that requires a high degree of receptive language may not be valid or appropriate to administer to children who demonstrate limited understanding of the English language.

In their discussion on the appropriateness of nonverbal tests for assessment of children who are culturally and linguistically diverse, Flanagan and Ortiz (2001) indicated that bias in testing may come from one of three characteristics of tests: the cultural content embedded in a test, the linguistic requirement in the test, and lack of representation within a normative sample of individuals from diverse backgrounds. Nonverbal tests are subject to these pitfalls as well. Nonverbal tests were developed to minimize the problems associated with administering verbally loaded psychological instruments, but many psychological instruments are purposely designed using methods that presume a particular level of language proficiency (receptively or expressively) to complete the tasks required (Cummins, 1984; Rhodes et al., 2005). Psychological tests typically reflect the culture of the majority group and the developers (Flanagan & Ortiz, 2001; Lonner, 1985). Therefore, interpretation of the results in a culturally and linguistically sensitive manner is imperative. Some practitioners interpret test results in a qualitative way that can incorporate the child's unique experiences. Many still, however, work closely with a more quantitative approach because they assume that the assessment is nonbiased when using a nonverbal instrument.

Bilingual and Multicultural Assessment Procedures

As the U.S. population becomes more culturally and linguistically diverse, there is a more pressing need for practitioners who are more knowledgeable and skilled in working with children and their families in schools, hospitals, and community clinics. A significant percentage of children who live under conditions of poverty are also culturally and linguistically diverse. Many scholars and practitioners in the field of psychological assessment and counseling have addressed this issue and proposed procedures that are nonbiased and nondiscriminatory, with various degrees of success (see Dana, 1993; Gopaul-McNicol & Thomas-Presswood, 1998; Padilla, 2001; Rhodes et al., 2005; Roseberry-McKibbin, 2002; Samuda, Kong, Cummins, Pascual-Leone, & Lewis, 1991; Suzuki, Ponterotto, & Meller, 2001b).

An assessment procedure that is nondiscriminatory when working with children from culturally and linguistically diverse backgrounds must be built on some fundamental concepts about psychological tests. These concepts have to do with patterns of bias that exist in standardized tests. Ortiz and Dynda (2005) fluently discussed these concepts that must be acknowledged if an assessment is to reach valid conclusions:

1. Understanding cultural influences (bias versus loading)
2. Understanding linguistic issues (bias versus demand)
3. Understanding norm sample issues (inclusion versus representation)

Assessors must understand that there is cultural information imbedded in any test, and performance on a test indicates the degree of exposure to this information or acquisition of those skills and abilities that are important in successfully completing the tasks on the test (Ortiz & Dynda, 2005). Research and test developers have addressed the psychometric appearance of bias as dictated by statistical differences in performance attributed to cultural difference. Individuals' lack of experience (i.e., acculturation) with a test's underlying cultural content (or loading), however, adversely affects performance on the instruments (Ortiz & Dynda, 2005).

Language presents a similar problem. Most practitioners accept that language development is characterized by an ordered and measurable developmental course greatly influenced by experience. In a similar manner, argued Ortiz and Dynda (2005), the items on standardized tests are sequenced and arranged developmentally, and the attenuating influence of language proficiency is not readily observed when comparing performances on any single test. It is the comparison between verbal subtests and nonverbal subtests, however, that reveals bias in test (Rhodes et al., 2005). Assessors must acknowledge and plan for the influence of language proficiency on tests of cognitive abilities because these tests assume a level of proficiency to understand and follow instruction, comprehend basic concepts, and develop and verbalize answers (Cummins, 1984; Rhodes et al., 2005). Bilingual children's language skills fall on a spectrum in regard to English and their native language that ranges from high proficiency in both languages to high proficiency in one and limited in another to limited proficiency in both languages. Given these basic concepts regarding tests items, linguistic demands (e.g., test activities' assumptions about language proficiency) and linguistic characteristics of bilingual children (i.e., differences in proficiency), it is easy to understand that grade- and age-based scores do not offer an appropriate comparison of performance for English language learners because such comparisons are made on the foundation of age- and grade-expected language developmental skills (Ortiz & Dynda, 2005).

Another concept relevant to the assessment of children who are culturally and linguistically diverse is their representation in the normative samples of standardized tests. Ortiz and Dynda (2005) emphasized that appropriate comparisons of performance are attained only when the individual's background and experiences are similar to those of the individuals that make up the norm sample. So, although test developers have been more diligent in obtaining a sample that is representative of the U.S. population in terms of race, ethnicity, age, socioeconomic status, and educational level, the fundamental problem of experience, variation in English language proficiency, and/or acculturation remains. Cognitive instruments that offer a norm sample composed of monolingual English speakers and/or monolingual native-language speakers are still inadequate for comparison purposes because bilingual speakers bring to the table background experiences that are different from the norm sample (Ortiz & Dynda, 2005). For test interpretations to be valid, practitioners must have a grounded understanding of these issues and make appropriate planning in their assessment procedures.

Based on these conceptual issues, Ortiz and Ochoa (2005) proposed a nondiscriminatory interpretive assessment approach to guide practitioners in determining the best approach to follow in the assessment of diverse school-age children that would lead to more valid results. The Multidimensional Assessment Model for Bilingual Individuals (MAMBI; Ortiz & Ochoa, 2005; see Figure 4.4) incorporates variables that are crucial to attaining valid results and appropriate recommendations for interventions:

Instructional program/history	Currently in a bilingual education program in lieu of, or in addition to, receiving ESL services								Previously in bilingual education program, now receiving English-only or ESL services								All instruction has been in an English-only program, with or without ESL services							
Current grade	K–4				5–7				K–4				5–7				K–4				5–7			
Assessment mode	NV	L1	L2	BL	NV	L1	L2	BL	NV	L1	L2	BL	NV	L1	L2	BL	NV	L1	L2	BL	NV	L1	L2	BL
Language profile 1 (L1 minimal/L2 minimal)	⊘	✓		✓	⊘	✓	✓	✓	⊘	✓		✓	⊘	✓	✓	✓	⊘	✓	✓*	✓	⊘	✓	✓	✓
Language profile 2 (L1 emergent/L2 minimal)	⊘	✓		✓	⊘	✓	✓	✓	⊘	✓		✓	⊘	✓	✓	✓	⊘	✓	✓*	✓	⊘	✓	✓	✓
Language profile 3 (L1 fluent/L2 minimal)		⊘				⊘	✓	✓		⊘				⊘	✓	✓						⊘	✓	✓
Language profile 4 (L1 minimal/L2 emergent)	⊘				⊘	✓	✓	✓	⊘		✓	✓	⊘		✓	✓	⊘		✓#	✓	⊘		✓	✓
Language profile 5 (L1 emergent/L2 emergent)	⊘	✓		✓	⊘	✓	✓	✓	⊘	✓	✓	✓	⊘	✓	✓	✓	⊘	✓	✓#	✓	⊘	✓	✓	✓
Language profile 6 (L1 fluent/L2 emergent)		⊘				⊘	✓	✓		⊘				⊘		✓								
Language profile 7 (L1 minimal/L2 fluent)																								
Language profile 8 (L1 emergent/L2 fluent)								⊘								⊘								⊘
Language profile 9 (L1 fluent/L2 fluent)								⊘		⊘				⊘		⊘								✓

Figure 4.4. Ochoa and Ortiz's Multidimensional Assessment Model for Bilingual Individuals (MAMBI). *Note:* CALP level 1–2 = minimal proficiency; CALP level 3 = emergent proficiency; CALP level 4–5 = fluent proficiency. NV = assessment conducted primarily in a nonverbal manner with English-language-reduced/acculturation-reduced measures; L1 = assessment conducted in the first language learned by the individual (i.e., native or primary language); L2 = assessment conducted in the second language learned by the individual, which in most cases refers to English; BL = assessment conducted relatively equally in both languages learned by the individual (i.e., native language and English). Shaded box = combinations of language development and instruction that are improbable or due to other factors (e.g., Saturday school, foreign-born adoptees, delayed school entry); circled checkmark = recommended mode of assessment that should take priority over other modes and which is more likely to be the most accurate estimate of the student's true abilities; regular checkmark = secondary or optional mode of assessment that may provide additional valuable information but which will likely result in an underestimate of the student's abilities; checkmark with asterisk = mode of assessment not recommended for students in K–2, but may be informative in 3–4, although results will likely be an underestimate of true ability; checkmark with pound sign = mode of assessment not recommended for students in K–1, but may be informative in 2–4, although results will likely be an underestimate of true ability. (From Rhodes, R.L., Ochoa, S.H., & Ortiz, S.O. [2005]. *Assessing culturally and linguistically diverse students.* New York: Guilford Press; reprinted by permission.)

89

1. Current degree of language proficiency in English and the native language

2. Current and previous types of educational programs (e.g., English as a second language, bilingual education, immersion programs)

3. Current grade level

These variables assist practitioners in identifying and selecting the assessment procedure appropriate for the bilingual child, such as

1. Reduced culture/language testing

2. Testing in native language

3. Testing in English

4. Bilingual testing

In many instances, the cultural and linguistic experiences of the child are such that a combination of several of the approaches better match the needs of the child. The MAMBI provides a comprehensive and systematic integration of all the critical factors important to determining assessment approaches with diverse children. Figure 4.4 illustrates the three central variables involved in the decision-making process: language profile, instructional programming/history, and current grade level, which are highlighted by the Ortiz and Ochoa (2005) model, and provides guidance as to the most appropriate assessment modality giving the child's characteristics. (For more details on this model, see Rhodes et al., 2005.)

School Neuropsychological Assessment Procedures

The most important contribution of a school neuropsychological approach is that it encourages an integrated explanation of behavior, blending hypotheses about distinct brain function with an understanding of a person's personality, life stressors, and social or family relationships (LaRue, 1992). A school neuropsychological assessment is guided by two rules: each student should be treated as an individual, and as such, the assessment should be tailored to the student's strengths and needs (Bernstein, 2000; Lezak et al., 2004). This perspective holds that many distinct cognitive functions work together smoothly in the intact brain so that cognition is experienced as a single attribute (Lezak et al., 2004). Therefore, to understand a child's achievement or behavioral difficulties, the diagnostician needs to test the integrity of these discrete cognitive factors that contribute to learning to better understand the problem so the results may be instrumental in informing instruction. The results of the assessment cannot be interpreted blindly. The interpretation must be done with the benefit of social history, behavioral observations, record review, and interviews, as well as an understanding of cultural, linguistic, and socioeconomic influences, because all of these not only affect scores and attitudes toward symptoms, but also provide insight into risk factors and help develop hypotheses (Hale & Fiorello, 2004). Psychological tests are said to be a means of enhancing observations (Lezak et al., 2004), so quantitative as well as qualitative data are essential to the process of hypotheses testing.

The critical learning or cognitive functions examined during a school neuropsychological assessment include executive functions, memory, language, motor output, sensory perceptual, attention, and social-emotional. Hale and Fiorello (2004) suggested conducting a screening battery that consists of a classroom observation, thorough social history, a measure of cognitive functioning, and a multidimensional achievement test. This screening battery would provide information on which to begin developing a hypothesis. If all data are within normal limits and the assessor feels it reflects the child's current level of functioning, then no further assessment is needed. If there are areas of concern, however, then additional testing more tightly tailored to the child is required to test the hypothesis for its validity and to make valid diagnostic decisions.

Hale and Fiorello (2004) proposed using the cognitive hypothesis-testing (CHT) model that focuses on examining the input, processing, and output demands of a test administered and then linking the findings to all other obtained data. For example, if the referral concern is lack of adequate progress in reading, then the assessor begins the process by gathering data from parents and teachers, observing the child, reviewing school records, and seeing the student's actual work in the classroom. Based on this information, the assessor begins to form some tentative hypotheses as to the problem at hand. A screening battery is conducted and yields results pointing to a decoding problem that prompts the assessor to develop more specific hypotheses about the areas of reading that are weak. The assessor then selects the instruments that would be most useful in investigating the hypotheses and whose format best suits the needs of the child. The assessor then begins to assess more intensely in the areas of learning that would most affect reading. Once all the data has been gathered during the hypothesis testing stage, a reexamination of the information gathered should occur to determine if the initial hypothesis was substantiated (Hale & Fiorello, 2004).

The next important step is to determine if the resulting data support what is occurring in the child's learning environment (i.e., ecological validity) by observing the classroom, reviewing data gathered, consulting with parents and teachers, and interviewing the student. This would help clarify any inconsistent data and give life to quantitative data and qualitative observation obtained during the assessment. Matching assessment data to classroom learning and performance and discussing these with teachers and parents sets the stage for developing interventions that are directly linked to assessment. Hale and Fiorello (2004) provided several recommendations to consider when designing intervention:

1. Interventions should be ecologically valid.
2. Intervention efficacy and treatment validity is required.
3. Interventions should be adaptable and flexible.
4. Interventions should be based on skills used in the classroom.
5. Interventions should be individualized and suited to the child's needs.

The last stage involves developing monitoring strategies that would help make decisions regarding changes and adjustments in the interventions implemented. The hypothesis testing continues even during the intervention stage. To determine the efficacy of the intervention, data gathering should continue. To evaluate the effectiveness of an intervention, the assessor must identify ways of measuring the outcome and collect baseline data for comparison. Consulting and collaborating with the teacher and other school staff is essential to monitoring and evaluating the effectiveness of the intervention implemented. (For more specific information on the CHT model, please review Hale and Fiorello, 2004.)

A school neuropsychological perspective in assessment is comprehensive, and results from comprehensive assessments provide a multidimensional view of the person. Abilities, achievements, temperament, motivations, experiences, and behaviors are all considered as factors that contribute to academic performance and influence the selection of appropriate interventions (Mather & Wendling, 2005).

Dynamic Assessment Procedures

Dynamic assessment has been described as another sensitive and appropriate assessment to be used with children from a background of poverty as well as those who are culturally and linguistically diverse. Dynamic assessment provides a nontraditional approach to assessment and a more direct route of linking assessment with intervention. Studies using dynamic assessment demonstrate the contribution of this approach in identifying gifted minority children (Lidz & Macrineb, 2001) and reducing test bias in the assessment of children who are culturally and linguistically diverse (Peña, Iglesias, & Lidz, 2001). Lidz (2003) described dynamic assessment as the inclusion of interaction to optimize the functioning of the learner during the evaluation process. Most dynamic approaches use a pretest-intervention-posttest format, and they emphasize learning process instead of product (Lidz, 2003). This approach yields diagnostic information such as the child's ability to benefit from instruction, the intensity of intervention required to improve the child's competence, the types of processes impeding optimal performance, and the kinds of interventions that show promise for improving the child's mastery of the work (Lidz, 2003). In order to be effective at this procedure, the practitioner must be specially trained. Dynamic assessment is not a substitute for standardized procedures, but added to a battery, it greatly enhances the usefulness and interpretive power of the information obtained. Dynamic assessment can also be administered alone to provide meaningful information about how a child learns and how to boost the learning process for a particular child.

Lidz (1991) discussed four main models of dynamic assessment: Feuerstein's approach (Feuerstein, Rand, & Hoffman, 1979), Budoff's standardized procedures (Budoff, 1987), Campione and Brown's graduated prompts (Brown &

Campione, 1994), and Lidz's curriculum-based dynamic assessment (see Lidz, 1991, for details). Feuerstein's approach emphasized intervention and analyzed the child's performance based on an extensive battery of Learning Potential Assessment Devices, which are adapted tests that included an intervention component. This approach to dynamic assessment required that the child's response be followed and matched with a degree of intervention needed for the child to progress. Lidz (2003) described this approach as clinical, intuitive, and requiring familiarity with Feuerstein's theory of cognitive modifiability and related concepts. The second model was designed by Budoff and was more standardized to accurately identify students who had mental retardation from those who lacked background experiences. The approach showed good validity, and it is used by some school districts in the United States. The Budoff approach employed a series of tests with a pretest-intervene-posttest format based on standardized teaching procedures that all children receive for task solution (Lidz, 2003). Campione and Brown's graduated prompts were developed based on Vygotsky's concepts and theoretical perspective. They operationalized Vygotky's concept of zone of proximal development (ZPD) using rubrics for counting the number of clues given to students to solve problems (Lidz, 2003). Students' learning is described by the number of clues needed to solve a problem. Campione and Brown have linked their model of dynamic assessment with academic task (Lidz, 2003), making it even more relevant to children's learning in the educational setting.

Lidz's curriculum-based approach is grounded in her work as a school psychologist. Recognizing the need to link assessment to valid interventions that guide instruction, Lidz (2003) selected activities from the classroom that reflected referral concerns (e.g., math, writing, reading). Assessment starts where most standardized tests end (i.e., ceiling), and an interactive approach (i.e., pretest-intervention-posttest) is added to the assessment. A neuropsychological perspective is incorporated by analyzing the mental process (e.g., critical learning areas: attention, perception, memory, metacognition/executive functions) required to work on the task presented, and the assessor documents how much it demands from the student (Lidz, 2003). The interventions selected are empirically based and demonstrate best teaching practices regarding the cognitive process required. Lidz's curriculum-based dynamic assessment can be used to enhance a comprehensive assessment and provide insight into a child's learning potential and style. It minimizes the effect of lack of experience, and it offers meaningful guides to inform classroom instruction. (For more detail of this model, please see Lidz, 2003.)

Interpretation of Data, Educational Implication, and Link to Intervention

Interpretation must be based on knowledge of typical cognitive development and educational progress. This knowledge is juxtaposed to the child's personal information gathered through social, medical, family, and school histories; interviews; and behavioral observations to determine if a problem might be present or to validate the referral question. Once all data are gathered and the assessment phase is complete, the assessor should look for patterns. The information resulting from cognitive and achievement measures is interpreted in light of the background information, interviews, behavioral observations, and knowledge of the typical developmental cognitive and learning process of children. Their match to ecological information determines the validity of the normative data or scores obtained from cognitive measures and achievement tests. This level of information gathering not only documents the severity of the problem and provides insight into possible interventions, but also helps make decisions as to whether the problem is important enough to require interventions.

During the analysis and interpretation of the data gathered, assessors should continuously make links to the possible implications for learning in a classroom setting and the contribution of background experiences or risk factors to the resulting data. Recommendations for intervention should consider learning strengths, social-emotional factors (e.g., motivation, self-efficacy), and protective factors because these are typically instrumental in the success of an intervention. Proposed interventions should specifically align with the resulting data of the assessment and answer referral concerns. Once interventions are implemented, ongoing assessment to determine the effectiveness of the intervention to improve the child's learning is required. Included in the recommendations should be specific plans for monitoring the child's progress. Most important to this process is to understand that assessment and intervention are two sides of the same coin (Bernstein, 2000).

5

Social-Emotional and Behavioral Assessment of Children from Poverty

A pessimist sees the difficulty in every opportunity; an optimist sees the opportunity in every difficulty.

Sir Winston Churchill

Healthy and adjusted children are those whose environments and person-level characteristics (e.g., strengths, personal competencies) offer enough positive experiences (i.e., protective factors) to counteract the negative effects of multiple risk factors. Indeed, children who were believed to be at risk for development of social and behavior disorders exhibited few or no indicators of pathology and frequently showed high levels of competence (Garmezy, 1974; Werner & Smith, 1982) due to the presence of protective factors. Current thinking on resilience emphasizes that problematic outcomes are predictable and considered a typical consequence of the deviations in developmental conditions because the processes that lead to problematic developmental outcome are the same as those that lead to favorable and positive ones (Felner, 2006). Elements of school, community, or home environments can help improve the match to the developmental needs and competencies in children (Felner, 2006). Social-emotional and behavioral assessment is a school element that can contribute significantly to the personal well-being of children referred for an evaluation because it can identify levels of need and challenges faced by children living in poverty; information gathered during the assessment can lead to the development of resilience-developing strategies for intervention. In Chapter 4, the authors presented a comprehensive model of assessment with a focus on cognitive and learning issues; this chapter is a continuation of that model but with specific emphasis on assessment of social-emotional and behavioral adjustment of children living in poverty.

Children who live in abject poverty and whose day-to-day lives unfold in environments characterized by chronic deprivation are at risk for developing emotional and behavioral difficulties. Research has documented that many environmental and familial factors as well as characteristics of the child and of the primary caregivers place children at higher risk for mental health problems (Dore, 1999; Kerker & Dore, 2006). Child factors that are typically linked to poor mental health include weak physical health, male gender, and difficult temperament (Williams, Anderson, McGee, & Silva, 1990). Family factors that are considered high risk are low-income status, marital conflict, single parenthood, large family size with children close in age, and family dysfunction (Offord, Boyle, Racine, & Fleming, 1992). Factors related to the caregiver that place children at risk include mental illness, limited education, violence in relationships, drug and alcohol abuse, and history of criminal behavior (Kerker & Dore, 2006; Offord et al., 1992). Other risks factors that should be considered are biological in nature and include familial history of mental illness, in utero exposure to drug and alcohol, and early trauma such as physical abuse (Leslie et al., 2000; Pilowsky, 1995; Shonkoff & Phillips, 2000). Children who exhibit emotional and behavioral difficulties in the classroom are often the most challenging to assess, educate, and manage. The complex nature of mental health creates a challenge for designing and implementing effective interventions (Roberts, Jacobs, Puddy, Nyre, & Vernberg, 2003). This chapter identifies effective practices in assessing the social-emotional and behavioral health of children from poverty.

Wagner, Kutash, Duchnowski, Epstein, and Sumi (2005) used data from the Special Education Elementary Longitudinal Study and the National Longitudinal Transition Study–2 to provide a national perspective on children and youth with emotional disabilities who receive special education services. Wagner et al. (2005) described the complex range of factors that explain the educational and social barriers children with emotional disorders face in school. The study revealed the following characteristics:

1. African American children were represented in a significantly larger percentage (27%) than is found in the general population (17%), and Hispanic children were underrepresented (12.1%) when compared with 16% of children in the general population

2. More than two thirds of children identified with an emotional disorder are boys

3. A high percentage of children who live in households with several risk factors for poor outcome are identified with emotional disorders:

    a.   Children living in poverty

    b.   Children living in single-parent households and whose head of household is unemployed and did not complete high school

    c.   Children living in a household where another member has a disability

4.   Receptive language difficulties

5.   Additional disability such as attention deficit disorder (ADD) or ADHD

6.   Significantly lower social skills than peers with other disabilities

7.   Receive special education services a year later than children with other disabilities

8.   More likely to have changed schools (four schools since kindergarten) than children with other disabilities; these changes in schools were due to reassignments and parents moving

9.   More likely to have been retained in a grade level than children in the general population

10.   Parents of children with emotional disorders are more likely to express dissatisfaction with their children's teachers, school, and special services than parents with children with other disabilities

11.   Parents of children with emotional disorders are more likely to help their children with homework than parents in the general population

12.   Children with emotional disorders demonstrate significant academic deficits similar to children with other disabilities

The overarching purpose of most psychological assessments is to achieve a better understanding of the student and to improve the student's quality of life by identifying problems and implementing effective interventions. According to Mash and Terdal (1997), there are four common purposes of assessment: 1) diagnosis: determining the cause of the difficulties, 2) prognosis: predicting future behaviors given certain conditions, 3) treatment design: gathering data to help in the development and implementation of effective strategies, and 4) evaluation: focusing on treatment efficacy. Understanding the problem is critical to determining the best method for measuring it (Kamphaus & Frick, 2004). Consequently, the assessment of children should be conducted within the context of a broad knowledge of developmental psychopathology (Kamphaus & Frick, 2004). Not surprisingly, developmental psychopathology argues that factors within the family and the environment play causal roles in the development of emotional and behavioral problems (Hetherington & Martin, 1986). Yet, at the same time, children's family context and environmental circumstances are only part of a complex puzzle in understanding challenging behaviors in children (Kamphaus & Frick, 2004).

DIAGNOSING SOCIAL-EMOTIONAL AND BEHAVIORAL DISORDERS IN THE SCHOOLS

School psychologists working in the schools are often responsible for identifying and diagnosing children with social-emotional and behavioral problems. They also provide counseling, design interventions, monitor progress, consult with teachers, work with families, and coordinate services with outside agencies (Roberts et al., 2003). School psychologists are guided by special education law, which uses a different nomenclature than mental health practitioners in diagnosing and categorizing children with emotional and behavioral disorders (Roberts et al., 2003).

An emotional disorder in the educational setting is identified based on Individuals with Disabilities Education Improvement Act (IDEIA) of 2004 prescribed procedures. This law, which was originally introduced in 1975, provides guidelines for identification of children with emotional or behavioral difficulties who are eligible for special education services. To offer school-based services, a psychological or educational evaluation must be undertaken. In addition, an educational need (i.e., a measurable effect on the child's ability to achieve) must be documented. The law requires that one or more of IDEIA's stated criteria must be met. IDEIA (2004) defines an *emotional disability* as follows:

> (4)(i) *Emotional disturbance* means a condition exhibiting one or more of the following characteristics over a long period of time and to a marked degree that adversely affects a child's educational performance:
>
> (A) An inability to learn that cannot be explained by intellectual, sensory, or health factors.
>
> (B) An inability to build or maintain satisfactory interpersonal relationships with peers and teachers.
>
> (C) Inappropriate types of behavior or feelings under normal circumstances.
>
> (D) A general pervasive mood of unhappiness or depression.
>
> (E) A tendency to develop physical symptoms or fears associated with personal or school problems.
>
> (ii) Emotional disturbance includes schizophrenia. The term does not apply to children who are socially maladjusted, unless it is determined that they have an emotional disturbance under paragraph (C)(4)(i) of this section.

Many professionals do not agree on the objectivity and validity of the federal definition to identify children with emotional disabilities (see Kaufman, 1997; Peterson & Ishii-Jordan, 1994). Others object to the exclusionary provision for children identified as "socially maladjusted." IDEIA does not define the term, and typically, children who are oppositional, who purposefully break rules, who live in environments where role models exhibit similar behaviors, and who display more externalizing behaviors as opposed to those who show more clinical or mental disorders (e.g., depression, phobias, obsessive compulsive, schizophrenia) are excluded from special education services (Forness, Kavale, & Lopez, 1993;

Kerker & Dore, 2006). Despite these shortcomings, IDEIA criteria continue to provide the framework for identifying children with significant emotional needs in school settings.

APPROPRIATE ASSESSMENT PROCEDURES FOR CHILDREN LIVING IN POVERTY

Social scientists now recognize that individuals operate within a complex set of environmental systems and that these systems influence people's psychological well-being at a fundamental level (Cauce et al., 2002). A body of research documented the emotional lives of children (see Brooks-Gunn, 1995; Cauce et al., 2002; McLoyd, 1998). This research indicated that the family, peers, school, neighborhood, and community play an important role in the life of the child, and this information should be included in a psychological assessment.

A framework for conducting comprehensive individualized assessments has been emphasized in Chapter 4, and it involves gathering data from multiple sources and using multiple methods. Standardized and objective behavioral testing procedures and projective measures, as well as parent, teacher, and child interviews; observations, and relevant background information (e.g., family, school/educational, and medical histories) should be considered when building an assessment procedure to secure a holistic view of the child.

1. *Interview with parent, child, and teacher.* Interviews are the cornerstones of the psychological assessment process. They help clarify referral issues, expectations, and refine concerns regarding behavior or emotional adjustment. They allow for history taking and enable practitioners to obtain information on the child's behavior from different perspectives. Also, they provide the opportunity to gather data on diagnostic symptoms; interventions tried; behavioral or emotional triggers; consequences of behaviors; environmental stressors; and severity, frequency, and duration of the problem. There are three types of interviews: structured, semistructured, and unstructured (Edelbrock & Costello, 1988). Structured interviews were developed to increase the reliability and validity of traditional child diagnostic procedures by decreasing interview bias (Sattler & Hoge, 2006). They provide a detailed description of the child's behavior (e.g., onset, duration, severity, frequency), level of impairment, and specific symptoms (Kamphaus & Frick, 2004). They are also linked to the American Psychiatric Association's *Diagnostic and Statistical Manual of Mental Disorders (DSM–IV–TR)*. Yet, they can be time consuming, overly dependent on *DSM–IV–TR* criteria and not on norm-referenced data, and susceptible to reporter bias (Kamphaus & Frick, 2004). Unstructured interviews are flexible, require good interviewing skills because there are no strict criteria to follow, and are helpful for clarifying issues of concern and following up on problem areas (Sattler & Hoge, 2006). Semistructured interviews do provide some guidelines, but they allow for investigating areas of concern and interpreting responses. These

types of interviews are best viewed as complementary techniques that yield valuable information during the assessment process (Sattler & Hoge, 2006).

2. *Background information/history taking.* Psychologists must frequently draw from their knowledge of child development, psychopathology, and poverty to move beyond the typical questioning on history forms and get at the specific needs of a child and his or her family. While gathering background information using an interview process, psychologists should explore the following issues:

    a.   Biological/medical: Developmental history (pre- and perinatal) and family history of illness, learning disabilities, mental illness, and so forth

    b.   Psychological/emotional assets: Coping style, personality characteristics (extrovert, introvert), self-image/self-esteem, impulse control, peer influence or relationships, and child's perception of family environment

    c.   Family history: Family perception or beliefs about the referral, parenting style and practices, discipline strategies, influence from members of extended family, marital conflict, mobility pattern, level of acculturation, parental adjustment, parental employment history or satisfaction, and family history of psychopathology

    d.   Educational history: Relationship with school professionals (positive/negative) or perception of them, history of achievement or performance, grade retention, academic strengths and weaknesses, schools attended, type of instruction and services provided in school, and relationship with peers

    e.   Social support and network: Relationship with community, extended family support, and peer influence

    f.   Spiritual/cultural/ethnic: Religious beliefs and their influence on views regarding behavioral concerns, disabilities, medical conditions, and educational and social choices

3. *Behavioral observation.* Observation procedures can provide valuable information on a child's behavior as it occurs and as it is influenced by events in the child's environment. It is a direct way of assessing target behaviors (e.g., antecedents and consequences; intensity, frequency, and severity of the behavior) and determining ecological validity of the data yielded by psychological instruments. *Ecological validity* refers to the functional and predictive relationship between the child's performance on objective measures and projective tests, and behaviors observed by parents and teachers in the child's natural environment (Sbordone & Long, 1996). Based on the behavioral concerns documented in the referral, the child can be observed in the classroom, at home, during recess or playtime, in the school cafeteria, on the playground, or during the actual testing session.

4. *Standardized, objective assessment instruments and projective measures.* Behavior rating scales and projective measures provide another level of social-emotional assessment that leads to a better understanding of the child's problems and the concerns expressed by the child's parents and teacher. Interpretation of projective measures and behavioral rating scales may present some limitations in that many psychologists misinterpret data due to inexperience working with children living in poverty. The key to using these procedures is adopting an interpretation framework that evolves within the appropriate bio-social-historical-political-experiential-psychological-linguistic context. For children whose experiences shaped their worldviews, social values, and behaviors, an understanding of their world is imperative to the interpretation of test data. For example, children may express safety concerns regarding violence in their communities or provide responses to test stimuli that reflect community values or expectations and not their own personal beliefs.

SELECTING APPROPRIATE MEASURES

Tests are administered to obtain in-depth assessment of the child's current emotional state, symptoms, interpersonal style, available internal coping resources, and environmental support (Wasserman, 2003). Psychologists may choose a combination of tests that include diagnostic, behavioral, and personality.

Nonverbal and Verbal Procedures

Children with emotional disorders tend to have difficulty with communication, specifically with understanding what others say (Wagner et al., 2005). A large percentage of children living in poverty are members of culturally and linguistically diverse groups who speak other languages. When English is not a child's first language, the assessor must consider a number of factors, such as the linguistic demands of the measures, when selecting tests as part of the assessment process. The degree of verbal demands of a test is dictated by how much language is required in the administration of the test for the individual to understand and follow instructions. Therefore, psychologists must be thoughtful of the following factors:

1. Reading demands: How much reading is required for the individual to complete the task? Tests that are heavily verbal and require considerable reading can interfere with the individual's understanding of directions and accuracy of response. If a psychologist is using a self-report measure that requires reading, then the reading level of the test should be on the child's independent reading level.

2. Expressive or spoken language demands: Extensive verbal responses can negatively affect the performance of a child whose language skills are limited.

3. Effect of linguistic demands: Do the linguistic requirements of the test limit the emotional expression of the child? The verbal demands of a test may require so much cognitive energy that it may limit the sharing of information that the test is intended to extract.

Wasserman (2003) identified three nonverbal assessment of personality techniques: drawing techniques (involve the reproduction of people, objects, or figures), object placement and play techniques (include arrangement of objects, toys, or figures in meaningful and interpretable ways), and self-rating/self-report techniques (rating pictures as they relate to oneself). Limitations for these techniques include weak statistical and theoretical underpinning, poor prediction of future behavior, and discrimination between contrasting clinical groups (Wasserman, 2003).

Behavior Rating Scales and Personality Tests

Self-rating and report measures that are verbally based are represented by broad band measures such as Behavior Assessment System for Children (BASC; Reynolds & Kamphaus, 2004) and narrow band tests such as the Child Depression Inventory (CDI; Kovacs, 1992). Other verbally mediated tests include projective measures such as the Thematic Apperception Tests (TAT; Morgan & Murray, 1935), Children Apperception Test (CAT; Bellak & Bellak, 1949); Tell-Me-A-Story (TEMAS; Costantino, Malgady, Rogler, 1988), and the Rorschach Inkblot Test (Rorschach, 1942). All these measures require considerable verbal responses and expressive language skills. As opposed to the achromatic and culturally bound pictures used by the TAT, the TEMAS was specifically developed for use with children and adolescents from a culturally and linguistically diverse background. Three sets of cards depict African American, Hispanic, and Caucasian characters interacting mostly in urban and familial settings, and the stimulus cards are culturally relevant and gender sensitive (Costantino, Malgady, Colon-Malgady, & Bailey, 1992). The TEMAS provides a way of addressing the disparity in multicultural assessment, and due to its multicultural construct, it has been used in other countries with good validity (Walton, Nuttall, & Vasquez-Nuttall, 1997). The Roberts–2 (Roberts & Gruber, 2005) is another popular test used with children who are culturally and linguistically diverse. It is a standardized test for evaluating children's social perception using stories elicited by stimulus pictures. The Roberts–2 offers three sets of test pictures or versions depicting three different ethnic groups: Hispanic, African American, and European American. Although it has the appearance of a projective test, Roberts and Gruber stated that it is not a projective test. Psychologists may also choose a combination of diagnostic and personality tests. Diagnostic tests are behavioral rating scales designed to diagnose disorders. They are developed to correspond with a diagnostic system such as the *DSM–IV–TR*. Tests such as the Beck Youth Inventories (BYI; Beck, Beck, & Jolly, 2003) and the Child Depression Inventory (CDI; Kovacs, 1992) are examples of diagnostic measures. Personality tests, such as the Personality Inventory for Children, 2nd Edition (PIC–2; Wirt, Lachar, Seat, & Broen, 2001), were developed to assess enduring underlying states and traits or dispositions such as introversion and extroversion. Although diagnostic and personality tests measure different things, the inclusion of both types of instruments in an assessment battery can lead to better understanding of the individual being evaluated. According to Kamphaus and Frick (2004), a diagnostic measure may provide information regarding the symptoms of a possible disorder, but a personality test can identify traits that may have implications for intervention or for the course or prognosis of the disorder.

Considerations in Selecting and Interpreting Behavior Rating Scales and Projective Tests

Research studies focusing on personality tests have long cautioned that practitioners should consider their interpretative points of reference because these are affected by a dominant cultural belief system (Dana, 1993; Pace et al., 2006; Thomas & Schare, 2000). Pace et al. noted that the scores of Native Americans on the Minnesota Multiphasic Personality Inventory–2 (MMPI–2; Butcher, Dalhstrom, Graham, Tellegen, & Kaemmer, 1989) will be meaningless unless placed in a holistic framework in which the scores are interpreted from a bio-psycho-social-cultural-historical-political-linguistic context. For example, researchers have argued that cross-cultural variation exists in the ages at which adolescent transition begins and ends and that it consists of a discrete period with distinctive tasks and tangible outcomes (Pace et al., 2006). Ethnographic studies suggested that African American youths who live in the inner city experience a number of factors such as age-condensed families, blurred intergenerational boundaries, accelerated life course, and structural inconsistencies in the definition of adolescent roles. All of these come together to place adolescents in adult-like or developmentally ambiguous roles from an early age. More revealing is that these roles are not evident in African American youths living in suburban areas with access to more economic resources (Burton, Obeidallah, & Allison, 1996; Pace et al., 2006). Other studies noted that for Native Americans, the end point of adolescence is not independence but dependence on the family (Red Horse, 1982). Yet other studies revealed cultural differences in gender expectations of East Indian youth in the United States (Saraswathi, 1999). Socioeconomic differences and cultural factors shape the understanding of adolescence and the developmental context it represents (Pace et al., 2006) and, hence, would affect interpretations of tests results.

   Cultural differences may also play a role in parents' acceptance of particular behavioral and emotional symptoms (Alegria et al., 1991; Cauce et al., 2002) and distress thresholds as it pertains to their children's problems (Weisz & Weiss, 1991). Acculturation is another factor that needs attention when working with parents who are immigrants. Level of acculturation is influenced by language proficiency, educational level, and exposure to majority culture. Parents might be asked to complete a form in a language that they do not fully comprehend; their level of literacy may affect their responses if they are expected to read or write, and their limited exposure to the mainstream culture may force them to rely on their culture as a frame of reference. Therefore, culture may affect whether parents define a behavior as problematic (Cauce et al., 2002).

Social or community norms may influence parents' identification of problem behavior. For example, parents and children are often asked to identify and rate symptoms on behavioral rating scales in terms of whether they occur "sometimes," "never," or "often," using the average same-age child as a reference (Cauce et al., 2002). Their responses may be predicated on the community context or on the common norms and values in their neighborhood. A parent may not identify a behavior as a problem if many of the children in the community engage in such behavior. Similarly, parents who struggle to meet basic day-to-day needs of their families may not see emotional distress in their children as problematic or may not even notice behaviors that are signs of psychological difficulties (Brannan, Heflinger, & Bickman, 1995).

Another area that psychologists must consider is the reliability and validity of many popular projective tests. Garb, Lilienfeld, Wood, and Nezworski (2002) recommended that projective strategies be used only if indexes have been demonstrated to be valid for their intended purposes. When making a decision regarding the inclusion of projective measures in an assessment procedure, psychologists should consider that:

1. The TAT has not been supported as a measure of psychopathology (Sharkey & Ritzler, 1985), and there is no set of pictures with emic and etic validity to be used with culturally and linguistically diverse populations (Costantino, Flanagan, & Malgady, 2001).

2. Studies using the TAT found that test–retest reliabilities typically reported were about .30 (Lilienfeld, Wood, & Garb, 2000).

3. Most clinicians used a subjective interpretative approach to the TAT that has no support in research (Ryan, 1985; Vane, 1981).

4. The CAT has no norms or evidence of reliability and validity.

5. Human figure drawing is typically interpreted via a sign approach (making diagnostic decisions based on isolated drawing features) or a global approach (making decisions based on all features of the drawing; Garb et al., 2002). The sign approach has been described as yielding inferences that have zero validity (Motta, Little, & Tobin, 1993; Thomas & Jolley, 1998). A global approach such as that used on the Draw-A-Person: Screening Procedure for Emotional Disturbance (DAP:SPED; Naglieri, McNeish, & Bardos, 1991) has shown that it can be used as a measure of global psychopathology (validity significantly better than chance; Garb et al., 2002).

6. Studies examining the Rorschach Comprehensive System suggest that it can be used in a multicultural assessment (Elliot & Ritzler, 1998). Although the Rorschach can be used in a multicultural assessment and can detect thought disorder and dependent personality traits, research does not provide evidence to support its use for diagnosing most mental disorders (e.g., conduct disorder, depression, panic disorder; Garb et al., 2002).

7. The TEMAS demonstrated low test–retest reliabilities in which the highest function correlation was r = .53, and correlational validity has not been fully established (Costantino, Malgady, & Rogler, 1988).

8. The Roberts–2 demonstrated test–retest reliabilities that are below .80 and based on a small sample, and the test manual does not provide data of construct or criterion-related validity studies (Sattler & Hoge, 2006).

Psychologists should be cautious in using projective measures with children who are culturally and linguistically diverse as well as with children living in poverty because statistical foundation in terms of reliability and validity are weak for some tests. Even for instruments that have been developed to be used with this population (e.g., TEMAS), reliability and validity data are weak. Moreover, although children from lower socioeconomic status are represented in the norms of tests such as the Roberts–2 (Roberts & Gruber, 2005) in accordance with their percentage in the general U.S populations, their unique experiences significantly affect interpretation of test results. Projective tests are better used as clinical tools to obtain information for treatment purposes or aid in exploration in psychotherapy and not necessarily as assessment devices to make educational decisions (Garb et al., 2002). When they are used with children living in poverty or who are culturally and linguistically diverse, administration and interpretation should be done by psychologists or examiners who are experienced and knowledgeable about cultural issues, linguistic demands, and historical and experiential factors and who are able to provide interpretation within a proper holistic and contextual framework.

The best way to understand emotional and behavioral functioning in children is within a comprehensive problem-solving framework that includes the influences of developmental processes (Rutter & Garmezy, 1983). A problem-solving approach that emphasizes assessment-to-intervention facilitates decision making that would benefit children and is typically less influenced by bias. Deno (2005) defined *problem solving* as the activities undertaken to reduce the perceived discrepancies between expected or desired level of performance and present or current level of performance. Bransford and Stein (1984) proposed a five-step model of problem solving. The IDEAL problem solving model is described as follows:

1. Problem-solving identification: Involving observing and recording the child's behavior to determine if a problem exists

2. Defining the problem: Qualifying the discrepancy between expected performance and actual performance by quantifying it to determine if the problem is important

3. Designing intervention plans: Investigating alternate goals and hypotheses leading to solutions

4. Implementing interventions: Monitoring and evaluating integrity of intervention and data gathering to determine if intervention is progressing as expected

5. Solving the problem: Reconsidering the data and allowing for the reevaluation of the discrepancy to determine if the intervention is resolving the original problem

Many schools employ a functional behavioral assessment (FBA) procedure, which utilizes problem-solving strategies, is widely used in many education systems, and is typically considered to embrace strategies that are less biased.

FUNCTIONAL BEHAVIORAL ASSESSMENT

FBA is a procedure developed to improve the quality of life of children by identifying behaviors that interfere with emotional and behavioral adjustment. This approach views behavior as rule-governed and as a means of communicating an emotional and behavioral need. This need is referred to as the *function* of the behavior. The environment plays a critical role in triggering and supporting inappropriate behaviors (Gresham, Watson, & Skinner, 2001). FBA involves the systematic gathering or collecting of data that is later analyzed to develop interventions that match the function of the identified behavior and provide positive behavioral support (PBS). One of the goals of FBA is to replace problem behaviors with appropriate ones that will answer the child's specific needs. By analyzing the data gathered, interventions are designed to teach the child more acceptable ways of addressing emotional needs. These interventions are meant to increase appropriate and adaptive behaviors and reduce inappropriate behaviors by teaching new behaviors, utilizing long-term strategies to reinforce and generalize appropriate behaviors to multiple settings, and to provide contextual support required for successful results. These interventions are generally referred to as PBS, which entails using a behaviorally based system to increase the capacity of schools and parents to develop workable environments that improve the connection between research-validated practices and the environments in which teaching and learning take place.

FBA became popular in the late 1990s when it was included in the reauthorization of the Individuals with Disabilities Education Amendment (IDEA) Act of 1997 as a scientifically based method of addressing behavioral concerns in children with emotional and behavioral challenges. The law required a functional assessment of behavior under certain conditions, such as suspensions of children with disabilities, but did not offer a specific model or guideline for conducting FBAs (Watson, Gresham, & Skinner, 2001).

FBA is based on a strong theoretical and empirical foundation, demonstrating that interventions based on the function of behaviors are more effective than those developed mainly on diagnostic descriptions (Steege & Brown-Chidsey, 2005). FBA is considered a collection of procedures for gathering information about antecedents, behaviors, and consequences to determine the function of the target behavior (Gresham et al., 2001). It is a multimethod approach based on observations, interviews, and review of records (Gresham et al., 2001), and as such, it is an appropriate procedure for most students, especially students from culturally and linguistically diverse backgrounds and children living in poverty.

There are two ways in which FBA can proceed: a direct and indirect way. When conducted in an indirect way, it requires gathering information from teachers, parents, and school personnel. FBA is direct when it includes behavioral observations of the child in different settings. Best practice, however, involves procedures that employ both direct and indirect methods. In general, the FBA approach consists of four stages: targeting problem behaviors and defining them in measurable terms; gathering information to determine severity, frequency, and duration of the problem; interpreting data based on its function; and developing and monitoring interventions that match the function of the behavior. One method for conducting FBA is the VAIL FBA model identified by Witt, Daly, and Noell (2000):

1. Validate: In this stage, the target problem behaviors are identified and information is gathered via interviews, anecdotal information, school records, and any other data documenting the problem. The identified behaviors are defined in concrete, measurable, and observable terms.

2. Assess: Behaviors identified through observations are analyzed for their level of severity, duration, and intensity. Other characteristics of the targeted behavior are described:

   - Antecedents (i.e., behaviors that occur before the target behaviors)
   - Consequences (i.e., behaviors that occur after the target behaviors)

   The antecedents and consequences influence the target behaviors. For example, the consequence that follows the target behavior helps identify the function of the behavior as well as possible replacement behaviors. Assessment methods used in this stage include observations, interviews, record reviews, and formal assessment data such as scatter plots, A-B-C records, behavior rating forms, and other documentation of formal observations. Data gathered can also be considered baseline to evaluate the effectiveness of interventions.

3. Interpret-Link: This stage includes the summary and interpretation of both formal and informal data. Other considerations are 1) weighing the value of the data, 2) identifying antecedents that are triggering the behavior and consequences that are reinforcing the behaviors, and 3) developing functional hypotheses regarding the behaviors. The literature in this area identified a set of functions of behavior, and although there might be differences in

terminology across researchers, most include the same functions with some minor differences. Witt et al. (2000) listed the following functions:

- *Power/control*: The goal of the misbehavior is to control a situation or event.

- *Escape*: The goal of the misbehavior is to avoid or escape a situation or event.

- *Attention*: The goal of the misbehavior is to seek or draw attention to self.

- *Sensory regulation*: The goal of the behavior is to regulate biological-based needs such as in a child diagnosed with ADHD. This child may need to work through his or her need for physical activity.

- *Revenge*: The goal of the behavior is to "settle a score" or get back at someone else to satisfy feelings of injustice.

- *Gratification*: The goal of misbehavior is to reward or please the individual.

- *Acceptance/affiliation*: The goal of misbehavior is to connect or be accepted by others.

4. Intervene, monitor, and reassess: Stages 1–3 assist in the understanding of antecedents and consequences triggering and maintaining the unwanted behaviors. This understanding of the student's behavior should lead to the development of behavioral interventions to address the function of the behavior and replace the inappropriate behavior with more appropriate ones. Once interventions have been selected, they are monitored and reassessed on an ongoing basis to establish their effectiveness.

FBA is a two-phase procedure: 1) data is collected and analyzed and 2) behavior improvement plans are developed. FBA is a process that emphasizes teaching appropriate behaviors to replace inappropriate ones. Assessment of problems such as low productivity, aggression, self-injurious behavior, attentional deficit, distractibility, disruptive behavior, noncompliant behaviors, anxiety, and other challenging behaviors are examples of common behaviors that may lend themselves to the analysis of maintaining conditions (Schill, Kratochwill, & Gardner, 1996). According to Stanger (1996), the connection between assessment and intervention takes place in three ways: 1) identifying and operationally defining specific and observable behaviors that become the targets of intervention, 2) targeting behaviors becomes critical to identifying interventions, and 3) reusing assessment methods similar to those employed during the collection of data throughout the intervention phase can help evaluate the effectiveness of the strategies implemented. When conducted appropriately, FBA and research-based interventions that are matched to the functions of the behaviors can be successful in improving challenging behaviors.

FAMILY- AND COMMUNITY-BASED ASSESSMENT

Family plays a central role to children's social-emotional adjustment as well as their performance in school. Children's emotional and behavioral functioning has been shown to be significantly influenced by the demands and stressors they encounter in their environment (Kamphaus & Frick, 2004). Contextual demands can influence the child's behavior in school. Obtaining an understanding of a child's psychological functioning entails assessing family and community context. Often, psychologists working in the schools limit their assessment to the child's characteristics and overlook other factors that may provide a richer understanding of the child's problem and that may help select interventions to address the child's emotional and educational needs.

Research has consistently documented a link between parent history of psychopathology and childhood disorders, such as ADHD, anxiety, bipolar disorder, schizophrenia, and eating disorders (Blum & Mercugliano, 1997; Frick, Silverthorn, & Evans, 1994; Geller, Fox, & Fletcher, 1993; Hay et al., 2003; Helzer, 1988). Assessing a child's family context is essential to the evaluation of the child's emotional and behavioral adjustment. Moreover, many instruments used to assess children utilize parents as informants. As a result, being able to ascertain the accuracy of parents' information is important to the interpretation of the information obtained.

Assessing the family helps school psychologists understand family-based problems and their effect on the child's school functioning. It can unveil contributing factors and help select strategies for intervention (Hinkle & Wells, 1995). Holman (1983) recommended four areas of evaluation as essential to assessing families: the problem, the family system, the family and its environment, and the family cycle. Hinkle and Wells noted that the most unobtrusive way of examining these issues is through an interview. School psychologists should consider assessing family functioning in the following areas: discipline strategies, parenting style, marital conflicts, and parental adjustment (Kamphaus & Frick, 2004). The degrees of assessment in these areas depend on the problem. Parent interview provides a rich source of information including familial history of psychopathology. Parent interview can be coupled with behavioral rating scales. Some popular scales such as the BASC–2 and the PIC–2 include scales that assess family relations. These scales, however, are very broad and contain a mixture of items evaluating different aspects of a child's family environment (Kamphaus & Frick, 2004). There are standardized measures of parenting behavior with adequate reliability and validity. The Parent–Child Relationship Inventory (PCRI; Gerard, 1994) assesses parents' attitudes toward parenting; the Parenting Stress Index–Third Edition (PSI–3; Abidin, 1995) measures parent–child problem areas; the Parenting Satisfaction Scale (PSS; Guidubaldi & Cleminshaw, 1994) measures parents' attitudes toward parenting and the parent–child relationship; and the Stress Index for Parents of Adolescents (SIPA; Sheras, Abidin, & Konold,

1998) identifies areas of stress in parenting adolescents. These rating scales, however, should be used with caution with diverse populations and parents who live in poverty because research documenting their use with these populations is limited.

Some questions that should be included in a parent interview targeting family history and functioning include

1. Status of parents' relationship

2. Home violence and conflict

3. Discipline practices and style and child response

4. Parents health and history of mental illness

5. Child relationship with siblings and caregivers

6. Parent involvement with school activities (e.g., PTA, teacher conferences) and child's school-related tasks (e.g., homework)

7. Recreation activities and affiliation with religious organizations

8. Extended family and support networks

9. Stress related to child rearing, marital relationship, financial status, acculturative stress, and so forth

10. Immigration issues (e.g., legal status, employment, migration story)

11. Expectations, concerns, and goals for children

12. Protective factors:

    a. Functional family life/relationship with parents

    b. Support network

    c. Access to social services

    d. Affiliation with religious organizations

    e. Parents' educational and employment status

    f. Role models

    g. Before- and after-school adult supervision

    h. Community resources

    i. Opportunities to be involved in ongoing enriching and stimulating educational experiences

Another area that should be assessed is the role of the community as it affects the child's adjustment and as it influences interpretation of test information. Brooks-Gunn, Duncan, and Aber (1997) and Leventhal, Fauth, and Brooks-Gunn (2005) highlighted the association between neighborhood-level socioeconomic factors and children's educational outcomes. Specifically, neighborhood influences seemed to affect the educational outcome of minority boys more readily than girls (Leventhal, Fauth, & Brooks-Gunn, 2005). Neighborhood norms in terms of what are considered expected behaviors play a role and influence how children behave in school. Children often get referred for special education assessment for behaviors that are tolerated in the community. Moreover, many conflicts in the community get carried over into the school settings. One way to assess for community influences is through interviews with parents, child, and relatives, with questions targeting community factors.

Some questions that should be included in a parent interview targeting neighborhood and community factors include

1. Resources available: Recreation activities, municipal responsiveness, and so forth

2. Neighborhood violence and parent concerns

3. Victims of violence in the community (e.g., robbery, assault, threat of physical harm)

4. Safety concerns

5. Involvement in the community (e.g., neighborhood watch groups, community meetings)

6. Support network in the community

7. Role models/gang influence

8. Perception of achievement in the community or by neighborhood peers

9. Relationship with neighborhood peers

INTEGRATING INFORMATION AND ARRIVING AT MEANINGFUL DECISIONS

The first goal in assessing children living in poverty is to develop an assessment procedure that can appropriately evaluate the concerns expressed by parents and teachers. Second, the assessment procedure must be nondiscriminatory. The assessment is nondiscriminatory if it addresses the child's native language; considers the child's unique experiences that may differ from norm groups included in standardized tests; makes decisions based on multiple factors; gathers information from many different sources and in different contexts; includes information on child developmental, family, medical, school, and psychiatric histories; utilizes tests that are valid and reliable for what they are being used to measure; and is conducted by examiners who are trained and knowledgeable in assessing the target population. The integration and interpretation of data should be made from a culturally and socially sensitive and responsive framework. Kamphaus and Frick (2004) recommended a strategy to integrate information obtained from the assessment process that has been adapted to be more culturally and socially responsive:

1. *Document all significant findings on the child's adjustment.* Note all clinically significant findings based on tests administered and interviews, observations, reports, and histories gathered.

2. *Look for convergent findings across sources and methods.* Identify similar and consistent findings and concerns across sources (e.g., parent, teacher, child) and methods (e.g., observations, interviews, rating scales) used.

3. *Try to explain discrepancies and interpret data from cultural, social, and experiential frameworks.* Attempt to explain discrepancies or differences. Often, discrepancies are due to differences in demands and expectations in various contexts in which the child functions. As such, they may reflect some real differences. Examiners should become familiar with the demands and expectations of different contexts or settings and the cultural or social explanation attributed to them.

One would expect to see agreement in data obtained from reporters in the same setting. When discrepancies are found in data obtained from reporters in the same setting, further analysis is required. One should consider the measure used and the behavior itself. Discrepancies may be due to the following reasons:

a.   Different measures or methods were used or reporters defined the problem differently using a different group as reference.

b.   The discrepancy might be due to a divergent score on a subscale as opposed to a global composite.

c.   The situational nature of the behavior (i.e., the behavior may manifest itself differently in different settings; for example, music class and math class).

d.   Responders might be using different frames of reference.

Explore different explanations for the problems identified. Padilla (2001) asserted that assessment is made culturally sensitive through an ongoing and active preoccupation with the cultural and social characteristics of the group or individual being assessed.

4. *Develop a hierarchy of problem areas.* Determine the child's areas of difficulty and establish which problem is primary and which is secondary based on degree of impairment, onset of the problem, and family history. Developing a profile noting how the target behaviors have affected other areas of functioning in school, home, and community assists the examiner in ascertaining the scope of the problem. On another level, one should also determine strengths and needs, based on data gathered. This level should begin the process of identifying possible interventions to address the behavioral and emotional concerns.

5. *Determine critical information to include in report.* The examiner reviews the data gathered and interpretation made to make decisions regarding what data should be included in the report and what should be deemed insignificant. Information that did not add to the formulation of the problem or development of the intervention should be considered irrelevant and not included in the report. According to Kamphaus and Frick (2004), this type of information can be omitted because when included it can detract from the case formulation. Selecting data

to be included in the report is considered part of the interpretation process and case conceptualization (Kamphaus & Frick, 2004).

6. *Develop interventions to address problem behavior.* Based on the data gathered, the analysis conducted, and interpretations considered, the examiner can begin developing interventions that address the referral questions or targeted behaviors. An important consideration is the social and cultural characteristics of the child and family, as well as protective factors. Family's strengths and weaknesses must be considered in the design of any intervention. Because it is important to any intervention that positive outcomes be generalized to other settings (e.g., playground, home, community), designing an intervention that facilitates parental involvement is essential. Included in the development of intervention are ways of measuring its effectiveness and monitoring its progress on an ongoing basis.

RECOMMENDATIONS FOR THE ASSESSMENT OF CHILDREN FROM POVERTY

The following recommendations should be considered when conducting assessments to address social-emotional and behavioral concerns in children living in poverty:

1. Gather information from multiple sources using multiple methods: This approach is more effective in capturing the child's unique experiences and their influence on the child's emotional adjustment.

2. Address acculturation issues in culturally and linguistically diverse children: A child's level of acculturation and that of his or her parents should be assessed because it influences the manner in which the child responds to the assessment process.

3. Language proficiency: The child's proficiency in English and the native language should be assessed to ensure that the child understands what is being required during the assessment and that the examiner is getting valid information.

4. Examiner should ensure that tests selected to be used with the child are reliable and valid.

5. Conduct an assessment that includes family and community factors.

6. Beware of cultural loading: Many tests reflect the cultural values and beliefs of the majority culture and do not reflect the unique experiences of children living in poverty or children from culturally and linguistically diverse populations.

7. Beware of linguistic demands on a test: Many tests expect a certain level of proficiency in English to understand the directions (receptive language) or to respond appropriately to the items (expressive language).

8. Interpret data from a cultural, social, and experiential framework: Interpret information gathered in light of background information and within the context of the child's social, medical, economic, familial, cultural, and linguistic histories. The goal of the interpretation is to tell the child's story in a culturally and socially responsive manner that will allow for the development of intervention that is effective.

By carefully considering these factors and incorporating these strategies when assessing children whose lives have been influenced by poverty, the assessment process is made more sensitive to the unique needs of these children, and the resulting product will provide accurate data on which to make instructional and programming decisions that can improve the educational lives of children.

6

Educational Strategies for Improving Children's Academic Achievement

No man can help another without helping himself.

Ralph Waldo Emerson

Education is pivotal to overcoming poverty; indeed, many children who receive a healthy start through early intervention and quality preschool programs have shown strong academic and social adjustment in school. Educational practices in the schools, however, often present roadblocks to achievement for children living in poverty. Educational practices, such as those leading to disproportionality in special education placement, have been of great concern to educators who work with children living in poverty and children from culturally and linguistically diverse backgrounds. Specifically, African American children and other ethnically diverse children are consistently overrepresented in special education categories of disability and underrepresented in programs for the gifted and talented (National Alliance of Black School Educators [NABSE] & ILIAD Project, 2002). At the same time, Hispanic, Native American, and Asian Pacific/Island children are underidentified for special education services. Overrepresentation as well as underrepresentation is a sign that children may not be receiving an appropriate education or being provided with access to general education or instruction that addresses their specific needs. Karoly et al. (1998) reported that close to 40% of adjudicated juvenile delinquents in the United States have reading difficulties and/or learning disabilities that were not addressed in school. Misidentification or mislabeling often leads to teachers having low expectations for academic performance for these children. Low expectation has been shown to negatively affect children's self-esteem and affect educational opportunities (NABSE & ILIAD, 2002).

The reason for disproportionality is rooted in systemic and society's bias and not primarily poverty (Losen & Orfield, 2002). Other prevalent reasons cited for disproportionality include problems designing and implementing instructional programs that address children's unique strengths and needs, ineffective methods and strategies employed to refer and classify children for special education, poorly trained teachers and lack of appropriate resources to support learning, and limited understanding of the problem (NABSE & ILIAD, 2002). Beside disproportionality, another alarming reality is that using very few factors, educators can predict with 90% accuracy children in the third grade who will not complete high school (Barr & Parrett, 2001). According to research, these factors include 1) children living in poverty who are enrolled in schools with a large student body composed of other children who live in poverty, 2) children who are reading a year behind by the third grade, and 3) children who have been retained a grade (McPartland & Slavin, 1990).

Schools that predominantly educate children from a background of poverty struggle to meet the children's needs because of the limited funding these schools receive. Schools serving children living in poverty do not have the same per-pupil expenditure as those in more affluent neighborhoods (National Research Council, 2002). Many schools receive funds based on property taxes. The tax base in communities characterized by poverty generally are lower due to diminished property value; as a result, schools that serve these communities receive insufficient funding that is typically unable to adequately provide the resources to appropriately support and address the educational needs of the children. This funding issue weighs on many areas of children's education: quality of teachers, a stable workforce, equipment and supportive instructional materials (e.g., books, computers), teachers' pay, condition of school buildings and classrooms, discipline and safety, and school climate (U.S. Department of Education, 2001).

Literacy is a risk factor for school dropout. Being unable to read has a deleterious and global effect on an individual's life. Reading difficulties affect students' ability to work independently on homework and class assignments, to perform in content areas that rely heavily on reading such as social studies and science, to follow written directions or to make notes, and to meet basic school expectations. Reading difficulties eventually affect children's self-confidence and behavior in school because a task that is so effortless for peers is a burden for them (Shaywitz, 2003). The effects are also apparent in an individual's ability to contribute to society. Karoly et al. (1998) pointed out some of the consequences of being unable to read:

1. Low reading levels are strong predictors of welfare dependency and prison incarceration.

2. Many individuals with a history of reading difficulties drop out of school.

3. Those who drop out of school have higher rates of unemployment and rely on low salary jobs.

4. More than half of the adults incarcerated have literacy levels below those required by the labor market.

Retention is another risk factor associated with high school dropout. Children are retained in a grade level as an educational remedy for underachieving. Teachers believe that it will provide opportunity to "catch-up" with peers (Jimerson, 2001). A century of research on retention, however, has failed to support it as an effective intervention for underachievement (Jimerson, 2001). Retention has a negative effect on children from culturally and linguistically diverse backgrounds and on boys because these children are retained more often than Caucasian children and girls (Jimerson, 1999). A significant number of studies indicate that retention is a powerful predictor of school dropout. As adults, individuals who were retained are more likely to obtain lower educational status, employment stability, and pay (Anderson, Jimerson, & Whipple, 2002; Jimerson, 1999). Other social difficulties such as truancy, chemical abuse, criminal involvement, and mental health problems are associated with retention (Anderson et al., 2002). The failure of retention to address children's academic difficulties can be explained by three important factors: 1) specific remedial or instructional strategies are rarely used to address academic, social, and cognitive problems; 2) the risk factors often associated with retention are not addressed (e.g., attendance, self-efficacy issues, ineffective instruction); and 3) children who are retained are older than their same-grade peers and this is associated with negative outcomes (e.g., stigmatization by peers, behavioral and social-emotional adjustment issues; Anderson et al., 2002).

The critical question is what kinds of educational practices increase the number of children who develop strong academic skills and complete school. Research supports a number of educational practices as effective in addressing the educational needs of children living in poverty, including early intervention programs, strong reading instruction programs, evidence-based instructional strategies (e.g., cooperative learning, peer tutoring), and parent involvement.

EARLY INTERVENTION

Early intervention has been shown to be effective in preventing the need for future special education services and minimizing the need for extensive programming. Research has demonstrated that early intervention programs can be effective in placing children on "the right track." Children who attend high-quality preschool programs typically enter kindergarten with stronger preacademic skills because they have been exposed to prereading and socialization activities, active learning, and educational activities that encourage creativity and support future learning and achievement. The implementation of preventive services and programs before children experience failure in school has been described as a public health priority by members of a panel of the National Institutes of Health (NIH; 2000). A substantial body of research gathered since the mid-1990s documents the power of prevention and early intervention and points to high-quality preschool programs as a means of improving children's quality of life. Furstenberg, Brooks-Gunn, and Morgan (1987) noted that it is essential for children to get "off on the right foot" in school because, on average, children who begin school as members of families at risk have worse outcomes than other children, even when the condition of their parents improves over time. Children who participate in high-quality preschool programs are less likely to be retained in school or to be referred to special education (Reynolds, 2001).

For children from poverty, high-quality preschool is critical. These types of programs benefit children from disadvantaged backgrounds academically and socially well into their adult lives (National Institute of Child Health and Human Development [NICHD], 2000). Unfortunately, children from low-income homes who need high-quality preschool programs the most are the least likely to obtain them (Espinosa, 2002). All too frequently, families are not able to afford the cost of high-quality preschool programs, are unaware of the characteristics of high-quality preschool programs when selecting a school, or find that these programs are located far out of their communities (Ispa, Thornburg, & Fine, 2006). Faced with these challenges, families enroll their young children in affordable programs that are close to home and offer extended hours of operation (Ispa et al., 2006). Many of these affordable preschool programs, however, are of poor quality and are typically associated with negative outcome. Children in poorly rated preschool programs tend to exhibit more aggressive and defiant behaviors in addition to delays in reading (Hausfather, Toharia, LaRoche, & Engelsmann, 1997).

What Is High-Quality Preschool

High-quality generally refers to those characteristics or features that are critical for the development of the child, family, and teacher. Espinosa (2002) indicated that preschools are typically rated on two important dimensions of quality: *process* and *structure*. These dimensions influence the kind of educational experiences children have in preschool (NICHD, 2000). According to Espinosa (2002), *process quality* refers to activities, interactions, materials, health and safety routines, and learning opportunities observed. It involves the experiences of children on an educational level, such as the curriculum and activities used to support the educational program; on an interpersonal level, such as teacher–child interaction as well as parent involvement; and related to health and safety routines. Curricula must contain activities and educational experiences that encourage growth in the cognitive and social development of children that are accomplished through teacher–child interactions and parent involvement (Espinosa, 2002; Peisner-Feinberg & Burchinal, 1997). Educational programs must also contain learning activities that have been shown scientifically to support early literacy and numeracy skills, language development, and scientific learning (Bowman, Donovan, & Burns, 2001; Gormley, Gayer, Phillips, & Dawson, 2005). *Structure quality* refers to adult–child ratio, size of each group, and education and training of members of the staff, including teachers. It involves structural characteristics such as teacher qualification and preparation, compensation of teachers and staff, square footage, and class size.

Critical features of high-quality preschool include

Process characteristics

- Comprehensive and age-appropriate curricula that include activities in the areas of cognitive, social, art, science, math, and music/movement (Katz, 1999)
- Strong parent involvement (Barnett, Robin, Hustedt, & Schulman, 2004)
- Screening and referral services (Rosman, Kass, & Kirsch, 2006)
- Positive relationship between teachers and children (Espinosa, 2002)
- Language-enriched activities and practices that encourage communication throughout the day with focus on reasoning and problem solving (Espinosa, 2002)
- Respect for diversity in all of its forms
- Sufficient equipment and materials to support the curricula (Espinosa, 2002)

Structural characteristics

- Qualified and certified teachers who receive ongoing staff development and supervision (Espinosa, 2002)
- Staff and teachers receive appropriate compensation (Whitebook, 2003)
- Ratio of no more than 10 children per staff member for children ages 3–5 (Barnett et al., 2004)
- Class size of no more than 20 children for children ages 3–5 (Barnett et al., 2004)

There have been a number of longitudinal studies that have fleshed out what is known about the power of high-quality preschool programs.

- The High/Scope Perry Preschool Program was initiated in Ypsilanti, Michigan, in 1962. The study followed 123 3- and 4-year-old African American children from a background of poverty who participated in the Perry Preschool Program. The preschool included a 1- to 2-year educational program, home visiting dimension, and a curriculum that encouraged active learning and creativity. The most current finding of this study indicated that by age 27, children who did not participate were five times more likely to become involved in crime and to become repeat offenders. Children who attended the program were more likely to stay in school, complete high school, and obtain higher annual salaries as adults compared with individuals who lived in the same community (Barnett, 1996; Reynolds, 2001; Rosman et al., 2006).

- The Chicago Child–Parent Centers (CPC) is a federally funded program that serves children ages 3 and 4. The center-based program has been providing comprehensive educational and support interventions to families from low-income and disadvantaged backgrounds since 1967. Services provided by the program include family and health services, half-day preschool at ages 3 and 4, full-day kindergarten, and school-age services in linked elementary schools at ages 6–9 (Reynolds, Temple, Robertson, & Mann, 2001). The study compared 989 children in the CPC program and 550 in a comparison group also attending full-day kindergarten, and results demonstrated that participants in the CPC program had higher rates of high school completion than those in the comparison group at age 20, had lower rates of school dropout, completed more years of education than the comparison group, had lower rates of grade retention and special education placement, and had lower rates of juvenile arrests (Reynolds et al., 2001).

- The Abecedarian Project is a longitudinal study program conducted by the University of North Carolina. This study followed children receiving early child care from birth into their early 20s. Children participating in the program received full-time high-quality education intervention from infancy to age 5. Children were offered individualized prescriptions of educational activities; engaged in activities focusing on social, emotional, and cognitive areas with emphasis on language development; and were followed up at ages 12, 15, and 21 (Carolina Abecedarian Project, 1999). Results of this study indicated that children who participated were retained less often than children who did not attend, were referred less to special education, were less likely to become teenage mothers, and tested a grade and a half ahead compared with their control group at age 15 (Carolina Abecedarian Project, 1999). In addition, their IQ scores were raised by 7–10 points, and they earned more as adults than those who did not attend the program (Carolina Abecedarian Project, 1999).

Other preschool programs that have been studied include Head Start, the Syracuse University Family Development Program, and the Minnesota Parent–Child Study. These programs document similar findings regarding high-quality preschool programs.

- Emotionally responsive caregiving, early competency in children, organized home environment, focus on developing language and cognitive abilities, and strategies to reduce children's level of stress are critical to resiliency (Barr & Parrett, 2001).

- Likelihood of criminal involvement is lower as well as an increase in high school completion, and improved academic performances are typical findings (Barnett, 1995).

- Economic self-sufficiency as adults is a common outcome in adulthood (Karoly et al., 1998).

A review study examining the long-term effects of high-quality preschool programs on cognitive development and school outcome found "sizeable" long-term effects on school performance, special education placement, grade retention, and social adjustment (Barnett, 1995).

LITERACY AND NUMERACY SKILLS

Being able to read is powerful for any child, but for a child from a background of poverty, reading is empowering. Although researchers have documented the critical role of preschool education, they also indicated that continued exposure to strong instructional programs in the early elementary grades was equally important to positive school outcome (Lang, 1992). Early school achievement is significant in predicting future educational performance (Chen, Lee, & Stevenson, 1996). Moreover, preschool cognitive skills as well as math achievement and reading performance during first through third grades tend to be maintained into early and late teenage years (Reynolds, 1994). Given this knowledge, it is imperative that teachers in the early grades target their instruction on the areas that lead to the development of strong reading and math skills. The significance is further emphasized by the knowledge that very few opportunities are present after the third grade to alter an academic trajectory (Downer & Pianta, 2006). Many counselors at the middle school level guide children from diverse backgrounds into remedial or undemanding courses. Once students fail to take the prerequisite courses for admission into more demanding courses, it becomes more difficult to enroll in higher-level or college-prep courses.

In 2000, the National Reading Panel (NRP), a group of leading scientists in reading research commissioned by Congress, published its findings on the status of research-based knowledge on reading and the effectiveness of a number of approaches to teaching reading. Research in reading has consistently supported a number of factors that are considered critical to effective reading skills: phonemic awareness, fluency, reading comprehension, and vocabulary instruction (Adams, 1990; McKenna & Stahl, 2003; NRP, 2000).

Phonological awareness is a broad class of skills that involves an awareness that speech can be segmented or sequenced into a series of discrete sounds, words, syllables, onset-rime, and phonemes (Mather & Goldstein, 2001). *Phonemic awareness* is a part of phonological awareness that involves processing phonemes (McKenna & Stahl, 2003), and it refers to the ability to recognize the smallest units that make up spoken language. Instruction on phonemic awareness usually entails teaching children to manipulate phonemes in spoken syllables and words. *Phonics* refers to teaching children how to use letter–sound associations to derive pronunciation of words and to spell words (NRP, 2000). Phonics involves activities such as matching words with the same initial sound and isolating, segmenting, blending, deleting, and substituting phonemes (McKenna & Stahl, 2003). Meta-analysis based on 52 studies indicated that instructing children to manipulate phonemes in words was highly effective in improving reading skills (NRP, 2000) and developing spelling skills (Bailet, 1991). Research focusing on the systematic instruction of phonics yielded significant advantages for children in kindergarten through sixth grades experiencing problems learning to read (NRP, 2000). Findings also revealed a positive effect on decoding and spelling, but not necessarily on comprehension. Reading is a multifaceted ability that consists of many other skills, and phonic skills must be incorporated and combined with the development of phonemic awareness, fluency, and text-reading comprehension skills (NRP, 2000) to develop good readers.

Another important aspect of reading is fluency, which is essential to reading comprehension. *Fluency* can be defined as the ability to read connected text rapidly, smoothly, effortlessly, and automatically with little conscious attention to the mechanics of reading, such as decoding (Meyer & Felton, 1999). It is that automaticity that contributes to skilled reading (Ehri, 1998). Children who decode words in a laborious manner have difficulty remembering what they read and making connections between the ideas reflected in the text and their background knowledge (McKenna & Stahl, 2003). Mastropieri, Leinart, and Scruggs (1999) noted that children whose decoding skills are not automatic (i.e., lack fluency) experience difficulty with reading in the following ways: 1) they read less text than other children and remember, review, and comprehend less of the information read; 2) they use more cognitive energy trying to identify individual words than other children; and 3) they may be less able to retain text in their memories. Analysis of the available research that included regular and special education classrooms and good and weak readers indicated that instructional practices to address fluency should consist of strategies such as guided oral reading and repeated reading procedures in which students receive direct guidance from teachers, peers, or parents. These strategies can lead to a positive effect on word recognition, fluency, and comprehension across grade levels (NRP, 2000).

Reading comprehension is the ability to understand what you read, and it is facilitated by good fluency and word recognition. Reading comprehension is grounded in several factors: fluent reading, background knowledge, vocabulary, and interest (Mather & Goldstein, 2001). Harris and Hodges (1995) described reading comprehension as intentional thinking in the process of constructing meaning through interaction with the text. Through extensive reviews of the research on reading comprehension, the NRP (2000) found the following three main themes:

1. Reading comprehension is a complex cognitive process that cannot be understood without a clear description of the role that vocabulary development and vocabulary instruction play in the understanding of what has been read.

2. Comprehension is an active process that requires an intentional and thoughtful interaction between the reader and text.

3. The preparation of teachers to better equip students to develop and apply reading comprehension strategies to enhance understanding is intimately linked to students' achievement in this area.

In summary, a strong, rich vocabulary supports reading comprehension; vocabulary instruction facilitates better understanding of what is read. Specifically, the use of computers in vocabulary instruction as well as deliberate instruction on vocabulary taught in the context of storybook reading or in listening to others is effective (NRP, 2000). Comprehension can also be improved by teaching specific cognitive strategies. The NRP, through its meta-analytic approach, identified the following instructional strategies as effective in improving reading comprehension when used in combination:

1. Comprehension monitoring, in which readers learn how to be aware of their understanding of the material

2. Cooperative learning, in which students learn reading strategies together

3. Use of graphic and semantic organizers (including story maps), in which readers make graphic representations of the material to assist comprehension

4. Question answering, in which readers answer questions posed by the teacher and receive immediate feedback

5. Question generation, in which readers ask themselves questions about various aspects of the story

6. Story structure, in which students are taught to use the structure of the story as a means of helping them recall story content in order to answer questions about what they have read

7. Summarization, in which readers are taught to integrate ideas and generalize from the text information

Writing is a component of literacy that is linked to reading. Hampton (1995) posited that in schools in the United States, children are given few opportunities to write, and those that are more in need of instruction and support in writing rarely get it. Children's ability to express their ideas in writing is influenced by several factors: fluent reading, background knowledge, vocabulary, and interest (Mather & Goldstein, 2001). Many effective strategies to improve children's writing are available, but they are used on a limited basis (Hampton, 1995). A number of strategies were identified based on research and experience in the field and these are recommended for accelerating children's writing abilities:

- Offering children opportunities to write routinely for various purposes and audiences
- Fostering writing as a meaning-making process and as an instrument for learning
- Encouraging children's independence via self-selected topics and self-evaluation
- Focusing on the quality of what is stated, rather than simply attending to presentational features
- Modeling the writing process and focusing on the need for systematic revision using conferencing
- Providing grading criteria or rubric to children before they start the writing assignment
- Instructing children on the conventions in the context of children's own writing
- Assessing children's work over time using a portfolio

Hallenbeck (1996) noted that having children focus on the purpose of writing, brainstorming, and expanding ideas improved children's abilities to generate and organize ideas. Englert (1992) outlined three principles that teachers may use for instructing children on how to write expository text: 1) engaging children in using strategies related to planning, organizing, revising, and editing text; 2) modeling their inner talk and reasoning involved in effective writing; and 3) learning about the social aspect of writing by collaborating with others and writing for authentic purposes.

Building strong literacy skills in children who are at risk is key to their success in school, and increasing math skills is of equal importance. Kloosterman and Lester (2004) reported that in 1990, data collected from the National Assessment of Educational Progress (NAEP) noted the disturbing differences in math achievement that fell along the lines of race, ethnicity, gender, and socioeconomic background. Today, the achievement gap is still troubling to educators. A more recent assessment indicated that, although African American and Hispanic children scored higher, they continue to achieve below the levels of Caucasian children (Perie, Grigg, & Dion, 2005). From the early grades, children's math curriculum should be designed to include the foundation knowledge that leads to the development of higher-order reasoning abilities and an appreciation for math and its application in life. Equally important is that the strategies incorporate procedures that are sensitive to individual differences in learning style, learning rate, and linguistic and cultural differences. Mullis, Dossey, Owen, and Phillips (1991) emphasized 10 keys to mathematics achievement:

1. Emphasizing reading as part of math
2. Linking math to everyday problems and situations

3. Developing children's reasoning and analytic skills

4. Teaching children how to more effectively communicate math ideas

5. Involving children in small-group and individual projects

6. Using technology (e.g., calculators, computers)

7. Providing instruction in pre-algebra and algebra

8. Encouraging parents to provide reading materials in the home

9. Using flexible, heterogeneous grouping practices

10. Employing anticipatory guides to improve reading comprehension of word problems

Research has identified three broad categories of strategies for teaching math effectively to children (D'Ambrosio, Johnson, & Hobbs, 1995):

1. Strategies that deal effectively with children's learning include reading, writing, and talking about mathematics, using technology (e.g., calculators, computers), building one's own mathematical knowledge, encouraging exploration and investigation, and using children's prior knowledge (Carter & Dean, 2006; D'Ambrosio, Johnson, & Hobbs, 1995).

2. The second category of strategies addresses content applications and integrations and consists of strategies such as relating math to the real-life experiences of children by using real-world problem-solving activities (e.g., taking surveys in class, writing math problems based on their personal experience, analyzing the results of community projects), integrating math with other content areas in a meaningful way (e.g., writing math autobiographies, describing math processes), and using culturally relevant materials (e.g., explore the numeration system from different cultural perspectives, games from different cultures; Carter & Dean, 2006; D'Ambrosio, Johnson, & Hobbs, 1995).

3. The third set of strategies target instructional approaches and encompass strategies such as

• Using technology (e.g., computer software, scientific calculators)

• Exploring mathematics concepts with hands-on materials and activities (e.g., using manipulatives to represent mathematics concepts)

• Encouraging oral and written expression (e.g., keeping a journal, writing a brief paragraph about a new understanding)

• Fostering collaborative problem solving (e.g., working on a long-term or a class activity or project with other students, reviewing homework assignments in a group, working together to review or prepare for a test)

Other equally valuable strategies include

• Using errors to encourage learning (e.g., teacher taking the role of facilitator and encouraging reflection on incorrect responses, emphasizing children's responsibility for their own learning, discussing children's progress with them individually)

- Employing direct instruction in reading comprehension (Kamil, 2004)
- Providing an enriched curriculum and challenging activities (e.g., moving curriculum beyond basic skills and incorporating challenging activities such as measurement, geometry, probability, algebra; using interdisciplinary activities that link science to mathematics; D'Ambrosio, Johnson, & Hobbs, 1995)

The goals of these strategies are to provide experiences that enhance children's appreciation for the value of mathematics, allow them to become confident in their abilities to do mathematics, teach them to communicate mathematically, and develop and reinforce reasoning mathematically (National Council of Teachers of Mathematics [NCTM], 1989). These goals generally lead to higher mathematics achievement, and they are more powerful when used in combination within a challenging and dynamic curriculum.

DIVERSE INSTRUCTIONAL STRATEGIES

Children from poverty often face a number of barriers to good and effective instruction. Teachers' low expectations for children living in poverty and the reliance on unchallenging and barren curriculum are significant road blocks to children's school success (Knapp & Shields, 1990). Low expectations for children often include inappropriate instruction that does not address the needs of the learners. Good instruction incorporates strategies that are diverse and targets the educational strengths and needs of most learners. The Association for Supervision and Curriculum Development (ASCD) Advisory Panel on Improving Student Achievement defined *good instruction* as "teaching that is engaging, relevant, multicultural, and that appeals to a variety of modalities and learning styles" (1995, p. 9). Kline (1995) identified a number of effective strategies used in instructing children from diverse backgrounds:

1. Provide opportunities for children to work together (Stover, 1993).
2. Use reality-based learning methods (Hollins, 1993).
3. Encourage interdisciplinary instruction and consider children's individual learning preferences (Carbo, 1987; Dunn & Dunn, 1992).
4. Engage students in learning (Hodges, 1994).
5. Involve teacher modeling of learning behaviors (Burroughs, 1993).
6. Allow children to explore and apply critical inquiry and reasoning (Carr, 1988; Dillon, 1984).
7. Encourage home–school collaboration (Epstein, 1995).
8. Employ multicultural teaching approaches (Banks, 1990; Hollins, 1993).

9. Involve accelerated learning techniques (e.g., using memory strategies to enhance learning; Rose, 1985).

10. Emphasize brain-compatible instruction (Carnine, 1990).

The following strategies have been deemed successful in educating children from diverse cultural, linguistic, and limited economic backgrounds.

Cooperative Learning

Cooperative learning is based on the idea that by encouraging children to learn together and by fostering opportunities for team effort, children would teach each other within the context of structured and small-group dynamic activities. Cooperative learning is a way of organizing small groups to encourage learning (Slavin, 1988). Cooperative learning emphasizes thinking skills, prepares children for working collaboratively with others, and has a positive effect on student achievement (Slavin, 1990). Although there are different approaches to cooperative learning, for it to be most effective, three components are central: team rewards, group goals and individual accountability, and equal opportunities for success (Slavin, 1988). Saravia-Shore and Garcia (1995) indicated that cooperative learning needs to be taught because children must be able to communicate, listen, give feedback, manage conflict, take leadership, contribute, and take responsibility for aspects of the activities in order to benefit from the process. It involves structuring children's needs to communicate, socialize, and work together. Teacher facilitation is imperative because cooperative learning requires more than having children sit next to each other working on a project (Saravia-Shore & Garcia, 1995). Cooperative learning approaches include assigning children to groups of five or six members, with each student having a specific task in the project that must be accomplished collaboratively. One student may read and set up the materials for the project, and another student may perform the experiment or carry out the procedure. A third student may be responsible for recording, a fourth student may illustrate the project, and a fifth student may read the recorded experience or report to the class (Saravia-Shore & Garcia, 1995). There is widespread agreement that cooperative learning strategies have a positive effect on students' achievement, especially at the elementary and middle school levels (Barr & Parrett, 2001; Slavin, 1988).

Direct Instruction

Direct instruction was designed to extend the learning gains of children living in high poverty areas who attended Head Start into elementary school (Barr & Parrett, 2001). This approach involves teachers following explicit directions for preparing, teaching, or instructing children. For example, a direct-instruction sequence to increase the probability that children will both correctly master and use effective academic strategies may include four major stages: 1) directly showing students how to use the selected skill or strategy; 2) students practice the skill under the teacher's supervision, and the teacher gives frequent corrective feedback and praise; 3) students use the skill independently in real academic situations; and 4) students use the skill in a variety of other settings to maximize generalization (Wright, 2001). Direct instruction has been shown to be effective in increasing children's performance on criterion-referenced and norm-referenced measures (Barr & Parrett, 2001; Carnine, 1994; Carnine, Silbert, Kame'enui, & Tarver, 2004).

One-to-One Tutoring and Peer Tutoring

Individual or one-to-one tutoring is described as the most effective form of instruction (Slavin, Karweit, & Wasik, 1992), and research findings support this contention (Center for Research on Effective Schooling for Disadvantage Students, 1990; Wasik & Slavin, 1993). Research on one-to-one tutoring notes that three key elements are essential to a successful outcome: tutors are trained, instruction is high quality, and amount of time in tutoring and incentive used match students' needs (Wasik & Slavin, 1993). These individualized tutoring sessions may involve tutoring the student for 20–30 minutes daily or less, based on educational needs. One-to-one tutoring provides many advantages when used with children who are at risk for school failure: improved achievement in higher grades, lower rates of retention, higher rates of school completion, and fewer referrals for special education services (Center for Research on Effective Schooling for Disadvantaged Students, 1990).

Peer tutoring is another dimension of one-to-one tutoring that has been shown to be effective for improving the skills of those who are tutored and for the tutors as well (Moll, Diaz, Estrada, & Lopes, 1992; Nath & Ross, 2001; Saravia-Shore & Garcia, 1995; Winter, 1986). Specifically, when peer tutors are used to help younger learners experiencing difficulty in reading, the reading skills of the tutees as well as the tutors improved appreciatively (Garcia-Vazquez & Ehly, 1995; Nath & Ross, 2001; Winter, 1986). The benefits of tutoring have not only been in reading, but also in the social-emotional adjustment of all students involved in the experience. Studies conducted with middle school students with a history of serious behavioral, academic, and attendance problems yielded findings that indicated that when middle school students worked with younger children as tutors, the middle school tutors learned as much as the children being tutored (Harvard Graduate School of Education, 1987). For these peer tutoring programs to be most beneficial to all participants, however, they must be structured and incorporate those components that have been shown to be effective in tutoring programs. Peer tutoring programs generally entail 20–30 minutes sessions two or three times a week. Garcia-Vazquez and Ehly (1995) identified important components of good peer tutoring programs:

1. Selecting peer tutor activities that complement classroom instruction
2. Providing comprehensive training to peer tutors in the important elements of the tutoring process
3. Ensuring that peer tutors have mastered the important elements of tutoring before working with the children being tutored
4. Adapting scientifically based instruction to improve the reading skills of children being tutored
5. Following up with periodic "tutoring integrity checks"
6. Evaluating and monitoring the effectiveness of peer tutoring

Computer-Assisted Instruction

Technology is becoming an essential aspect of children's learning in school. Computer programs and Internet access can be used to enhance classroom instruction, promote independent learning, support cooperative learning activities, encourage research, and improve literacy and math skills. Many schools who serve high poverty areas, however, often lack the resources to provide students with the benefits that come from effectively using computers to enhance classroom instruction. There is a recognized gap in the use of and access to technology between families of limited resources and affluent families (Lieberman, 1999).

Studies have found that computer-assisted instruction can benefit children significantly, especially children who are at risk. *Computer-assisted instruction* can be defined as tutorial, drill-and-practice, and simulated activities that complement a teacher-directed instructional program (Cotton, 1991). Mioduser, Tur-Kaspa, and Leitner (2000) studied the contribution of computer-based instruction when compared with more conventional modes of instruction (i.e., teacher instruction with textbooks) to early reading skills acquisition. The study found that children at high risk who received the reading intervention program with computer materials significantly improved their phonological awareness, word recognition, and letter-naming skills relative to their peers who received a reading intervention program with only printed materials and those who received no formal reading intervention program (Mioduser et al., 2000). There are several computerized reading programs that have been effective in improving children's reading skills such as Earobics and Fast ForWord (Mioduser et al., 2000). Research on the effectiveness of using computer-assisted instruction indicated that when used as part of a comprehensive instructional program, computer-assisted instruction is effective in improving achievement, especially for children from disadvantaged backgrounds and children who are having difficulty achieving (Cotton, 1991).

Culturally Responsive and Linguistically Appropriate Pedagogy

Respect for cultural and linguistic experiences is essential to learning, especially for children from diverse backgrounds. Tharp (1992) affirmed that teaching and learning are most effective when they are framed and contextualized in the experiences, skills, and values of the community and when learning involves dynamic activities with peers and teachers. Studies focusing on learning and culture found that children's academic achievement increased when certain aspects of their home cultures were incorporated into the classroom (Jordan, Tharp, & Baird-Vogt, 1992). Saravia-Shore and Garcia (1995) distilled six key instructional practices that respect the experiences and perspectives of students who are diverse:

1. Integrating the home culture (e.g., students can interview parents, research cultural practices)

2. Capitalizing on children's backgrounds (e.g., semantic webbing)

3. Employing culturally relevant curriculum materials and activities (e.g., books, stories)

4. Identifying and dispelling stereotypes (e.g., identify racist and sexist language and depictions and discuss with students)

5. Building culturally compatible learning environments by recognizing children's language, home–community culture, and learning style

6. Using cooperative learning strategies to incorporate diverse learning styles, teach about cultural practices, and build on personal and group experiences

Recognizing the value of language and providing students with activities and opportunities to build both languages are critical to the success of students who are linguistically diverse. English language learners struggle to obtain basic reading skills and are referred to special education programs because they are not provided with a curriculum that recognizes their language differences and builds on their native language. Indeed, the lack of appropriate instruction has been recognized as a reason why children who are culturally and linguistically diverse struggle to meet academic success (Cummins, 1983).

Two types of bilingual education programs have consistently been shown through research to improve children's achievement and proficiency in English: maintenance and dual language programs (Thomas & Collier, 2002). Maintenance programs offer instruction in the child's native language for part of the day (different programs have a specific ratio for the extent of time children receive instruction in their native language and English) and children remain in this program for 4–6 years. The purpose of maintenance programs is to keep and build children's native language while they are learning English. Dual language programs consist of both English language learners and English speakers. In this program, students participate for 4–6 years, typically beginning in kindergarten. The extent of time children are exposed to English and the native language differs based on the model being employed (50:50 or 90:10). Dual language offers English language learners the opportunity to learn English while continuing to make gains cognitively and academically in their native language, and English speakers are provided the opportunity to learn a second language proficiently.

Although research supports these two programs as effective and successful in helping English language learners close the achievement gap while learning English, they are the least used in schools (Rhodes et al., 2005).

Rhodes et al. (2005) indicated that several components have been recognized in effective learning environments for English language learners: 1) instruction in a student's native language is provided, 2) content-based instruction in English is provided, 3) children are engaged in active learning, 4) children's culture and language are recognized, 5) interaction with monolingual English-speaking peers is facilitated, and 6) the bilingual education program stands as an essential and recognized part of the school. Because development of children's cognitive skills is facilitated by continued language development in their native language, good bilingual or dual language programs are imperative to children's achievement. Saravia-Shore and Garcia (1995) recommended the following teaching strategies that have been shown to increase English language learners' achievement in school:

1. Including dual language strategies (integrate English speakers with English language learners in an academic setting where children are systematically exposed to research-based instructional strategies in both languages)

2. Creating strong bilingual classrooms where teachers offer literacy and content instruction for children in their native language while they are learning English

3. Instructional strategies should match children's level of language proficiency

4. Using subject matter or content to teach language

5. Utilizing cooperative learning strategies to problem solve and practice English

6. Using peer tutors and computers

7. Employing thematic and interdisciplinary teaching by using subject matter and learning English via themes

Parent Involvement

Parent involvement plays a pivotal role in children's achievement. Research findings underscore the significant contribution of parents to children's school achievement when they work collaboratively with schools (Christenson & Sheridan, 2001). Parents in the schools provide students with an important connection—school and home—and this links these two very important contexts in children's learning (Christenson & Sheridan, 2001). Parents can become involved in their children's schools on many different dimensions. They can participate in school activities, support teachers' instruction by helping with homework or volunteering in the classroom, and become partners with school staff in decision making at the school or district level (Epstein, 1995; see Chapter 9).

Children living in poverty have a high rate of school failure because schools and the larger society have failed them. Society as reflected in school staff and administrators can begin to change the tide of low expectation and poor school performance by providing effective instruction. Researchers have found that children living in poverty can achieve in the face of negative family background and life circumstances and that factors such as the school's mission, expectations, leadership, instructional practices, environment, and family involvement play a significant role in preparing children for success in life (Comer, 1999). Consistent with what researchers have found regarding children from poverty, Cartledge and Lo (2006) presented a list of school practices that reflects these findings:

- Providing a curriculum and instructional program tailored to the specific population and that upholds high expectations
- Providing a well-trained and committed staff
- Placing the focus on children and learning
- Offering ongoing professional development
- Teaching with a sense of urgency and keeping students academically engaged in learning activities in which their progress is monitored
- Using effective academic interventions and strategies and establishing schoolwide programs of instruction
- Teaching to prevent, starting with high-quality preschool programs
- Having adequate materials and resources
- Affirming and nurturing students and reinforcing their strengths
- Developing positive, collaborative relationships with families
- Establishing schoolwide behavioral programs

These practices, many of which were discussed in this chapter, are key to educating children living in poverty. Effective instruction improves the quality of life of children living in poverty, and students with strong academic skills are better equipped to gain access to resources and open doors to opportunities that are essential to rise above poverty (Cartledge & Lo, 2006). In the same manner that a free and appropriate education is a civil right for children with disabilities, effective and appropriate instruction is also a civil right for children living in poverty.

7

Social-Emotional and Behavioral Strategies for Improving Children's Adjustment and Achievement

From the standpoint of everyday life ... there is one thing we do know; that man is here for the sake of other men—above all, for those upon whose smile and well-being our own happiness depends, and also for the countless unknown souls with whose fate we are connected by a bond of sympathy. Many times a day I realize how much my own outer and inner life is built upon the labors of my fellow men, both living and dead, and how earnestly I must exert myself in order to give in return as much as I have received.

Albert Einstein

Research in the area of resilience has been successful in translating negative risk factors into positive action that would strengthen the development of children (Krovetz, 1999). There are three powerful factors working together to affect children's adjustment in school and subsequent quality of life: achievement, learning, and positive social interactions. The school experience can become a negative one for children who experience difficulty in learning, achieving, and behaving. McEvoy and Welker (2000) asserted that not understanding and acknowledging the relationship between these three factors has led to the failure of many well-meaning programs in school. Programs often focus on individual attributes of children and do not take into consideration all the risk factors and circumstances that predict academic underachievement and behavioral and emotional difficulties (McEvoy & Welker, 2000).

Living in poverty exposes children to multiple risk factors that can affect their emotional well-being. The likelihood of adverse child outcomes is significantly increased when economic deprivation coexists with other risk factors such as severe marital conflict, community violence, limited access to health and mental care, large family size, paternal criminality, and maternal mental illness (Luthar, 1999). Moreover, although these factors individually do not increase the likelihood of an adverse outcome, when they coexist (i.e., two or more risk factors), the result is an increased chance of the presence of social-emotional adjustment difficulties and low academic performance (see Luster & McAdoo, 1994; Rutter, 1979; Sameroff, Gutman, & Peck, 2003; Sameroff, Seifer, Zax, & Barocas, 1987).

Many studies have underscored the relationship between a disturbed family climate and children's behavior problems (see Cummings, Davies, & Campbell, 2000; Parke & Buriel, 1998). Negative and conflicted familial relationships can have a detrimental effect on children in general, but children living in more affluent homes have protective factors that mitigate to some extent the effect of their negative family climate (Luthar, 1999). The stability of an ordered school environment, access to trained school counselors and psychologists, safe schools, supportive teachers, positive role models, and effective instruction all serve as protective factors. Yet, in the presence of limited protective factors, many children living in poverty grow up to be well-adjusted adults, while others are burdened by multiple risk factors and, in many cases, consumed by them.

Research on characteristics of effective schools provides evidence that schools have a significant effect on children's development (Johnson, Schwartz, Livingston, & Slate, 2000). Indeed, schools have the power to contribute substantially to the emotional adjustment and well-being of children living in poverty when they provide an atmosphere that fosters resiliency. Doll, Zucker, and Brehm noted that "truly resilient children are vulnerable children who benefited from the caring, sustenance, and guidance of a community" (2004, p. 1). The community of the schools can foster an atmosphere of resiliency by providing safe environments where children can focus on learning; having adults that are caring and responsive to children's emotional, behavioral, and social needs; and promoting high behavioral and academic expectations. School-based protective factors include positive school climate, cultural sensitivity and inclusionary values and practices in the school, clear and high performance expectations for all children, student participation and parent involvement, strong children bonding with the school environment, schoolwide conflict resolution practices, and opportunities for skill acquisition and social development (Sprague & Walker, 2005). Researchers have found that schools that offer effective instruction tend to be safer schools with more positive climates (Gottfredson, Gottfredson, & Czeh, 2000). Behavioral and emotional adjustment in children is undoubtedly improved by the provision of effective instruction and a sense of academic accomplishment. Chapter 6 addressed instructional strategies that lead to improved academic achievement. This chapter discusses the types of social and behavioral interventions and educational practices that promote students' achievement and that are conducive to improved social-emotional adjustment in children. These strategies or educational practices fall into four broad categories: establishing a positive core of school-based values, establishing and communicating schoolwide rules and behavioral expectations, addressing peer influence and challenges, and establishing support for children who are at risk (Sprague & Walker, 2005).

Children spend most of their time in school where they learn and socialize under the guidance of teachers and other school staff. Teachers are in a position to empower children by helping them develop the behaviors needed to be productive, disciplined, and socially competent individuals in society (Cartledge & Lo, 2006). Sprague and Walker (2005) affirmed that schools can begin to establish an atmosphere that is positive, safe, and fosters resiliency by establishing and sponsoring school-based positive values about how to interact and treat others that incorporate civility, caring, and respect for the rights and property of others; establishing and communicating schoolwide rules and behavioral expectations and identifying specific applications of them (e.g., in hallways, classroom, playground, school bus); addressing peer influence and challenges; and establishing support for children who are at risk.

ESTABLISHING A POSITIVE SCHOOL CLIMATE

Addressing the needs of the entire school population sets the platform for preventing problem behaviors and enables school staff to intervene early with students whose behaviors are indicative of mental health concerns. By teaching behaviors that support civility, caring, and respect for others, school staff help reduce some of the negative influence of peer culture that can affect school safety (Sprague & Walker, 2005). Organized and well-managed classrooms minimize problem behaviors, but equally important, classrooms can become resilient communities that offer significant support and guidance so that children who are exposed to negative life circumstances can learn and experience success in a safe and nurturing environment (Doll et al., 2004).

Classroom-Based Strategies

Deci and Flaste (1995) postulated that children are more predisposed to persevere and work when faced with a challenging activity and when teachers create a school atmosphere where three basic needs are satisfied: the need to feel connected, the need to feel autonomous, and the need to feel competent. Deci and Flaste suggested that satisfying these needs can lead to more resilience in children. Classrooms can be managed and run in ways that provide effective contexts for learning. According to Doll et al. (2004), research in the areas of risk and resiliency in children who are vulnerable, academic success in children who live in urban environments and are at high risk, and conditions that facilitate inclusion of children with disabilities, have yielded similar findings that identified a number of classroom practices as conducive to high achievement and positive emotional and behavioral adjustment. Doll et al. (2004) used these findings to identify six characteristics that defined resilient classrooms and described the classroom practices that facilitate academic and interpersonal success:

1. *Academic efficacy*: This term refers to the beliefs children have regarding their academic skills. Children's willingness to persist at a task, their level of effort and their frustration tolerance in the face of a challenging task, and their implementation of work behaviors conducive to academic success are all influenced by academic efficacy (Patrick, Hicks, & Ryan, 1997). Researchers know that several classroom characteristics facilitate academic efficacy:

   a. Classrooms that provide the opportunity for children to undertake challenging work with supportive instruction and guidance from teachers

   b. Classrooms that allow children to see peers succeed at the same tasks

   c. Classrooms where children receive frequent feedback and affirmation regarding their ability to learn successfully

   d. Classrooms where children receive recognition and celebration of their success (see Bandura, 1986; Doll et al., 2004)

2. *Academic self-determination*: This term is defined as having personal goals for learning and the skills to accomplish, monitor, and revise the goals as needed. According to Doll et al. (2004), resilient classrooms promote academic self-determination by offering children practice and direct instruction in academic goal setting, problem solving, self-evaluation of academic skills, and decision making. Research shows that self-determination is associated with many positive learning behaviors and outcomes that include responsibility and ownership for learning, higher academic achievement and engagement in learning (Masten, 2001), increased persistence when working toward goals, and higher level of academic self-efficacy and conceptual learning (Ames, 1992; Deci, Hodges, Pierson, & Tomassone, 1992).

3. *Behavioral self-control*: Children's ability to control their behavior and impulses in the classroom is essential to developing a classroom environment where learning is the focus. In a classroom, children must be able to focus, attend, and concentrate; work independently or with little teacher guidance until the work is complete; follow teacher directions; and work collaboratively with others. Doll et al. (2004) defined *behavioral self-control* as present when children's behaviors and conduct are appropriate for learning whether the teacher or adult authority figures are in the classroom. Students should be provided with behavioral information that increases their awareness of the

effect of their decisions on their lives and that of others (Cartledge & Lo, 2006). Students must be taught to manage their own behaviors in such a way that they have the skills to make self-corrections and solve problems even when adults are not available to direct them. When students are taught problem-solving skills and are reinforced for implementing these strategies independently and in different contexts, they are most likely to internalize these behaviors (Lazarus, 1993).

4. *Effective peer relationships*: Positive peer relationships are the foundation of healthy adult friendships. Peer relationships offer young children a developmentally based opportunity to begin learning how to collaborate, maintain friendships, manage conflicts, forgive minor offenses, and evaluate the value of a friendship. Positive peer relationships bring great emotional satisfaction to children, and this is incredibly apparent when working with children who have difficulty relating to others. Less popular children are typically shunned by peers and are afforded fewer opportunities to learn from social experiences (Cartledge & Milburn, 1996). Peer relationships are critical to the development of social competence and the promotion of academic success (Doll et al., 2004; Wentzel, 1991). A classroom promotes effective peer relationships when activities, routines, values, and rules foster conflict resolution, peer inclusion, and collaboration. Instructional practices such as cooperative learning activities and peer tutoring help build more positive relationships between children.

5. *Effective teacher–student relationships*: Research in effective schools has consistently pointed to positive and authentic teacher–student relationships as one component contributing to a positive school climate (Comer, Haynes, Joyner, & Ben-Avie, 1996; Gottfredson et al., 2000). Others have reported that preparing teachers to communicate more effectively with children (e.g., talking and listening to students) and to establish a warm and caring classroom atmosphere (e.g., helping and nurturing students) influence children's attitudes toward school and have an effect on children's relationship with teachers (Brown, 1999a). Teachers create and promote authentic teacher–student relationships when they are responsive to students' needs; are warm and caring; engage the class in activities that encourage positive social connections; affirm students' learning abilities and celebrate their success; run an organized and structured class with routines, predictable rules, and consistent limits; provide reassurance when students face challenging work and engage students in learning; and provide clear and high behavioral and academic expectations (Doll et al., 2004).

6. *Effective home–school relationships*: From a broad perspective, home–school relationships may include home-based activities that are associated with student learning as well as school-based events in which parents participate in school activities (Cartledge & Lo, 2006). There is an extensive knowledge

base to support the fact that parent involvement is associated with increased achievement and school success (see Christenson & Sheridan, 2001; Comer et al., 1996). It is important that school staff understand parents' circumstances because this affects parents' level of involvement in school. Some parents are able to participate at the home-based level, whereas others are able to contribute at the school-based level. By providing parents with support and encouragement at the level that they are able to contribute to their children's education, schools may foster more participation, guide parents into participating in the areas where their involvement can have the most beneficial result, build more positive relationships between families and school, and encourage a more resilient school atmosphere.

Social Skills Training

Social skills training can be defined as a positive, preventive effort to decrease problem behaviors, correct existing problems, or stop inappropriate behaviors from worsening (Cartledge & Lo, 2006; Cartledge & Milburn, 1996). When children are provided with the tools to conduct themselves socially in more acceptable ways, the results are behaviors and conduct that create and sustain more nurturing, safe, and inclusive schools. Social skills are developmentally based, so there are social skills curricula designed for students in kindergarten through secondary school that may incorporate developing problem-solving skills, self-control, coping strategies, and anger management skills (Sprague & Walker, 2005). Social skills instruction is generally based on a social modeling paradigm and tends to consist of the following components: 1) identifying and providing rationale for the skill, 2) modeling the skill, 3) offering guided practice, 4) allowing independent practice, and 5) planning and facilitating for behavior generalization (Cartledge & Lo, 2006). The skills are typically taught within the context of a small group and rely on role plays and activities to foster students' active participation (Sprague & Walker, 2005). These programs can be effective in teaching children to resolve interpersonal conflicts in more socially appropriate ways (Shure & Spivac, 1982); use problem-solving strategies and anger coping skills to decrease aggressive responses in interpersonal problems (Lochman, Coie, Underwood, & Terry, 1993); and apply self-managing, perspective-taking, and self-monitoring skills (Lochman, Burch, Curry, & Lampron, 1984). Social skills training also helps develop more resilient children who demonstrate more flexibility, adjustment to different instructional situations, acceptance of corrective feedback, empathy and caring, communication skills, interpersonal skills, and positive relationships with peers (Bernard, 1991; Krovetz, 1999). Cartledge and Lo (2006) indicated that for social skills instruction to be most effective, several components should be considered: 1) social skills training should begin early, 2) social skills instruction should be ongoing from elementary through secondary school, 3) social skills should be taught to mastery, and 4) teachers instructing social skills should be trained.

ESTABLISHING AND COMMUNICATING RULES AND BEHAVIORAL EXPECTATIONS

School climate plays a significant role in maintaining safe and orderly schools. Schoolwide intervention programs are set up to communicate and enforce behavioral expectations and establish an atmosphere of academic and behavioral competence and mutual respect in the school building (Sprague & Walker, 2005). Schoolwide level programs that focus on improving classroom management, using effective instructional strategies, building school capacity to initiate and sustain innovation, and grouping youth who are at risk into "school-within-schools" to create more supportive interaction and flexibility in instruction have been shown to be preventive and even more effective than group counseling in reducing aggressive, antisocial, and violent behaviors in individual students (Gottfredson et al., 2000). Programs that are designed to disseminate information, produce fear, appeal to moral values, and focus on affective education are not very successful in reducing antisocial behaviors or substance use (Gottfredson et al., 2000). School-based programs, however, that are ongoing and that focus on comprehensive instruction on social competency skills such as stress management, social skills instruction, anger management, social problem solving, and communication skills have been shown to be effective in decreasing inappropriate social behaviors (see Gottfredson et al., 2000).

Schoolwide Positive Behavior Support

Although there are a number of empirically strong and effective programs that advocate a schoolwide approach to enforcing consistent behavioral expectations such as the Schoolwide Ecological Intervention (Nelson, 2000), Second Step Violence Prevention Curriculum (Frey, Hirschstein, & Guzzo, 2000), and the Best Behavior Staff Development Program (Sprague & Golly, 2004), this book focuses on the Schoolwide Positive Behavior Support program (SWPBS; Horner, Sugai, Lewis-Palmer, & Todd, 2001) because it is a program used by many schools.

Most schools rely on deficit models in which an individual child is identified as lacking the skills to adjust or behave appropriately in school. All other risk factors that are contributing to the child's problems are typically ignored. The child is often identified for school counseling and/or disciplinary procedures such as school suspension (e.g., in-school, out-of-school), school detention, and withdrawal of privileges (e.g., recess, computer time) to address behavioral offenses. Unfortunately, many of these practices and procedures are "band-aid" approaches and associated with negative outcomes. For example, repeated suspensions and exclusions are associated with negative school attitude, academic underachievement, poor self-image, grade retentions, poor peer interactions, hostile feelings toward school staff, and school dropout (Shingles & Lopez-Reyna, 2002). In essence, the child is seen as the problem and little recognition is given to the school environment and peer influences that may also be contributing to the problem. As noted earlier, schools play a significant role in improving children's ability to adjust by providing an atmosphere that instructs and supports skills that are conducive to resilience. SWPBS allows schools to create and implement empirically proven strategies to address schoolwide, classroom, and individual problem behaviors (Lewis & Sugai, 1999).

SWPBS incorporates multiple dimensions that target a continuum of behavioral support in drawing out positive changes in the school system (e.g., routines, structure, policies), school physical structure, students, and school staff behaviors (Sugai et al., 2000). The purpose of SWPBS is to 1) create a positive school atmosphere, 2) establish and teach behavioral expectations at a whole-school level, and 3) teach to mastery and encourage demonstration of behavioral skills (e.g., following school rules, respectful and responsible peer interactions, academic engagement; Sprague & Walker, 2005). The ultimate goal, though, is to create and sustain a responsive school atmosphere that supports schooling for all children (Walker, Irvin, & Sprague, 1997). The program provides several levels of support, incorporating universal (primary prevention), specialized group (secondary prevention), and individual student (tertiary prevention) strategies with a continuum of instructional and behavioral support to encourage the advancement of all students (Sprague, Sugai, Horner, & Walker, 1999). Moreover, when parents are included in this process, they too may learn from the strategies and reinforce desired behaviors at home.

SWPBS is defined by key practices that include (Lewis & Sugai, 1999)

1. Team-based problem solving and planning: A comprehensive whole-school approach requires that all staff be involved in the process and collaborate.

2. Administrator and staff commitment and support: Because it is a schoolwide approach, the majority if not all school staff must be committed to supporting the programs. Sprague and Walker (2005) noted that at least 80% of school staff must be committed to monitor, support, coach, and implement the intervention over a long term.

3. Systematic assessment of disciplinary practices and processes: There must be a procedure to systematically measure and monitor the effectiveness of the interventions, so assessment measures (pre- and post-) must be identified and implemented.

4. Continuing staff development: School staff must receive ongoing training, feedback, support, consultation, and coaching in the effective implementation of strategies essential to the success of the program by a designated trained staff member or a consultant.

5. Data-based decision making: Ongoing review and evaluation of school-generated data such as office referral, school report, and student attendance should be conducted as a means of monitoring students' behavior, guiding decision making and planning, evaluating the effectiveness of interventions, and making revisions if needed (Cartledge & Lo, 2006).

6. Establishment of clear policies and agenda: School staff must establish a clear set of disciplinary policies that include defined, expected behaviors as well as problem behaviors and consequences for all students and staff. Students should be clear about appropriate and inappropriate behavior, and staff members should be trained on responding to inappropriate and appropriate behaviors. School staff must be trained on fairly applying rules and providing incentives and motivational strategies to promote and support appropriate student behavior. Maximum focus is placed on positive reinforcement as a means of increasing desired behavior. Students also receive ongoing instruction and booster sessions on academic and social strategies to bring about the behavioral changes necessary.

7. Adoption of evidence-based practices: The program calls for the implementation of researched-based instructional and behavioral strategies that include social skills training, academic instruction, individual behavioral plans, and parent involvement and training (Cartledge & Lo, 2006).

8. Application of functional assessment: For students who exhibit behaviors that need more targeted responses, a functional behavioral approach is advocated. Here, the function of the child's behaviors are identified by a team of staff members who interact with the child, and a behavioral intervention plan is developed, implemented, and monitored for effectiveness.

Cartledge and Lo asserted that "the impulse to exclude misbehaving students so as to free up time for those who welcome instruction is strong" (2006, p. 176), especially in schools that serve children living in poverty. These practices, however, lead to the very outcomes schools are trying to prevent: school dropout and antisocial behaviors. Whole-school behavioral programs such as SWPBS have been shown to provide school staff with more effective ways of promoting appropriate social behaviors and increasing student achievement. Equally important, teachers who participate in these programs tend to be more satisfied and motivated because these schools are safer, conducive to learning, and the relationship between student and teachers is more positive.

ADDRESSING PEER INFLUENCE AND CHALLENGES

Peer influence in and out of school affects children's behavior in school. The effect of neighborhood contexts where violence may be advocated by adults and peers alike is of significant concern. Much too often these behaviors are brought to school as children try to belong to a peer group and believe that they must show bravado to be safe in school and not be rejected by peers. Schools must address the issue of peer influence and culture to begin changing the climate of the school and focus students' attention on learning.

Education researchers (Frey et al., 2000; Horner et al., 2001; Sprague, Sugai, & Walker, 1998) agreed that students must be an integral part of changing the climate of the schools, and the implementation of programs that address bullying, violence in the school, and anger management are a critical part of any school plan. Creating a peer culture of respect, caring, and civility in which disagreements are solved reasonably and problem-solving strategies are utilized naturally are fundamental to safe and effective schools but also to a peaceful society. Sprague and Walker (2005) emphasized five strategies that can transform the destructive peer culture that exists in many schools that serve children living in poverty:

1. Implement one of the empirically based school violence prevention programs (e.g., Second Step Violence Prevention Curriculum; Frey et al., 2000).

2. Bully proof the school by implementing antibullying programs aimed at neutralizing the power of bullies (e.g., The Olweus Bully Intervention Program; Olweus, 1993).

3. Expose students to and teach anger management and conflict resolution techniques.

4. Ask students to sign a pledge not to bully, offend, and tease others (this has been shown to have an effect on students' behavior).

5. Identify and refer children who are seriously emotionally troubled for mental health services.

Moreover, there are programs that have successfully combined the principles of SWPBS with bullying prevention strategies and have produced significant reductions in aggression in students (Orpinas, Horne, & Staniszewski, 2003). The bottom line is that the influence of peer culture cannot be ignored and must be systematically addressed to change the climate of a school.

PROVIDING SUPPORT FOR CHILDREN AT RISK

The adoption and implementation of whole-school behavioral programs that target behavior and academic achievement allows school staff to more effectively identify students who are experiencing learning problems and/or behavioral difficulties that require more intensive attention. Students whose behavior has not changed despite positive behavior strategies and support provided by school staff, and whose behaviors are "red flags" for more serious emotional concerns, should be identified and referred for more intensive therapeutic interventions.

LeBlanc (1998) advocated for a three-level screening approach that is multimethod, multisource, and multisetting for identifying children at risk. This model included screening approaches that incorporated multiple informants, from different settings, using different methods. Sprague and Walker (2005) discussed three strategies of identification: 1) training teachers to identify warning signs, 2) screening to identify children at risk, and 3) reviewing school records and involving parents. Teachers and other school staff must be trained to identify signs of serious behavioral difficulties in children. These signs should include, but are not limited to, threatening to harm self and/or others, social withdrawal, aggression, uncontrolled anger, being a victim of violence, drug and alcohol use, gang affiliation, academic underachievement or learning problems, feelings of rejection and social isolation, depression, and bullying behavior. School staff that recognize signs of emotional trouble in a student should notify school administrators and trained mental health staff (e.g., school psychologists, social workers, school counselors). The second strategy involves universal screening in which students' emotional states are rated using instruments that measure internalizing or externalizing behavioral difficulties (e.g., depression, aggression, social skills). Teachers and parents rate students using measures such as the Drummond Student Risk Screening Scale (SRSS; Drummond, 1993) or Social Skills Rating Scale (SSRS; Gresham & Elliot, 1990). The third strategy requires trained mental health staff to review records of students who have been identified by teachers and through screening methods as being at risk. Trained staff review records looking for three areas of school adjustment: academic underachievement (e.g., low grades, grade retention, remedial services), class or school disruption (e.g., discipline referrals, school suspensions), and individual variables (e.g., number of schools attended, days absent, special education placements and services). The information gathered (e.g., screening data, teacher and parent ratings, record review) is reviewed as a whole by a school team that includes mental health staff (school psychologist, social workers, or school counselors), parents, teachers, and school administrators to make decisions regarding the level of intervention required (e.g., individual counseling or therapeutic services; small, structured therapeutic and educational settings; family therapy and other clinical or psychiatric services).

Children at risk must be provided with intensive and ongoing therapeutic services that involve parents' participation. Some schools have adopted "full-service school" models in which schools offer health clinics and mental health services that address the family's needs. This type of connection allows for closer work between school staff, mental health providers, and parents, to the benefit of children and families. Ultimately, however, children must not only be identified as at risk but also must receive the services that would bring about changes necessary to improve their quality of life. Schools must play a more decisive role in helping parents identify these services when they are not available in the schools.

Understanding the connection between academic underachievement, learning problems, and behavioral and emotional difficulties is critical to children's adjustment in school. Effective behavioral strategies must include strategies aimed at addressing children's learning problems and behavioral needs in order to successfully improve their emotional adjustment and achievement in school. Schoolwide behavioral approaches that are comprehensive and long term have been the most effective in changing children's behavior and improving children's academic performance.

8

The Influence
of School Climate

People who soar are those who refuse to sit back, sigh and wish things would change. They neither complain of their lot nor passively dream of some distant ship coming in. Rather, they visualize in their minds that they are not quitters; they will not allow life's circumstances to push them down and hold them under.

Charles R. Swindoll

Schools in low-income communities often exhibit problems with school climate, and these problems are concomitant with difficulties in students' achievement and socialization (Esposito, 1999). *School climate* refers to the social and educational atmosphere of a school (Comuntzis-Page, 1996). It also has been defined by Tagiuri as a "relatively enduring quality of the internal environment of an organization that (a) is experienced by its members, (b) influences their behavior, and (c) can be described in terms of the values of a particular set of characteristics (or attributes) of the organization" (1968, p. 27). In addition, Moos (1979) defined *school climate* as a learning environment in which students have educational and social experiences based on a set of procedures or expectations set up by the teachers and administrators. Moos discussed three categories of social environments: 1) relationship—related to affiliation with other individuals in the classroom and includes teacher and staff support; 2) personal growth/goal orientation—refers to personal or individual development and growth of all members of the learning environment; and 3) system maintenance and system change—refers to the organization of the learning environment, the clarity of rules and expectations, and the diligence of the teacher and other school personnel in enforcing the rules. School climate is influenced and further defined by the presence of factors that include parent involvement, school safety, teachers' expectations for students, quality instruction, pleasant working and learning conditions, teachers' morale, and strong leadership. Lareau (1987) asserted that a school's climate is particularly relevant to families that have traditionally felt marginalized by institutions in the United States. Schools with a negative school climate are the ones linked to low achievement, school dropout, low attendance, staff turnover, school violence, and low parent involvement (see Barr & Parrett, 2001; Brown, 1999a; Nelson, Covin, & Smith, 1996).

CHARACTERISTICS OF A POSITIVE SCHOOL CLIMATE

Many studies identified factors that are associated with children becoming at risk, and a large percentage of these factors identified life in the home, the community, and a background of poverty. Research examining the complicated problems related to children living in poverty, however, shows that school factors further exacerbate these problems (Barr & Parrett, 2001). Purkey and Schmidt (1996) asserted that schools must be "inviting places," and schools that have a positive climate are those in which

- Parents, teachers, administrators, and children perceive the school staff as warm, caring, and concerned.
- Teachers, school staff, and administrators see children as valuable and treat children with respect even when their behavior is not appropriate.
- School policies (discipline, grading, and promotion) are developed and administered so they promote personal and educational achievement.
- Educational programs in the school including curricula are designed to be inclusive (ethnically, culturally, linguistically, and socioeconomically).
- Educators recognize children's accomplishments and encourage them to fulfill their potential.

Littky (2004) emphasized that relationships are the foundation of school climate and trust and respect provide grounds to cultivate relationships between teachers, children, and families. Other scholars noted the importance of teachers and school administrators as instrumental to providing a fertile ground to develop a positive school atmosphere. Delisio (2005) reported that signs of a positive school climate include

- Teacher stability and common goals define the school.
- Curricular and instructional components are clearly defined.
- Schoolwide celebrations recognize stakeholders.
- School staff are recognized for their contribution to the school.
- Open communication is encouraged between school staff.
- School administrators offer tangible support.

A number of teacher factors have been discussed as contributing to positive school climate. Brown (1999a) reported that factors such as training teachers to communicate more effectively with children, develop effective disciplinary procedures, and establish a warm and caring classroom atmosphere influence children's attitudes toward school; this in turn improves school climate. Barr and Parrett (2001) emphasized addressing myths about children exposed to multiple risk factors as a step to improving school climate.

1. *Slow instructional pace benefits these children.* Studies have documented the benefit of high expectations and enriched learning environment in the education of children from a background of poverty. Accelerated and enriched curriculum has been shown to lead to higher achievement for all children (see Levin & Hopfenberg, 1991).

2. *Retaining children at risk in the early grades prepared them to move on.* The benefit of retaining children has not been proven. Meta-analytic studies and educational research conducted over a century have not supported retention as an effective intervention (Anderson et al., 2002; Jimerson, 2001). Retention has been associated with school dropout and other negative outcomes. Moreover, for children with multiple risk factors, retention may increase the chances of school failure (Barr & Parrett, 2001). Children retained tend to have a history of absenteeism, numerous school changes, large family size, low parental education, low family involvement in addition to poor academic achievement, and low standardized test scores (Anderson et al., 2002). Studies focusing on children's emotional adjustment and achievement through the secondary grades reported negative outcomes related to retention that include low levels of academic adjustment, failure to complete high school, and low education and employment status in adulthood (Jimerson, 1999). Moreover, retention was found to be the most powerful predictor of school dropout, with retained students 2 to 11 times more likely to not complete high school than promoted students (Anderson et al., 2002).

3. *Schools that educate poor children can do so with the same funding as schools with a smaller number of families from a background of poverty.* Many educational scholars have discussed inequity in school funding and its devastating effect on poor children. Inequity in school funding adds to the difficulty schools experience in meeting the needs of the students and their families, and this inability to meet basic educational needs contributes to a negative school climate. Barr and Parrett clearly illustrated this point:

> "In spite of decades of civil rights litigation and legislation that has fought segregated schools and even concluded that "separated but equal" was not in fact equal, property tax funding and local control of schools have combined to stratify U.S. public education into the haves and have-nots. It is clearly recognized that poor children who attend school with other poor children have an enormous challenge to overcome if they are to succeed in school. The existence of poverty in the home and community is too often matched by poverty in the

school setting, which directly contributes to the failure of so many at-risk youth. Too often the students who are so in need of enriched, accelerated education are subjected to the schools with the worst financial support, the most poorly paid teachers, the most dilapidated buildings, the worst equipment, textbooks and instructional materials, and they respond accordingly by failing, leaving, or giving up." (2001, p. 51)

4. *Classroom teachers can effectively address the needs of these children without additional training.* The educational and emotional needs of children from a background of poverty are better addressed by teachers who are trained to understand their needs and to intervene effectively. Haberman (2005) and Levine (2005) strongly emphasized the need to have teachers that are specifically trained to work with children who are diverse and living in poverty. Young, inexperienced, and ill-prepared teachers are more likely to quit the field when placed in poor urban schools than mature teachers. Teacher research reports that 1 in 10 young teachers (under age 26) who choose to work in urban schools would remain in the schools long enough (3 years) to become effective teachers for this population of children (Haberman, 2005) and then leave. Levine noted that the faculty in teacher education programs have little experience working with children and families who live in poverty. Therefore, the faculty is not prepared to train teachers to instruct and nurture children in schools with a high concentration of families from low-income homes. Lack of prepared teachers contributes to the high teacher turnover and low stability in the teacher force intended to develop and support these children's learning.

5. *Reduced class size is the most effective way to improve instruction.* Although small classroom size can be effective in improving student learning, it is successful only when other factors are present such as high expectations and effective instruction. What appears to be important is good instruction and student involvement. When these factors are present, class size does not matter (Taylor, Pearson, Peterson, & Rodriguez, 2003).

6. *Children experiencing difficulty achieving need special education services.* When teachers are not effective in managing classroom behavior or in instructing children who have academic needs, the best course of action is generally perceived to be a referral to special education. The direct consequence of this belief is the overrepresentation of children from a background of poverty and children from culturally and linguistically diverse backgrounds in special education programs. Although racism may also play a role in overrepresentation, another factor is a school's inability to address the educational and emotional needs of these children. Not all children who are having difficulty achieving have a disability. Strong instructional strategies that are research-based and coupled with ongoing targeted assessment and monitoring can address the learning needs of poor children. Special education services should be the last step considered for children who have not made adequate academic progress and who are suspected of having a disability.

The myths and false beliefs that school administrators and teachers have about children and families who live in poverty must be addressed and confronted to begin building a positive school climate. Studies have emphasized that teachers often have low expectations for children living in poverty and children from culturally and linguistically diverse backgrounds (Zemelman, Daniels, & Hyde, 1998). A school climate that shows sensitivity and respect for individual differences and diversity encourages the capabilities and focuses on the worth of children and their families (NABSE & ILIAD, 2002). Eliminating harmful forms of bias and ensuring cultural competence is critical to establishing a positive school atmosphere (NABSE & ILIAD, 2002). Ongoing staff development for teachers is important to dispel the myths and harmful bias teachers hold about children and families living in poverty. Equally important is the fact that teacher involvement in the planning of staff development and in the implementation of programs in the schools further reinforce teachers' critical role in the education of children.

PROVIDING A POSITIVE SCHOOL CLIMATE

Schools identified as having a positive school climate are those that are successful in creating a safe, supportive school atmosphere that offers schoolwide behavioral and academic expectations, encourages parent involvement, and provides preventive programs (e.g., bully proofing, social skills development, conflict mediation), behavioral and emotional support (e.g., counseling services, connection to community outreach programs), and ongoing staff development.

Families must feel that their children are safe in schools, and schools must implement programs that prevent violence and provide children with a sense of security. Children must feel that they can reach out to teachers and school principals when they feel in danger and that action will be taken to address their concerns. Katz (1997) pointed out that children are more motivated when they feel that someone is listening to their concerns. Schoolwide discipline, social skills, and bullying programs help set the behavioral expectations for all children. They are the foundation of effective prevention and they develop the framework for school-based efforts to support effective parenting (Sprague & Walker, 2005). Promoting school environments that build self-esteem and improve resiliency and protective factors are key to school safety. Children who are involved in meaningful school activities are less likely to become involved in school violence (Stephens, 1995). Promoting schoolwide prosocial activities and establishing behavioral expectations help school order and safety. The effective implementation of schoolwide discipline programs has been shown to improve school climate (Sugai & Horner, 2002; Sugai & Lewis, 1999; see chapter 7).

Effective instructional programs that lead to the development of strong academic skills are essential to improving school climate. Many children who are not successful academically develop behavioral problems that further exacerbate their learning difficulties. Early intervention programs and strong reading programs that address the components of reading have been shown to be critical to the development of good readers (see chapter 6 for more information on effective academic strategies).

Parent involvement is another dimension to improving school climate. Parents who are involved in their children's school feel more positive about the school. They are invested in the decision-making process, they participate and help plan activities, and they support their children's learning. Children whose parents are involved in the school perform better academically and behaviorally (Christenson & Sheridan, 2001).

School must have a way of addressing children's behavioral and mental health issues and must have trained staff to identify problems and provide support. School psychologists, social workers, or counselors may provide counseling services required to address children's emotional needs and may provide guidance and education to parents and teachers. In addition, developing relationships with community agencies and coordinating services with outreach programs are also effective ways of providing further support to children and families. Families can be referred to these agencies, or community-based programs can be invited into the school to provide services.

Developing and nurturing a positive school climate also includes ongoing staff development for teachers and school staff. Teacher and staff involvement in planning and implementing instructional and behavioral programs in the school is imperative. Because teacher and staff input and cooperation is important to the effective implementation of most programs, many programs call for teacher commitment. Research found that securing commitment from at least 80% of the teachers and school staff is important to the effective implementation of a new program (Sprague & Walker, 2005). According to Sprague and Walker, the following school practices contribute to the development of school problems in children who are at risk:

- Poor instruction that leads to school failure

- Reliance on punitive classroom and behavioral-management practices

- Limited opportunity for students to learn and practice appropriate interpersonal and self-management skills

- Behavioral rules and expectations that are not clear and consistent

- Inconsistent correction of rule violations and failure to reinforce adherence to them

- Lack of individualized instruction, failure to differentiate instruction, and limited recognition or accommodation of individual differences (e.g., linguistic and ethnic differences)

- Failure to help students from a background of poverty connect to the school process

- Lack of agreement between teachers, school staff, and administrators regarding the implementation of disciplinary strategies

Many of the previous practices are teacher related and can be changed by not only securing teacher commitment, but also teacher involvement in the selection, development, and implementation of new programs, including ongoing staff development needs. Teacher involvement, however, also requires teacher respect and acceptance of the administrator's leadership and ultimate responsibility for the school's operation. A relationship between teachers and school administrators grounded in the goal of improving children's academic success and emotional adjustment should be the guiding force.

A positive school climate is the coordination of a number of factors that include creating a safe environment where students feel accepted and welcome and where they have clear behavioral, social, and academic expectations. In schools with positive climates, students receive the instructional and emotional support they need to be successful, their parents feel invited into the school, and their participation is welcomed and encouraged. Teachers and other school staff have a collaborative relationship with parents and administrators. They are part of the decision-making process in the school, and although the school is far from perfect, all stakeholders feel that they are working together toward a common mission—educating children.

9

Working Effectively with Parents

The impact of privilege on our vision
- The more privilege we have, the harder it is to think about how our own actions have affected others with less privilege.
- We take our privilege for granted—our right to safety, acknowledgement, being heard, being treated fairly, being taken care of; our right to take up the available time, space, and resources, etc.
- The more power and privilege we have, the harder it is to think about the meaning of the rage of the powerless.

McGoldrick, Giordano, & Garcia-Preto (2005, p. 34)

The purpose of family involvement in children's education is not solely to engage families in the school process, but to link important contexts (school and home) for strengthening children's learning and overall development (Christenson & Sheridan, 2001). Studies have found that the larger the discontinuity between home and school, the more children's academic achievements decline (Hansen, 1986). Continuity and consistency between both the home and school environments mutually influence children's performance in school. The connection between schools and families has been identified as a significant protective factor for children, especially for those who live in an environment characterized by multiple risk factors (Weissberg & Greenberg, 1998), and an emphasis on developing shared meaning across home and school contexts can interrupt the cycle of failure in children (Pianta & Walsh, 1996). The first step in establishing a workable relationship between schools and families is developing an understanding of families and the factors that may present barriers and those that may facilitate their involvement in the schools.

System theory provides a paradigm for understanding human behavior as it unfolds within family relationships. According to system theory, to understand an individual, one must study how each member of the individual's family relates to every other family member (Becvar & Becvar, 1999). The components of a family system are interrelated and as such, each family member's behavior cannot be understood and treated as an isolated unit. The family is a component or a subsystem of a larger system (e.g., neighborhood, culture, society; Becvar & Becvar, 1999). System theory offers a framework for understanding the reciprocal influence of the many ecosystems of the developing child (Christenson & Sheridan, 2001). From this perspective, when evaluating a child's behavior and academic needs, the focus is placed on understanding the contributing factors and not the causes of the child's difficulties (Christenson & Sheridan, 2001). Understanding the contribution of the school and home is viewed as critical to helping the child. Pianta and Walsh (1996) emphasized that children grow and learn in the context of the family, and, consequently, shared meaning must be developed over time between the child/family system and the school/schooling system.

Hanson and Lynch viewed a *family* as "any unit that defines itself as a family including individuals who are related by blood or marriage as well as those who have made a commitment to share their lives" (1992, p. 285). The definition recognizes that families are diverse on many different dimensions. Families have been affected in multiple ways by societal changes, including political agendas, maternal employment, single-parent families, blended families, family mobility, economic trends in the United States, and unemployment rates.

CULTURAL DIVERSITY IN PARENT-SCHOOL INTERACTIONS

School psychologists and other professionals in the schools must recognize changing family patterns and the diversity that characterizes today's American family and must establish responsive programs for students and their families (Simpson, 1996). Of utmost importance is developing programs that respect parents and include them in decisions about their children's learning. Simpson asserted that school-based practitioners, such as school psychologists, social workers, counselors, and others, must understand his or her values and attitudes and be prepared to suspend judgment on behaviors, worldviews, and lifestyles of others that conflict with his or her personal beliefs. School-based practitioners must develop a certain posture in order to work productively with families who live in poverty. This posture should facilitate the process of collaborative interaction with families. Harry, Kalyanpur, and Day (1999) offered a framework that advocates a two-way process of information sharing and understanding that should set a road map leading to cooperation and collaboration. The process, intended to be an ongoing activity, is conducive to self-awareness, cultural responsiveness, respect for diversity, and enhanced communication between professional and family. People tend to interpret situations based on their past experience, and the interpretations are rarely culture free (Lynch, 2004). Being able to suspend judgment, as Simpson recommended, is a difficult if not unrealistic task because culture and class influences are an integral part of individuals' lives and they are frequently invisible and elusive (Lynch, 2004). The following framework is a four-step process that is initiated by the professional when working with families from diverse backgrounds. The model of Harry et al. (1999) has been adapted and is described next:

1. *Identify the cultural and social values that are rooted in one's interpretation of a student's difficulties.* The school-based professional examines the values embedded in his or her recommendations or decisions and explores what aspects of his or her personal identity may have influenced the interpretation of the child's difficulties (e.g., culture, class, political affiliation, age, gender, religion, family structure, sexual orientation). This exercise is meant to uncover the source of one's beliefs and reveal how those beliefs may affect a person's perspective on a problem and hence affect one's interaction with families different from oneself. The goal is self-awareness because when an individual is not in tune with his or her own cultural and class values and the influence of these values on day-to-day decisions, including professional decisions, it is difficult to work effectively with families who are diverse (Lynch, 2004).

2. *Determine if the family one is serving ascribes to the same values. If not, determine how their values are different from one's own.* Once a person has examined the interpretation of the presenting problem and the recommendations to determine his or her cultural value input, then he or she should explore with the family how these are consistent or incongruent with their view or position. Harry et al. (1999) suggested that this be undertaken with much respect for the family and a genuine desire to understand.

3. *Acknowledge and give respect to any cultural differences recognized, and explain the cultural basis of one's assumptions.* This step has the capacity for being educational from both sides: that of the school practitioner and of the family. In this stage, the practitioner explains to the parent the basis for his or her decision. The decisions may reflect one's personal belief, mainstream values, and/or professional training (Harry et al., 1999). This allows the decision-making process to become more transparent and can become educational to parents by letting them in on the belief system used by the school to explain behavior and make recommendations.

4. *Via the discussion and collaboration process, determine the most effective approach of adjusting one's professional interpretation and/or recommendations to accommodate the value system of the family.* Through respectful dialogue with families, a person can work out solutions to problems that have the potential for creating conflict between the school and the family. Families that feel respected and heard are more willing to work with schools and even trust decisions made

by school staff. Simpson (1996) noted that conflicts between families and school practitioners emerge from the failure of both groups to understand each other's values and expectations. The goal of the four-step process is to help school practitioners do the following: 1) become more comfortable and successful in their interactions and relationships with families whose life experiences are different from those of mainstream school personnel, 2) develop interaction patterns that enable families from diverse life experiences and cultural backgrounds to feel positive about their relationship with the school staff, and 3) arrive at a decision that accommodates the family's goals and expectations (Lynch, 2004).

Researchers such as Epstein (1995) offered six kinds of family–school involvement that broaden the typical expectations regarding parent involvement and participation and include activities at home that help connect parents to schools. Programs that incorporate activities in all six types are the most comprehensive and successful. The six types of family–school involvement consist of the following:

1. Parenting: Entails the school working with families in areas such as understanding the child and adolescent development, enhancing parenting skills, and assisting families in creating a home environment that fosters and supports learning (e.g., develop a parent resource center that offers information on child development and realistic behavioral expectations; disseminate information on how a parent, regardless of educational level and income background, can help children succeed in school)

2. Communicating: Entails purposely developing communication strategies that facilitate a two-way process of communication regarding children's progress and their needs (e.g., share school policies with parents, offer flexible schedules for parent conferences)

3. Volunteering: Entails schools actively recruiting, organizing, and training families to participate and support children learning in school (e.g., using parents' skills and talents in the school, including parents on field trips)

4. Learning at home: Entails school personnel developing and providing activities that encourage working with parents at home to enhance children's learning (e.g., homework, offering parent resources to use at home)

5. Decision making: Entails assisting families in becoming involved in school and district-level decision making that affects practices and even policies (e.g., training parents to be leaders, creating parent committees to address relevant issues in the school)

6. Collaborating with the community: Entails organizing and coordinating activities, resources, and services to families, children, and schools to augment children's learning in school (e.g., developing partnerships with community businesses and agencies, organizing activities that involve children working in the community and the community contributing to schools, developing mentorship programs)

Building trust is an important aspect of developing collaborative relationships with parents. Families must feel that they can trust schools to make decisions that are truly for the benefit of their children. School practitioners can begin to promote trust by employing activities that will facilitate this process. Margolis and Brannigan (1990) suggested the following: 1) accepting parents as they are; 2) sharing information and resources; 3) emphasizing parents' aspirations, concerns, and needs; 4) following through with recommendations, or keeping one's word; 5) discussing objectives openly; and 6) preparing for meetings. Christenson and Sheridan (2001) noted that employing structured problem-solving approaches and communication strategies is also important.

MODELS FOR PARENT AND FAMILY INVOLVEMENT

Parent involvement can be defined as family participation at school and at home (Christenson & Sheridan, 2001), and it is linked to many positive outcomes for school children. Parent involvement has been associated with improvement in reading achievement, grades, math performance, behavior, disposition or attitude toward work, self-esteem, homework, school attendance, decrease in school dropout, and classroom participation (see Clark, 1993; Comer, 1988; Epstein, 1986; Kellaghan, Sloane, Alvarez, & Bloom, 1993; Rumberger, 1995; Sattes, 1985). Although there seemed to be a moderate to strong correlation between income level and children's school performance when data is aggregated, the correlation is weaker when other family factors are considered (Christenson & Sheridan, 2001). Other family factors in the context of the home play a greater role in children's school achievement than income level. For example, a study conducted by White (1982), in which 102 studies were analyzed, revealed factors such as parents' participation in learning activities; parents' guidance, attitude, and expectations for their children; and parents' participation in cultural activities had a significant effect on children's performance in school. Parents' ability to provide pro-educational resources for children is much more conducive to higher achievement and educational growth than family structure (Milne, 1989). Moreover, parents who are able to socialize their children for the schooling process and encourage children's persistence and focus on effort when facing difficulty have been shown to positively support children's learning (Bempechat, 1998).

When researchers directed their inquiry on similarities and differences between low-income high achievers and low-income low achievers, they found that parents of both groups had high aspirations for their children. High achievers, however, were more involved in learning activities that included reasoning activities and they received constructive and supportive feedback from an adult or peer in their environment (Clark, 1990). Parents of high achievers engaged in frequent conversations with their children, had regular communication with the school and were involved in school activities, strongly supported and encouraged academic pursuit, established clear and consistent limits and expectations, and steadily monitored how their children used time (Clark, 1990). Having available resources at home (e.g., books), however, had a significant effect on continuing children's achievement during the summer months (Entwisle, Alexander, & Olson, 1997). Research shows that low- and high-income high achievers made similar gains during the school year, but children who were high achievers from low-income families fell behind during the summer when children from high-income families continued to grow (Christenson & Sheridan, 2001).

Collaborative efforts between schools and families designed to be comprehensive are the most effective in increasing children's school performance. Programs that include activities for parents that address multiple levels of partnership such as structure, philosophy, attitudes, student performance, and day-to-day practices improve student achievement to standards similar to those of children from middle-class families (see Comer, 1995; Comer et al., 1996; Yale School Development Program [SDP] Staff, 2004). Moreover, high consistency in message between school, home, and community plays an essential role in children's social development and scholastic success. Christenson and Sheridan (2001) argued that schools often do not consider home–school collaboration a critical aspect of students' academic success and should not develop programs in which home–school collaboration is treated as an appendage. Christenson and Sheridan further emphasized that programs designed to be comprehensive hold the promise of closing the achievement gap, and the authors suggested that school staff must communicate a message affirming that children's academic and behavioral performance depends not only on the curriculum of the school, but also on the curriculum of the home. A two-way communication between the school and home can augment consistency across settings and address conflicts between home and school.

Over the years, there have been three comprehensive and researched parent involvement programs: the SDP, Robert Slavin's Success for All Project (SFAP), and Henry Levin's Accelerated Schools Project (ASP). These programs have been used successfully to implement local school restructuring in low-income communities. The core belief of these university-based programs is that a student's background cannot be used as an excuse for school failure. They emphasize high expectations for students, stress changes at the school-building level, insist on a collaborative approach to bring about change, and include parent involvement (Ascher, 1993).

Yale School Development Program

The Yale School Development Program (SDP) is also known as the Comer Process, for James Comer who led the Yale Child Study Center team that intervened for 2 years in two inner-city public schools in Connecticut (SDP, 2004). This collaboration began in the late 1960s between the Yale University Child Study Center and two New Haven public schools. These schools were described as serving predominantly African American children, having more than 80% of students receiving free and reduced lunch, struggling with a low-achieving and low-attending school population, having a poor school climate (difficulty between students, teachers, and parents), and having low staff morale (Ascher, 1993). The goals of the program were to develop a school atmosphere where children felt valued, comfortable, and secure; rebuild ties between home and school; encourage children to form positive attitudes about school and healthy emotional bonds with school personnel and parents; and foster and support healthy overall development to promote learning (Coulter, 1993). According to Haynes and Comer (1990), the goal of SDP is to strive to make communities cohesive and tightly interwoven in mutual respect, so that "even in the face of the potentially deleterious effect of poverty, their integrity and strength are maintained" (p. 109).

SDP emphasized healthy child development as the cornerstone of academic success and stressed six developmental principles as the basis for all learning:

1. Child rearing, development, and learning are connected.

2. Development begins early and is an ongoing process.

3. Meaningful learning happens in children when positive and supportive bonds with nurturing adults are formed.

4. Children's first teachers are their parents.

5. Collaboration among parents, staff, and community members has contributed significantly to children's academic success despite their social and economic status.

6. Schools promote growth on all developmental domains: physical, ethical and moral, cognitive, social, language, and psychological.

The Comer Process is described as an operating system defined as a way of managing, coordinating, and integrating school activities. It offers a structure and process for encouraging adults to support children's learning and overall development (SDP, 2004). According to SDP, three structures encompass the framework that guides the operating system:

1. School planning and management team: Members consist of principal, assistant principal, teachers, support staff, and parents. Functions include development of a comprehensive school plan; establishment of academic, social, and community relations' standards; and organization of school activities.

2. Student and staff support team: Members consist of principal, school personnel with knowledge of child development and mental health (e.g., psychologist, social workers). Functions include encouraging favorable and positive social atmosphere and relationships, linking student services, assisting in the sharing of information, focusing on student needs, gaining access to resources in the community, and designing prevention programs.

3. Parent team: Members consist of parents in the school. Functions include developing activities that foster parent participation in the school's social and academic programs.

This operating system is guided by three principles (Comer & Haynes, 1991):

1. No-fault: Embrace an atmosphere that encourages an attitude of personal responsibility that helps keep the focus on students' needs, problem solving, and accountability.

2. Consensus: Decisions are made through consensus via dialogue and understanding.

3. Collaboration: All teams work together in the spirit of collaboration and agree not to paralyze the principal (Ascher, 1993).

The program encourages multilayer parent involvement activities by including parents in the classroom; on school planning and management teams; and in supporting activities such as fairs, fashion shows, graduation ceremonies, and workshops (Ascher, 1993). The purpose is to involve parents in the school and foster a positive relationship between parents and school staff because they are instrumental to children's success in school. Another important component of the Comer Process is an ecological approach that addresses the mental health needs of the children. For example, a problem with violence is viewed first as a problem in the school and second as a problem with the child, when modifying the system fails to resolve the problem (Ascher, 1993). The student and staff support team is actively involved in developing strategies and implementing programs to address the mental health needs of the children. The SDP philosophy is one that focuses on building relationships between students, teachers, school administrators, and parents as a way of developing comprehensive school plans that positively affect student achievement. Schools are certified as SDP schools after undergoing training, meeting established behavioral requirements, showing knowledge of the SDP philosophy and approach, and completing a full 5-year implementation cycle of the program (SDP, 2004).

Studies evaluating the outcomes of the SDP have shown positive results. Studies examining achievement levels, attendance rate, and performance on standardized assessments have shown significant gains when SDP schools are compared with non–SDP schools (see Becker & Hedges, 1992; Comer, 1988; Comer & Haynes, 1991, 1992; Cook, Murphy, & Hunt, 2000; Hall & Henderson, 1990; Millsap et al., 2000; Noblit, Malloy, & Malloy, 2001).

Success for All Project

The Success for All Project (SFAP) was developed in the late 1980s by Robert Slavin and a team of researchers at Johns Hopkins University's Center for Effective Schooling for Disadvantaged Students. SFAP emphasized offering ethnic minority children from low-income families specific social and academic resources that have been proven through research to be effective in improving achievement in students who are at risk (Ascher, 1993). The program includes instructional strategies such as cooperative learning, peer tutoring, language skills building, and early intervention approaches. Schools interested in implementing SFAP must agree to use the following practices essential to the program:

1. Prekindergarten and/or kindergarten classes must focus on developing language skills by using the Peabody Language Development Kits and other curriculum supplements (Ascher, 1993).

2. There should be heterogeneous groupings of children, except for reading, in which children should be grouped by reading ability for 90-minute sessions. Groups are reevaluated every 8 weeks.

3. A reading curriculum in the kindergarten and first grade should be used. This curriculum should emphasize relevant components of reading that include reading comprehension and are linked to writing. Strategies such as cooperative learning, teaching activities, and partner reading are implemented.

4. A schoolwide attendance program with an attendance monitor is required if the attendance rate is less than 95%.

5. Daily individual tutoring for eligible students should be provided by a certified teacher/tutor for 20-minutes sessions.

6. A family support team is developed to provide parents with support in implementing strategies at home that promote learning such as increasing attendance, reading at home, connecting parents to community agencies and social services, and preparing parents to be volunteers in the school.

7. Establish an agreement to commit to the SFAP evaluation process and sharing of district data.

8. Develop a building advisory team to assist in shaping program policy and guide program development. Members of this team consist of the principal, teachers, and parents (Ascher, 1993).

SFAP requires buy-in by 80% of school staff, commitment from district decision makers (e.g., superintendent), and personnel involved in the implementation must be certified. Staff receive training with detailed manuals and follow-up support that involves coaching, monitoring, and participating in group discussions.

Studies measuring the effectiveness of SFAP have yielded results suggesting positive outcomes as indicated by improvements in school performance and retention rates and reduced special education placements. Comparisons between control students and SFAP students have shown that on the average, SFAP students exceeded control students in reading, and the most significant or profound improvements were noted for students with the most needs and risk factors (see

Bodilly, Purnell, Ramsey, & Keith, 1996; Madden, Slavin, Karweit, Dolan, & Wasik, 1992; Ross et al., 2001).

Accelerated Schools Project and Accelerated Schools Plus

Accelerated Schools Project (ASP) is a program born out of the concerns for the educational experiences of children who were disadvantaged and attending low-performing schools in the late 1980s. Henry Levin and his colleagues at Stanford University developed ASP to address the organizational needs of low-performing schools; the organizational principles employed are believed to have a positive effect on children's academic performance. The project is now located at the University of Connecticut and renamed Accelerated Schools Plus and operates in partnership with Neaq Center for Gifted Education and Talent Development.

The goal of the ASP is to enhance and enrich the instruction of children who are at risk based on schoolwide community's view of learning. All children are expected to achieve at high levels and all stakeholders are involved and engaged in building and fulfilling the school's vision (Biddle, 2002). The ASP framework emphasizes employing with all students instructional procedures that have been used primarily with gifted and talented students. This strategy is believed to accelerate children's learning while providing them with the academic foundation they need. Schools adopting the ASP framework engage in a five-stage Inquiry Process to begin solving their organizational or academic problems (Ascher, 1993).

1. Focusing on the problem

2. Brainstorming solutions

3. Creating a synthesis

4. Administering pilot test for experimental program

5. Evaluating and assessing the pilot to determine if it is effective

This collaborative process leads schools to make changes in their organizational structure and/or curriculum. ASP places emphases on organizational principles, decision-making process, and school governance (Ascher, 1993). Levin and Hopfenberg (1991) identified three guiding principles at the core of ASP:

1. Unity of purpose: Developing a common vision

2. Empowerment and responsibility: All stakeholders (parents, teachers, and administrators) share in decisions about instructional practices, personnel selections, and so forth

3. Building on strength: Using the strength of school personnel, students, and parents to improve the school and children's achievement

Parent involvement is part of the governance structure that includes three levels: steering committees (members include principal, school staff, teachers, and parents), cadres (organized around specific areas—parent involvement, school assessment, reading, behavior empowerment), and the school as a whole (involved in all decisions made about instruction, curriculum implementations, resource allocation; Hopfenberg, Levin, Meister, & Rogers, 1990).

Research in the effectiveness of ASP has demonstrated positive outcomes. Schools have shown improvements in reading, language, and math (McCarthy & Still, 1993. Studies also show improvement in students' attendance, parent involvement, and even teachers' attendance (see Bloom et al., 2001; McCarthy & Still, 1993; Ross, Wang, Sanders, Wright, & Stringfield, 1999).

SUCCESSFUL PARENT INVOLVEMENT ACTIVITIES

Epstein (1995) identified six types of family–school involvement, and they illustrated ways in which parents can be drawn into being active and positive influences in schools. Many schools throughout the nation have instituted different activities to involve parents in the schools. Some activities developed to foster the participations of families in the schools are described next.

Parent Resource Centers

Many schools developed resource centers that house information that includes books, DVDs, kits, magazines, computers, current technology, and other information on a variety of topics (e.g., parenting, child development, discipline, reading, learning disabilities, résumé writing). Parent resource centers may also sponsor parent workshops on a variety of topics from discipline strategies to special education issues. Some centers have staff that accompany parents to parent–teacher conferences and serve as advocates. Many of these resource centers are run by trained staff that may include teachers, parents, and other school staff. The staff at these centers, in addition to providing information to parents, may also link parents to resources in the school system and in the community.

After-School Programs and Homework Centers

Schools establish partnerships with local universities and colleges, teacher's unions, local businesses, and parent associations to staff homework centers. Teachers, parent volunteers, or undergraduate or graduate students may volunteer as tutors to help children with homework. Some schools have teachers on-call to respond to parents' questions about homework; others have teachers available online to help students and parents.

Family Literacy Program

Schools offer training to parents with children in early grades to support students' reading and writing at home. Parents work with their children in school and at home, with guidance from trained staff, or they use different materials and computer programs to enhance children's literacy skills. Emphasis is placed on enhancing learning and cognitive skills and training parents on how to support their children's learning skills.

Flexible Schedule

Many schools offer parents flexible time for scheduling parent–teacher conferences and school visits. Some schools set up parent–teacher conference days where the teachers' school day begins in the afternoon and ends mid-evening to accommodate working parents' schedules. Some schools have an open-door policy in which parents can visit anytime and may conference with the child's teacher; these schools provide class coverage by another teacher during the conference time.

Family Night Out

This activity involves families attending nightlong activities in the schools that start on Friday evening and end on Saturday morning. Families bring sleeping bags to spend the night in the school building. School staff assists in organizing and managing the activities, which can include table games, sports, and movies.

Computer Check-Out Program

These kinds of programs allow families to borrow laptops to take home. Families often receive training and are offered computer programs (e.g., reading, math) and materials that will support their children's learning. Families can borrow computers for a specified amount of time. These programs work well in getting parents of children in higher grades involved in school. National studies of computer use in the United States note that there is an increase in the percentage of households owning computers, but this is not true of all socioeconomic levels (Picciano, 2006). Families of limited resources have less access to the Internet and are less likely to own computers (Picciano, 2006). Therefore, programs that allow families to have access to technology play a role in leveling the experiential gaps between children with economic resources and those with limited resources.

Parent Education Courses

Parent education courses engage parents in the learning process by providing instruction on computer literacy, GED, physical and mental health, college credit classes, and other personal improvement courses. These courses emphasize lifelong learning and engage parents in the school and the community.

Family Technology Night

This activity involves the development of a series of workshops for families to learn how to use different computer programs (e.g., desktop publishing), how to access the Internet to obtain information, and how to use this kind of technology to support their children's school performance.

The Little Things

There are many little things schools can do to support parents and encourage their involvement in the school, including

- Calling parents to give good news: Teachers call parents to inform them of the child's improvement in grades or behavior. School staff call parents to invite them to meetings and note the good news that will be shared about the student. This strategy can be effective in getting parents of children with disabilities to attend multidisciplinary team and IEP meetings.

- Sending personal letters or notes home relating all the ways the student has improved and/or thanking parents for supporting the student

- Offering to help parents navigate social services agency bureaucracy

- Being ready to listen when parents disagree with a decision, reflect their concerns, and actively consider their point of view

- Being culturally responsive and demonstrate respect for economic diversity in all school activities

- When working with families with a child with a disability, assigning a staff member to work closely with the family, sit with the family during meetings, explain procedural safeguards, and advocate for the family

- Organizing homework helpers and babysitters and providing a meal on parent–teacher conference days or evenings

- Preparing monthly or weekly newsletters with articles written by parents, students, teachers, and the principal, highlighting positive activities, student accomplishment, parent involvement, and other information that connects parents to what is happening in school

HELPING PARENTS BECOME ADVOCATES FOR THEIR CHILDREN

Training parents to become advocates for their children can prove to be an effective way of getting parents involved in their children's education. Moriarty and Fine noted that

"With the low priority often placed on services for children as a group, even less emphasis on providing services for children on an individual basis, and ever-shrinking resources for programs tied to the welfare of children, it has become apparent that parental responsibilities must be more far reaching than that of protector and provider." (2001, p. 316)

Many parents are not prepared to serve as their children's advocate and require training to learn the skills associated with effective advocacy: problem solving, negotiation, conflict management, knowledge about educational issues, and assertive and tactful communication (Moriarty & Fine, 2001; Simpson, 1996).

Schools are in the best position to train parents as advocates because the relationship between parents and school staff can be conflicting when it is related to children's academic performance and behavior. By training parents to be advocates for their children and giving them a sense of efficacy, the relationship between schools and parents can be improved as they are invited as partners into the school's decision-making process. The Merriam-Webster dictionary defines an *advocate* as one that supports or promotes the interest of another. Parents often feel inadequate as advocates because they do not have in-depth knowledge about educational procedures and law, their time and resources are limited, and sometimes their closeness to the issues at hand interfere with their objectivity and hence their advocacy effort (Moriarty & Fine, 2001). In an effort to encourage families to participate in their children's education, Moriarty and Fine identified a six-stage model aiming at training parents to be advocates in the school.

Stage 1: Establishing a Partnership

The purpose of this stage is to begin developing a collaborative partnership with families by orienting all parties to a solution focus; shared communication; and mutual respect, responsibility, and ownership of the issues of concern. Strategies that lead to these goals are presented to families. Strategies such as thinking before speaking, apologizing immediately when an error or misunderstanding occurs, entering the conference with a spirit of cooperation, and engaging in polite and thoughtful communication are taught and reinforced (Moriarty & Fine, 2001).

Stage 2: Sharing Information

The goal of this stage is to share information that would assist all parties to identify major and minor issues; understand areas of concern; recognize values, beliefs, and expectations; note areas of disagreements; and clarify confusion and misunderstandings. This is accomplished by teaching families active listening skills that include attending, following, and reflecting (Stewart, 1986).

Stage 3: Finding Agreements

The purpose of this stage is to actively engage in activities that provide the opportunity to reach a place of agreement or where the issues of concern are perceived in similar ways. Parents are taught conflict management skills and assertive communication strategies to facilitate the process of arriving at equitable solutions. Conflict management skills entail identifying the signs of conflict, focusing on issues of concern, remaining open, and acting in the spirit of collaboration (Moriarty & Fine, 2001; Verderber & Verderber, 1989). Assertive communication is the process of understanding one's feelings, desires, and wants and being at ease expressing these in an appropriate and respectful way to others (McFarland, 1986). Families who are skilled in communicating their thoughts and feelings in ways that affirm their rights and respect others, and those that understand how to manage conflicts, are better prepared to advocate for their children.

Stage 4: Exploring Alternatives

The main goal of this stage is to begin determining possible alternatives and related resources, to evaluate the implications of those alternatives, and to reach a consensus between parents and teachers (Moriarty & Fine, 2001). Both parties listen and consider each other's contribution, and families participate in brainstorming and exploring options and negotiating to develop plans that would effectively address concerns. This all constitutes a learning process for both parents and teachers and establishes mutual responsibility for the development of a plan.

Stage 5: Making a Plan

In this stage, a plan of action is developed, or time lines for formulating a plan later are established. The planning process includes responsibilities for implementing and monitoring the plan. The process undertaken (Stage 1–5) is summarized to reinforce the collaborative journey and the things accomplished (Moriarty & Fine, 2001).

Stage 6: Following Up

This stage entails evaluating and monitoring the plan formulated, considering any new concerns, and deciding the next course of action. Following up on decisions made, evaluating the course taken, and determining whether to continue or change plans are important to the collaborative process, and it keeps families and schools working together in the interest of the child.

Preparing families to be advocates provides them with the skills to establish a collaborative relationship with schools by placing them on equal footing in the problem-solving and decision-making process. Simply, it empowers parents. Successful communication between families and school staff inspires a sense of shared purpose, is bidirectional and ongoing, and works toward mutually benefiting solutions to problems (Christenson & Sheridan, 2001). Parents who are advocates accept the responsibility of working on behalf of their children, and partnering with school staff contributes to school success.

10

Implications for Training and Educational Policy

If you want one year of prosperity, grow grain.
If you want ten years of prosperity, grow trees.
If you want one hundred years of prosperity, grow people.

Chinese Proverb

This book began with an exploration of how poverty affects all levels of children's lives. It examined how unfavorable environmental conditions begin to exert influence from inside the womb and, if left unattended, continue throughout a child's life. Following Section 1 were chapters that addressed practical issues regarding assessment and promising interventions. The goal of these chapters was to illustrate how to use knowledge of a child's environmental condition to make decisions about assessment, interpret results from a comprehensive and integrative perspective, and implement learning and behavioral strategies that have the potential for improving children's quality of life and future outcomes.

Poverty is indeed a very powerful confounding variable. Education has always been seen as the single most significant factor that can change the course of children's lives by minimizing if not eliminating the detrimental effects of situational and generational poverty. Society's past, present, and future lie on the basic educational capabilities of its members (Barona & Garcia, 1990). The political forces as well as the social and economic structures in the United States, however, have erected roadblocks that have interfered with the socioeconomic advancement of the most disadvantaged groups in the population, making them vulnerable to failure in a changing society. Historically, children living in poverty have been the most vulnerable and unsuccessful in the educational system. A large percentage of these children are from culturally and linguistically diverse groups. Their life circumstances press them into visiting and revisiting, in some cases, from generation to generation, conditions that facilitate negative life outcomes. These children have lower school-completion rates, lower paying jobs as adults, higher teenage pregnancy rates, and higher health care needs than their middle-class counterparts. The mere notion that conditions such as unequal schooling, inadequate instruction, low teacher expectations, low-paying jobs, deficient health care, inadequate housing, and socially disordered neighborhoods exist point to a sociopolitical atmosphere that condones the very state of affairs it generally condemns. As others have eloquently stated, education is the engine driving the future of the country and of our children (Levine, 2006), and as such improving it should be our utmost priority.

EDUCATIONAL PRACTICES THAT PREDISPOSE CHILDREN TO FAILURE

For more than 20 years, Haberman (2005) conducted research to identify the educational conditions that lead to children's success in school, including teacher attitude and values (see Haberman, 2004, 2005). Haberman asserted that schools with a population predominantly of urban children who live in poverty fail because teachers, principals, and staff members teach values and skills that predispose children to fail in society. These skills are intended to get children through middle school and high school, but set children up to fail as productive citizens of society. According to Haberman, these skills, belief systems, and values influence children's ability to be successful in schools and function in the workplace. He noted that these practices constitute an "ideology of unemployment." Haberman pointed to these practices as a lowering of expectations for students living in poverty and hold that teachers contribute to this by focusing on the following values and practices.

Nownes

Nownes refers to disconnected learning and day-to-day teaching units that stand alone as an effort to address the need of a transient student body. This practice stands in stark contrast to what is known about effective instructional practices (e.g., thematic interdisciplinary teaching). One strong effect poverty has on schools is student mobility and turnover (Zemelman et al., 1998). A study by the Center for School Improvement (CSI; 1996) reported that only two of every five students stay in the same school from first to sixth grade. Moreover, many children change schools four to six times, including switching schools during the academic year (Consortium on Chicago School Research, 1994). This slows down the progress of the class and forces readjusting class lessons and rebuilding class cohesion (Zemelman et al., 1998). Therefore, in many middle schools in urban systems, the focus has been placed on stand-alone lesson plans and may not include homework or a connection to previous teaching units to reinforce learning (Haberman, 2005). This strategy, however, has unintended effects—students are uninvolved, they are not required to prepare or pursue learning in other ways, and this fosters no commitment to learning and growing as part of the educational process.

Showing Up

Many teachers accept students' attendance and inactivity as sufficient for a passing grade. If students attend class, are not disruptive, and allow the teacher to complete the lesson planned for the day, then learning is assumed. By rewarding attendance, not expecting involvement, and tolerating a detached presence, however, teachers are communicating that just showing up is sufficient to succeed (Haberman, 2005).

Investment

Some students perceive the schools as authoritarian institutions where decisions are made by those in control: superintendent, principals, and teachers. By not dispelling these perceptions and allowing students and parents to be spectators, schools foster the belief that learning is the teacher's responsibility and not the students' (Haberman, 2005). School policies should be made with the involvement of students or their families; failure to include the appropriate stakeholders communicates to families that they are not accountable or important in the process. Children and their families must be invested in the educational process, the school building, and the community (Gutman & McLoyd, 2000).

Excuses

In the low expectation atmosphere of urban schools, many teachers show tolerance for chronic lateness and absences by accepting excuses and giving offending students passing grades. The value being communicated is that a good excuse is equivalent to not being at fault for the behavior (Haberman, 1997).

Noncooperation

Encouraged by neighborhood values, many students come to school with conflict resolution strategies that emphasize asserting control and force. Consequently, principals and teachers often find it easier to separate students who do not get along instead of teaching and engaging students in ongoing positive conflict resolution strategies and activities. According to Haberman (2005), students have come to expect that it is reasonable not to work with others they do not like (this includes teachers and peers). By not actively teaching positive conflict resolution skills and infusing these throughout children's curriculum, principals and teachers support the ideology set that includes a lack of appreciation for working out conflicts and differences in a respectful and responsible way.

Respect

In a study of violence and teenagers living in poverty, Haberman and Dill (1995) surveyed students who noted that respect is afforded to individuals perceived as powerful. Basically, the belief is that individuals have power when they have the potential to inflict physical or psychological harm directly or indirectly. Respect is not given based on following school rules, completing school assignments, having a position of authority, or attaining educational accomplishment. According to Haberman (2005), school policies reinforce these values by using disciplinary strategies that are negative and coercive. By using PBS systems to manage children's behavior, uphold higher behavioral standards, and empower students from the early grades, teachers and principals can change a value system based on control and force to one based on respect.

Authority and Ignorance

Families living in poverty are more likely to have negative experiences with institutions exerting authority (e.g., health care system, welfare agency, housing department, justice system), which are carried over to school officials. Teachers and administrators reinforce this negative interaction with authority by not working collaboratively with parents; relating to them in an authoritative and legalistic manner; and using, from the early grades, simplistic external rewards and punishment to control children's behavior as opposed to strategies that empower children and emphasize intrinsic values. Haberman (2005) noted that by not using behavioral strategies that empower children to behave appropriately and by not using reinforcement strategies that are intrinsic, the motivation for knowing the rules and behavioral expectations are not internalized. According to Haberman (1999), students learn that if they are not aware of the rules, then they are not responsible for them.

Peer Influence

As discussed earlier in this book, peer pressure plays a significant role in the lives of children, including children from poverty. The friendships in the neighborhood can support a value system that is antithetical to success in school. Haberman (1999) noted that the behavior of many inner-city children can be best described as "passive resistance" because schools have failed to actively engage them.

Messing Up

By implementing policies that allow students with behavior or achievement problems to be moved from school to school, to be placed in special schools or in special education classes, and by not implementing school academic and social-emotional programs that improve children's achievement and behavior, schools continue to unintentionally reinforce in children the value of not assuming responsibility for their actions (Haberman, 2005).

Explaining Success

According to Haberman (1999), children surrounded by poverty often evaluate their experiences from an external locus of control. They account for their success as a matter of luck, social connections, or innate abilities, but rarely do they attribute their success to effort. Teachers further promote this value orientation by using instructional strategies that do not engage students in active effort but emphasize right answers.

Relevance

When students learn only that which is presently understandable, he or she becomes hostage to and not beneficiary of personal experience (Haberman, 1999). Although connecting new concepts to children's experiences is a powerful instructional tool, it should be broad, inclusive, and with real-world application. Learning from the experiences of others is just as important. Children living in poverty are often limited in their experiences compared with children from more economically advantageous backgrounds, so teachers should instruct in a way that enriches these children's experiences and maintains high standards and expectations.

Purpose

To benefit from the educational process, students must accept that learning involves effort and preparation. Teachers must communicate to students that good learning leads to accomplishment and involves effort, persistence, focus, and repetition.

According to Haberman (1999), altogether, these practices basically constitute a lowering of academic standards and expectations and lead to an ideology about employment that is antithetical to success in the workplace. It limits children's opportunities by not providing the proper academic foundation and work ethic that brings about success in school and the workplace. Haberman's perspective can appear critical of school professionals and current educational practices in urban schools that serve children living in poverty. His work emphasizes engaging children actively in learning and developing their interest to facilitate social mobility and ultimately improving their quality of life. He developed an interview survey to select teachers and school administrators that is used in many urban schools in the United States, including the District of Columbia, and a body of knowledge on the ideology and behavior of effective teachers for diverse children and youth living in poverty (Quirk, 2005). Haberman (2004) posits that teachers who are successful in teaching children living in poverty create a community of learners that value the following practices:

- *Modeling.* Teachers guide children's learning through active demonstration of learning principles; students see teachers as learners, not only as teachers.
- *Continual sharing of ideas.* Teachers share ideas with one another regarding issues of equity, instruction, curriculum, testing, and school organization.
- *Collaboration.* Teachers become involved in team teaching and other collaborative efforts in program development, writing, problem solving, and research.
- *Egalitarianism.* Families, students, and community members are involved in decision making in the school.
- *High productivity.* Teachers are involved in the creation of new programs, developing and adapting curriculum, researching textbooks, and training and working with parents.
- *Community.* Teachers make decisions for the school that are based on the best interests of the students and their families and not on what is best for the faculty.
- *Practical applications.* Teachers continually evaluate their practices to make sure that they are serving the educational needs and developing the social emotional well-being of children.

Haberman's work has been noted for not including information on how to implement effective teaching practices, changing the ineffective teaching practices of current teachers, and dealing with the shortcomings in urban schools that serve children living in poverty (e.g., limited resources, ineffective organizational structure; Brown, 1999b). More specifically, Haberman's research is based on decades of teacher and student interviews, but his writings have not explicitly provided a description of his research methodology (Brown, 1999b).

The future of the nation lies in the quality of the education of our children. Society is responsible for the education of all children, and for this reason, many politicians are put in office to address issues relating to education. At the front end are teachers, school administrators, supportive/consultative school staff (e.g., school psychologists, counselors, speech-language pathologists), and parents, who are directly responsible for the instruction of children.

TEACHER PREPARATION PROGRAMS

Teachers have been given the responsibility of educating children who arrive in school with diverse educational experiences. Some come from homes where they have been read to, talked to, and provided with enriching cognitive and linguistic experiences, but there are others who come from backgrounds with inadequate resources and significantly limited enriching or educationally growth-producing experiences. Many have had very challenging starts in life and have deep educational needs. Levine (2006) presented a policy report based on a 4-year study of education schools, or colleges that train and prepare teachers; the quality of teachers being trained; and the factors that affect the education of teachers. The study was seen as essential, given the need for more and better qualified teachers to meet the ever-increasing educational needs of America's children and the current failure of public schools to address issues related to educational inequity or to raise student achievement. Teachers are instrumental to and have the most critical effect on children's achievement and learning. The study recognized the weaknesses of teacher education programs, including vague curricular goals that do not address the instructional and emotional needs of school children, faculty disconnected from practice, low admission and graduation standards, large differences in institutional quality, and deficient quality control (Levine, 2006). These weaknesses are instrumental in producing teachers unprepared to meet the needs of today's school children. Levine proposed five recommendations:

1. Schools of Education should focus on classroom practice and the educational needs of today's school population.

2. Schools of Education should focus on student achievement as a chief measure of teacher education program success.

3. Schools of Education should be reconstructed to reflect the skills and knowledge that promote classroom learning, and teacher preparation programs should last 5 years.

4. Schools of Education should create effective procedures for teacher preparation quality control.

5. Failing teacher preparation programs should be closed. Good programs should be strengthened, excellent programs should be expanded, and incentives should be offered to strong students and career changers interested in education to enter doctoral programs.

By strengthening teacher preparation programs, teachers are better prepared to deal with the realities of the schools. Poor teacher quality cheats children of the opportunity for a better future (Levine, 2006).

Other recommendations to improve the quality of teachers and improve their ability to meet the needs of children are to emphasize in all programs the need to develop cultural competence and an understanding of second language acquisition processes, diversify student teachers' experiences in terms of exposure to children from different backgrounds (socioeconomic status, disabilities, ethnicity, and language proficiency), develop competency in instructional strategies that are evidence based, focus on good classroom management skills, and emphasize working collaboratively with other school professionals (e.g., school psychologists, speech-language pathologists, counselors, social workers).

Zemelman et al. (1998) noted that almost 100% of teachers are from the middle class, whereas many of the children in inner-city schools and impoverished rural areas are from lower socioeconomic backgrounds. This divide brings about many assumptions and misunderstandings that are rooted in misinformation. Research has found that teachers at times underestimate the willingness of parents to work collaboratively with them to help children succeed (Allen & Mason, 1989), and others have come to expect the worst of these children (Zemelman et al., 1998). Teacher preparation programs must include information and experiences that instruct teachers how to work with children who live in poverty. They must learn how to motivate, generate interest, and engage children in the learning process. Based on a review of research on effective teachers working with children in high poverty areas, Haberman (2005) extended seven observations about teacher preparation programs:

1. The current teacher candidate selection criteria used by many universities and colleges have no predictive validity. They identify teachers who will quit and fail in these schools rather than teachers who will be effective.

2. The preparation of teachers to work with children who are diverse and living in poverty requires recruiting groups of teacher candidates who are prepared to teach in particular settings for communities with specific characteristics.

3. Mature college graduates from diverse fields of study with work and life experience have been shown to be more successful in teaching children who are diverse and living in poverty than young undergraduates who majored in education.

4. Training is not as important as choosing and preparing the right candidate. This strategy is more effective than selecting an individual and expecting that, through education, he or she will become an effective teacher in an urban or rural setting.

5. True preparation of teachers occurs in the schools where the teacher is the teacher of record, rather than a teacher candidate not responsible for students' learning.

6. The faculty in teacher preparation programs are often not experienced themselves in working with children who are diverse and living in poverty. The best mentors and faculty are those who have worked as classroom teachers and have been effective with this group of students.

7. Teachers' licenses should be granted after 1 year as an intern and after candidates have served as the teacher of record, demonstrating their potential to be effective working with children who are diverse and living in poverty.

Teachers working with children from diverse backgrounds living in poverty must be accountable for the children's learning and achieving despite these children's challenging life conditions and lack of parent involvement typically found in more affluent homes. Before teachers can be effective, however, they must first be able to genuinely engage children without judgment. As Littky (2004) noted, one cannot know a child whose voice one does not listen to, whose interest remains a mystery, whose family is excluded, and whose feelings are dismissed as irrelevant to the education process.

SCHOOL ADMINISTRATOR LEADERSHIP TRAINING PROGRAMS

In today's diverse school environments, principals and superintendents are required to do more than just supervise teachers. They are expected to lead their school in the development of goals, priorities, financing, staffing, curriculum, pedagogies, learning resources, use of time and space, assessment methods, and technology (Levine, 2005). In addition, they need to recruit and retain quality teachers and staff members, educate new and veteran educators with appropriate staff development programs, prepare and support parents and students for new social demands, and engage in continuous evaluation and school improvement, while fostering a sense of community and building morale in a time of increasing changes (Levine, 2005). In many urban and suburban schools, principals fight against a woefully dysfunctional bureaucracy that works against children. School boards composed of individuals with little knowledge of education, teacher's unions for whom children's achievement is not a priority, budgetary decisions that disrupt children's educations, and human resources staff who at times take away the staffing decisions from principals to keep ineffective teachers employed. In a survey conducted in 2003 of principals and superintendents, more than 30% reported that their programs did not prepare them to work with a diverse school population or with students from low socioeconomic backgrounds, handle the bureaucracy and politics in schools, deal with parents, or address the changing demands toward student testing and accountability (Farkas, Johnson, Duffett, Syat, & Vine, 2003). School leaders noted insufficient funding as a big challenge, followed by school politics and ineffective tenured teachers (Farkas et al., 2003) who are almost impossible to remove even though their deficiencies hurt children.

In a 4-year study of America's schools that focused on the training of school leaders, a number of deficiencies were identified: 1) a large percentage of the programs described as inadequate, 2) curriculum disconnected from the needs of the leaders and their schools, 3) ill-equipped faculty to educate school leaders, 4) inadequate attention and focus on clinical education and mentorship by successful practitioners, and 5) degrees awarded that did not meet the needs of today's schools (Levine, 2005). Some of the problems in the quality of these programs stemmed from the fact that school leadership programs cater to three groups of educators: current and future school administrators, future researchers and scholars, and teachers earning a degree mainly for salary enhancement (Levine, 2005). A small number of these candidates go on to become professors and a great

number enter these programs for promotions or to enhance their salaries. Unfortunately, curricula has been watered down to meet the needs of the majority. In
his study, Levine (2005) offered six recommendations:

1. School districts and states need to create other ways of granting raises and
    not rely on the accumulation of credits.

2. Universities must foster high standards for school leadership programs by
    implementing financial practices that strengthen those programs.

3. Programs that are weak should be improved or closed.

4. Programs should create more challenging curriculum to prepare effective
    school leaders.

5. The doctorate of education degree should be eliminated and replaced by a
    degree equivalent to an M.B.A. (master's in business administration) such
    as an M.E.A. (master's in educational administration) because a doctorate
    of education degree is not needed for developing competency as a school
    leader.

6. The doctor of philosophy degree in school leadership should be reserved for
    the preparation of researchers.

The role of school leaders is essential to the development of a school atmosphere
in which teachers can uncover the academic potential of all their students. They
are often forced, however, into adversarial positions with teachers because many
do not receive the support (financial, administrative, and emotional) they require
to make schools work for the benefit of children and their parents. School principals are often caught between the decisions of a superintendent (including his or
her central office staff and the board of education) and the teachers. Haberman
(2005) asserted that school leadership is the process of putting the best interest
of school children ahead of the convenience of the adults. Haberman discussed
the ideology of "star principals" serving children from a background of poverty.
The ideology is summarized as follows:

- Security is a prerequisite for learning to occur.

- Principals' goals are to improve students' learning.

- Connecting parents and children to health services must occur to improve
  learning in students who live in poverty.

- Principals are accountable and responsible for the effectiveness of the school
  as a whole.

- Classroom management is a necessary condition but not enough. Student
  learning is the criterion for determining teachers' competency.

- Parents are sources of useful information and partners in meeting the needs
  of children.

- Everyone that enters the school should be treated with respect.

- *Leadership* is defined as empowering others and helping them demand what is in their best interest, not acceding to what they want.

- Recognizing weaknesses in one's program is the beginning of finding solutions; cover-up reinforces shortcomings.

- The greatest benefit given to a school is removing ineffectual teachers.

- Principals must be involved in the selection of teachers to be accountable for instruction.

- Important decisions should be made with others.

- It is the principal's job to keep the school focus on children and their educational needs and to protect the school from the chaos that results from state mandates, school board politics, central office confusions, temporary superintendents, and yearly implementations of "new programs."

SCHOOL PSYCHOLOGY PROGRAMS

The work of psychologists in the schools is greatly influenced by their training, federal law, and pressures in the schools themselves. These influences are mostly visible in assessment practices. Training guidelines for psychologists require inclusion of diversity and individual differences in the curriculum or training models.

Both the National Association of School Psychologists (NASP) and the American Psychological Association (APA) recognize the significance of developing diversity competence or understanding of cultural and linguistic diversity as well as socioeconomic differences in their candidates. The knowledge and skills required to develop appropriate competency in the practice of school psychology are outlined in the *Standards for Training and Field Placement Programs in School Psychology* (NASP, 2000). Domains for training and practice in school psychology call for specific training in the understanding of children's diversity in development and learning. In its *Guidelines and Principles for Accreditation of Programs in Professional Psychology*, APA (2000) requires that programs acknowledge the significance of cultural and individual differences and diversity in their training of psychologists. Indeed, many training programs require at least a course addressing multicultural issues. Many trainers typically supplement individual courses (e.g., assessment, counseling) by including chapters or articles addressing cultural diversity and individual differences in the reading assignments of candidates. For this type of information to have a meaningful effect on candidates' subsequent practice, however, it should also be infused into every aspect of the candidates' training (e.g., coursework, practicum, internship).

The development of multicultural or diversity competency in assessment or counseling requires a continued effort to update and reevaluate one's understanding and practices. Suzuki, Ponterotto, and Meller (2001b) indicated that for assessment procedures to be appropriate in a diverse context, there must be a continued focus on understanding the purpose of the assessment, the level of cultural and linguistic loading on selected tests, alternative methods and procedures, and the level of experience assumed by the instrument. Suzuki et al. (2001b) encouraged the following direction in the training for a more multicultural and diverse assessment practice:

- Infusing multicultural issues into all assessment and counseling courses in the training of psychologists

- Focusing on the development of alternative assessment measures and procedures

- Increasing sensitivity to issues of equivalence as well as cultural divergence in understanding psychological and educational construct (i.e., tests reflect what is valued in a particular group or society)

Because a lot of what psychologists are asked to do in the schools involves assessment, a closer look at the practices of psychologists is essential. Kamphaus, Petoskey, and Rowe (2000) reported that the Wechsler scales were the most used instrument by school psychologists. The Wechsler scales are not always the most suitable instruments for some children, however. Fortunately, today, psychologists have a larger pool of tests from which to select, so psychologists need to become more comfortable selecting tests that fit the needs of the individual child and not that of the examiner.

At a very basic level, Sattler (2001) discussed the four pillars of assessment (standardized tests, informal assessment, interviews, and observations). This method is comprehensive, especially when the data obtained is interpreted in light of the child's unique experiences and background. School districts place pressure on psychologists to complete a particular number of assessments a year, which forces many psychologists to streamline their practices and to rely on what Hale and Fiorello (2004) have referred to as a *screening* (a cognitive test, an achievement test, and a visual motor test) to make life-changing educational decisions for children. Given the complexity of the assessment process with children from diverse backgrounds, critical information may be overlooked in the interest of time (Suzuki et al., 2001b). It is in the best interest of all children, and especially children from a background of poverty, to receive comprehensive assessments and not mere screenings. These comprehensive assessments should generate results that are linked to interventions that are research based. For psychologists to continue to be relevant to the instructional process and educational programming of children, they must be able to work collaboratively with teachers and parents to offer assessment products that are integrative.

Crespi and Cooke (2003) noted that since the mid-1980s, there has been a growing trend in professional psychology recognizing the contribution of a brain-behavior framework as it relates to children's learning and social-emotional adjustment. The impetus for such a trend is an increasing understanding through research and sophisticated imaging techniques that show connections between children's behavior and learning and brain functioning. Another reason is that the comprehensive and integrative framework of this perspective has the potential of providing powerful information regarding intervention when coupled with the knowledge base school psychologists bring to the table about learning and behavior in schools. School psychologists already work with children with a variety of biologically based disabilities (e.g., TBI, fetal alcohol syndrome, autism, ADHD), so school psychology training programs would serve these practitioners well if more emphasis is placed on developing assessment skills that include an understanding of reading, writing, math, and behavior from a brain-behavior perspective. Becoming aware of other knowledge-based assessment and interpretation frameworks allows for a more flexible and comprehensive approach to assessment of children.

NO CHILD LEFT BEHIND

The education of children has been affected by the No Child Left Behind (NCLB) Act that was signed into law in 2001. NCLB is the federal government's effort to support and reform the education of elementary and secondary school children. There are four principles that are the cornerstones of this law: stronger accountability for results, greater flexibility for school districts and states in the use of federal funds, more choices for parents of children from a background of poverty, and an emphasis on teaching strategies that are evidence based (U.S. Department of Education, 2002). The impetus behind this law was the achievement gap between Caucasian and minority children and rich and poor children. The law places great emphasis on reading in the early grades, improving the quality of teachers, and ensuring that children learn English. Cornerstones or principles of the NCLB act include

- Accountability: States are required to assess and measure students' skills in reading and math in third through eighth grades based on high academic standards that are aligned with the assessments used to measure performance. In this way, parents, states, educators, and the general public can track students' performance. Moreover, schools are required to break down the data by race, ethnicity, poverty levels, limited English proficiency, and disabilities, with the goal of identifying any child who requires further support. Schools are also required to report on school safety and to generate an annual "report card" that offers comparative information on the quality of schools (U.S. Department of Education, 2002). Such information can then be used by parents to make decisions about their children's education. Schools that do not meet academic yearly progress are targeted for corrective or improvement plans and/or restructuring. Schools that perform above the standards are eligible for academic recognition.

- Flexibility: By submitting to greater accountability, states and schools presumably gain more control over how they may use federal education funds. School districts can move up to 50% of their federal formula grant to any other federal programs such as Educational Technology, Improving Teacher Quality State Grant, Safe and Drug-Free Schools, or Title I programs without any special permission. Title I funds are the largest federal investment to schools to provide educational support to children who are poor or at risk for academic failure (U.S. Department of Education, 2002). It is believed that this kind of flexibility allows states and schools to use the funds to address the specific needs of their school population.

- Parental choice: With this law, parents who have children in schools ranked as low performing for 2 consecutive years have the option to transfer their children to a higher performing public school or charter school. The home school district then must provide transportation. Moreover, children from low-income families who are enrolled in low-performing schools for at least 3 years are eligible to receive additional educational help including tutoring, summer school, or after-school programs (U.S. Department of Education, 2002). Children who attend schools where they do not feel safe or children who may have been the victim of crime may choose to transfer to a safer school within the district boundaries.

- Focus on research-based strategies: NCLB specifically highlights the allocation of federal funds to educational programs (e.g., reading, math, drug and violence prevention) that have been proven to be effective in the scientific literature. The focus is on instructional methods that have been shown to lead to improved student learning and performance. NCLB (2002) defined *scientifically based research* as that which applies rigorous, systematic, and objective methods to obtain valid knowledge relevant to reading development, reading instruction, and reading difficulty.

On the surface, NCLB seems to address many of the significant maladies that plague public schools, especially schools that serve children who live in high poverty areas, who are English language learners, and who are ethnically diverse. NCLB specifically addresses issues such as the achievement gap between rich and poor, which mirrors the gap between Caucasians and other ethnic groups; quality instruction; and teacher qualification. Its focus on school accountability, scientifically proven strategies, and parent choice seemed to finally provide the long-awaited action educators and parents were hoping for to turn around public education as it affects schools that serve predominantly students from low-income households and those who are culturally and linguistically diverse. Significant pitfalls, however, were revealed on close examination of NCLB regulation. The federal law as written and implemented has the most devastating effects on the very schools it purports to help.

Sizer (2004) noted that there are trends that threaten today's education:

- Inadequately funded or equipped schools.

- Reliance on local taxation, which cannot support adequate schooling in communities characterized by poverty. Moreover, state and federal equalization formulas do not cover the cost of differences between poor and wealthy school districts.

- Access to public education is a function of one's neighborhood in most states. Families with more economic resources have access to schools with larger funding than do families with limited income. As a consequence, segregation based on class and income has become prevalent.

- The authority of school administrators and teachers has been eroded.

Throughout this book there has been repeated mention of the deleterious effect of poverty on children, families, communities, and schools. More specifically, researchers have noted that schools that serve mostly children living in poverty are the ones most likely to hire less experienced and noncertified teachers, have higher teacher turnover and a larger percentage of substitute teachers, function with fewer resources (e.g., computers, books, materials, labs) and technology, have poorly maintained buildings (e.g., old heating and cooling systems), have larger class sizes, and depend on unequal funding (Darling-Hammond & Post, 2000; Gorski, 2005; Kozol, 1992; Levine, 2006). The following are a series of shortcomings with NCLB:

1. NCLB is underfunded, and placing more demands on schools in poor neighborhoods that were unequally funded from the start marks these schools for failure (Darling-Hammond, 2004).

2. Its focus on assessment without first addressing the factors in society that lead to the achievement gap unfairly penalizes schools that serve children living in poverty.

3. NCLB mandates the hiring of qualified teachers but does not set forth a policy that delineates or supports this expectation or provide adequate funding to sustain such a plan (Darling-Hammond, 2004).

4. NCLB does not specifically deal with issues such as the high percentage of school dropout. Moreover, some educational researchers assert that children are retained in grades and others pushed out of school by the unrealistic demands of NCLB. School staff encourage (e.g., encourage their absence, move them to other schools) students who are low performers or truants to leave schools in order to meet the standards or annual yearly progress. This is said to happen to students with little power or knowledge to assert their rights (Wood, 2004).

5. A subsequent study by McNeil and Valenzuela (2001) in schools where the NCLB assessment model was used revealed that

    a. Instruction was aimed at low-level skills to the detriment of higher-order learning skills.

b. Schools diverted funds from curricular resources to test-preparation materials.

c. Teachers used teaching strategies that focus on test-preparation practices and not those linked to good instructional practices.

6. The adequate yearly progress (AYP) formula promoted by NCLB fails to give schools acknowledgement for appropriate improvements in student achievement. Its implementation prohibits schools from presenting valid and reliable evidence of student progress, and the interventions for schools that do not meet AYP are considered punitive and not scientifically based (American Federation of Teachers, 2004).

7. The procedure used to identify AYP has school districts comparing this year's grade level with next year's grade level and not comparing students to themselves. Comparing children to themselves provides more powerful information about learning and achievement (Center for Educational Policy [CEP], 2004).

8. Some requirements of NCLB are considered unworkable, overly stringent, and unrealistic (CEP, 2004). Specifically, the testing requirement for children with disabilities and English language learners. Children identified with disabilities are expected to perform on grade level, similarly to their typically developing peers. Some children with disabilities have significant cognitive and learning deficits. These children learn at a different rate than children without disabilities, and they require specialized instruction to support their learning. NCLB holds these children to the same standards as children without disabilities (CEP, 2004), however. English language learners are expected to reach 100% proficiency in English within a period of time that is inconsistent with research in second language acquisition. Moreover, because English language learners are not being compared with themselves but to a new set of students each year, it is difficult or even unreasonable to expect students to achieve 100% proficiency in English within a short period of time.

Children living in poverty have vastly more barriers to overcome than their more affluent counterparts. Schools that service these children must offer a variety of services that support not only the education of the children, but also educate parents so that they can support their children's learning. In addition, schools are finding it necessary to address mental health issues in children and their families. Although children living in low-income homes have the ability to learn like other children, many do start from further behind and require trained staff that understand their needs. By not providing realistic measures to correct the root problems in schools that serve children and families living in poverty, a system is set up that further negates these children their right to an appropriate education.

References

Aaron, P.G. (1997). The impending demise of the discrepancy formula. *Review of Educational Research, 67,* 461–502.

Aber, J.L., Bennett, N.G., Conley, D.C., & Li, J. (1997). The effect of poverty on child health and development. *Annual Review of Public Health, 18*(1), 463–483.

Abidin, R.R. (1995). *Parenting stress index* (3rd ed.). Lutz, FL: Psychological Assessment Resources.

Abrams, E.J., Matheson, P.B., Thomas, P.A., Thea, D.M., Krasinski, K.K., Lambert, G., & Shaffer, N. (1995). Neonatal predictors of infection status and early death among 332 infants at risk of HIV-1 infection monitored prospectively from birth. *Pediatrics, 96,* 451–458.

Adams, M.J. (1990). *Beginning to read: Thinking and learning about print.* Cambridge, MA: The MIT Press.

Alegria, M., Robles, R., Freeman, D.H., Vera, M., Jimenez, A., Rios, C., et al. (1991). Patterns of mental health utilization among Puerto Rican poor. *American Journal of Public Health, 81,* 875–879.

Alexander, K.L., Entwisle, D.R., & Thompson, M. (1987). School performance, status relations, and the structure of sentiment: Bringing the teacher back in. *American Sociological Review, 52,* 665–682.

Allen, J.B., & Mason, J. (1989). *Risk makers, risk takers, risk breakers: Reducing the risks for young literacy learners.* Portsmouth, NH: Heinemann.

Alper, S. (2001). Alternate assessment of students with disabilities in inclusive settings. In S. Alper, D.L. Ryndak, & C.N. Scholl (Eds.), *Alternative assessment of students with disabilities in inclusive settings* (pp. 1–17). Boston: Allyn & Bacon.

Alpern, L., & Lyons-Ruth, K. (1993). Preschool children at social risk: Chronicity and timing of maternal depressive symptoms and child behavior problems at school and at home. *Development & Psychopathology, 5,* 371–387.

Alvidrez, J., & Weinstein, R.S. (1999). Early teacher perceptions and later student academic achievement. *Journal of Educational Psychology, 91*(4), 731–746.

American Academy of Pediatrics, Committee on Drugs. (1995). Treatment guidelines for lead exposure in children. *Pediatrics, 96,* 155–160.

American Academy of Pediatrics. (1997). Breastfeeding and the use of human milk. *Pediatrics, 100*(6), 1035–1039.

American College of Obstetricians and Gynecologists (ACOG; 2000, July). *Breastfeeding: Maternal and infant aspects* (ACOG Educational Bulletin No. 258). Compendium of Selected Publications (pp. 210–225). Washington, DC: Author.

American Federation of Teachers. (2004, July). *NCLB: Its problems, its promise.* AFT Teachers Policy Brief, Number 18.

American Psychiatric Association. (2000). *Diagnostic and statistical manual of mental disorders* (text revision). Washington, DC: Author.

American Psychological Association. (2000). *Guidelines and principles for accreditation of programs in professional psychology.* Washington, DC: Author.

Ames, C.A. (1992). Achievement goals and the classroom motivational climate. In D.H. Schunk & J.L. Meece (Eds.), *Student perceptions in the classroom* (pp. 327–348). Mahwah, NJ: Lawrence Erlbaum Associates.

Anderson, G.E., Jimerson, S.R., & Whipple, A.D. (2002). *Children's ratings of stressful experiences at home and school: Loss of a parent and grade retention as superlative stressors.* Manuscript prepared for publication. Available from authors at the University of California, Santa Barbara.

Apfel, N., & Seitz, V. (1997). The firstborn sons of African-American teenage mothers: Perspectives on risk and resilience. In S.A. Luthar, J.A. Burack, D. Cicchetti, & J.R. Weisz (Eds.), *Developmental psychopathology: Perspectives on adjustment, risk, and disorder* (pp. 486–506). New York: Cambridge.

Aponte, J.F., & Barnes, J.M. (1995). Impact of acculturation and moderator variables in the intervention and treatment of ethnic groups. In J.F. Aponte, R.Y. Rivers, & J. Wahl (Eds.), *Psychological interventions and cultural diversity* (pp. 19–30). Boston: Allyn & Bacon.

Artiles, A.J., & Trent, S.C. (1994). Overrepresentation of minority students in special education: A continuing debate. *Journal of Special Education, 27,* 410–437.

Ascher, C. (1993). *Changing schools for urban students: The school development program, accelerated schools, and success for all.* New York: ERIC Clearinghouse on Urban Education. (ERIC Document Reproduction Service No. ED355313)

Association for Supervision and Curriculum Development (ASCD) Advisory Panel on Improving Student Achievement (1995). Barriers to good instruction. In Association for Supervision and Curriculum Development (Ed.), *Educating everybody's children* (pp. 9–18), Alexandria, VA: Author.

Astley, S.J., & Clarren, S.K. (1996). A case definition and photographic screening tool for the facial phenotype of fetal alcohol syndrome. *Journal of Pediatrics, 129,* 33–41.

Atkinson, D., Morten, G., & Sue, D.W. (1989). *Counseling American minorities: A cross-cultural perspective.* Dubuque, IA: W.C. Brown.

Aylward, G.P. (1996). Environmental risk, intervention and developmental outcome. *Ambulatory Child Health, 2,* 161–170.

Aylward, G.P. (1997). *Infant and early childhood neuropsychology.* New York: Plenum Press.

Bailet, L.L. (1991). Beginning spelling. In A.M. Bain, L.L. Bailet, & L.C. Moats (Eds.), *Written language disorders: Theory into practice* (pp. 1–21). Austin, TX: PRO-ED.

Bandura, A. (1986). *Social foundations of thought and action: A social cognitive theory.* Upper Saddle River, NJ: Prentice Hall.

Banks, J.A. (1990, Fall). *Preparing teachers and administrators in a multicultural society.* Austin, TX: Southwest Development Laboratory.

Barnett, W.S. (1995). Long-term effects of early childhood programs on cognitive and school outcomes. *Future of Children, 5*(3), 25–50.

Barnett, W.S. (1996). Lives in the balance: Age-27 benefit cost-analysis of the High/Scope Perry Preschool Program. *Monographs of the High/Scope Educational Research Foundation, 11.* Ypsilanti, MI: High/Scope Press.

Barnett, W.S., Robin, K.B., Hustedt, J.T., & Schulman, K.L. (2004). *The state of preschool: 2004 state preschool yearbook.* New Brunswick, NJ: National Institute for Early Education Research.

Barnhart, H.X., Caldwell, M.B., Thomas, P., Mascola, L., Ortiz, I., Hsu, H.W., et al. (1996). Natural history of human immunodeficiency virus disease in perinatally infected children: An analysis from the pediatric spectrum of disease project. *Pediatrics, 97,* 710–716.

Baron, I.S. (2004). *Neuropsychological evaluation of the child.* Oxford, England: University Press.

Barona, A., & Garcia, E. (1990). Preface. In A. Barona & E. Garcia (Eds.), *Children at risk: Poverty, minority status, and other issues in educational equity* (p. xiii). Washington, DC: National Association of School Psychologists.

Barr R.D., & Parrett, W.H. (2001). *Hope fulfilled for at-risk and violent youth* (2nd ed.). Boston: Allyn & Bacon.

Barton, P.E. (2003). *Parsing the achievement gap: Baselines for tracking progress.* Princeton, NJ: Educational Testing Service.

Barton, P.E. (2004). Why does the gap persist? *Educational Leadership 62*(3), 8–13.

Batshaw, M.L., & Conlon, C.J. (1997). Substance abuse: A preventable threat to development. In M.L. Batshaw (Ed.), *Children with disabilities* (4th ed., pp. 143–162). Baltimore: Paul H. Brookes Publishing Co.

Beck, J.S., Beck, A.T., & Jolly, J.B. (2003). *Beck youth inventories.* San Antonio, TX: The Psychological Corporation/ Harcourt Assessment.

Becker, D.J., & Hedges, L.V. (1992). *A review of the literature on the effectiveness of Comer's School Development Program.* Unpublished manuscript prepared for the Rockefeller Foundation.

Becvar, D.S., & Becvar, R.J. (1999). *Systems theory and family therapy* (2nd ed.). Lanham, MD: University Press of America.

Beeghley, L. (2005). *The structure of social stratification in the United States* (4th ed.) Boston: Allyn & Bacon.

Beker, T., Farber, A.F., & Yanni, C.C. (2002). Nutrition and children with disabilities. In M.L. Batshaw (Ed.), *Children with disabilities* (5th ed., pp. 141–164). Baltimore: Paul H. Brookes Publishing Co.

Bellak, L., & Bellak, S.S. (1949). *The Children's Apperception Test.* New York: C.P.S.

Bellinger, D., & Dietrich, K.N. (1994, November). Low-level lead exposure and cognitive function in children. *Pediatric Annals, 11,* 600–605.

Bempechat, J. (1998). *Against the odds: How "at-risk" students EXCEED expectations.* San Francisco: Jossey-Bass.

Bergan, J.R., & Kratochwill, T.R. (1990). *Behavioral consultation and therapy.* New York: Plenum Press.

Bernard, B. (1991). *Fostering resiliency in kids: Protective factors in the family, school, and community.* Portland, OR: Northwest Regional Educational Laboratory.

Bernbaum, J.C., & Batshaw, M.L. (1997). Born too soon, born too small. In M.L. Batshaw (Ed.), *Children with disabilities* (4th ed., pp. 115–142). Baltimore: Paul H. Brookes Publishing Co.

Bernstein, J.H. (2000). Developmental neuropsychological assessment. In K.O. Yates, M.D. Ris, & H.G. Taylor (Eds.), *Pediatric neuropsychology: Research, theory, and practice* (pp. 405–438). New York: The Guilford Press.

Biddle, J.K. (2002). *Accelerated schools as professional learning communities.* Paper presented at the Annual Meeting of the American Educational Research Association, New Orleans, LA (ERIC Document Reproduction Service No. ED468300).

Birenbaum, A. (2002). Poverty, welfare, reform, and disproportionate rates of disability among children. *Mental Retardation, 40,* 212–218.

Blanc, A., & Wardlaw, T. (1995). Monitoring low birth weight: An evaluation of internal estimates and an updated estimation procedure. *Who Bulletin, 83*(3), 178–185.

Bloom, H.S., Ham, S., Melton, L., & O'Brien, J., with Doolittle, F.C., & Kagehiro, S. (2001). *Evaluating the Accelerated Schools Approach: A look at early implementation and impacts on student achievement in eight elementary schools.* New York: Manpower Demonstration Research Corporation.

Blum, N.J., & Mercugliano, M. (1997). Attention-deficit/hyperactivity disorder. In M. Batshaw (Ed.), *Children with disabilities* (4th ed., pp. 449–470). Baltimore: Paul H. Brookes Publishing Co.

Bodilly, S., Purnell, S., Ramsey, K., & Keith, S.J. (1996). *Lessons from New American Schools Development Corporation's demonstration phase.* Santa Monica, CA: The RAND Corporation.

Boisjoly, J., Harris, K., & Duncan, G. (1998). Initial welfare spells: Trends, events, and duration. *Social Service Review, 72*(4), 466–499.

Bouchard, T.J., Jr., & Segal, N.L. (1985). Environment and IQ. In B.B. Wolman (Ed.), *Handbook of intelligence: Theories, measurements, and applications* (pp. 391–464). New York: John Wiley & Sons.

Bowers, C.A. (1993). *Educational cultural myths, and the ecological crisis: Toward deep changes.* Albany: State University of New York Press.

Bowman, B., Donovan, S.M., & Burns, S. (2001). *Eager to learn: Educating our preschoolers.* Washington, DC: National Research Council. Retrieved December 1, 2006, from http://www.nap.edu/readingroom/books/

Bradley, R.H., Whiteside, L., Mundfrom, D.J., & Blevins-Kwabe, B. (1995). Home environment and adaptive social behavior among premature, low birth weight children: Alternative models of environmental action. *Journal of Pediatric Psychology, 20,* 347–362.

Brannan, A., Heflinger, C.A., & Bickman, L. (1995). *The Burden of Care Questionnaire: Measuring the impact on family living with a child with serious emotional problems.* Unpublished manuscript.

Bransford, J.D., & Stein, B.S. (1984). *The IDEAL problem solver.* New York: Freeman.

Brantlinger, E. (2003). *Dividing classes: How the middle class negotiates and rationalizes school advantage.* New York: RoutledgeFalmer.

Briggs, X. (1998). Brown kids in white suburbs: Housing mobility and the many faces of social capital. *Housing Policy Debate, 9*(1), 177–213.

Brodal, P. (1992). *The central nervous system: Structure and function.* New York: Oxford Press.

Brody, G.H., Stoneman, Z., & Flor, D. (1996). Parental religiosity, family processes, and youth competence in rural, two-parent African American families. *Developmental Psychology, 32,* 696–706.

Brody, N. (1992). *Intelligence* (2nd ed.). San Diego: Academic Press.

Bronfenbrenner, U. (1979). *The ecology of human development: Experiments by nature and design.* Cambridge, MA: Harvard University Press.

Bronfenbrenner, U. (1986). Ecology of the family as a context for human development: Research perspectives. *Developmental Psychology, 22*(6), 723–742.

Brooks, J.S., Brooks, D., & Whiteman, M. (2000). The influence of maternal smoking during pregnancy on the toddler's negativity. *Archives of Pediatric and Adolescent Medicine, 154*(4), 381–385.

Brooks-Gunn, J. (1995). Children in families and communities: Risk and intervention in the Bronfenbrenner tradition. In P. Moen, G.H. Elder, & K. Luscher (Eds.), *Examining lives in context* (pp. 467–519). Washington, DC: American Psychological Association.

Brooks-Gunn, J., & Chase-Lansdale, P.L. (1995). Adolescent parenthood. In M.H. Bornstein (Ed.), *Handbook of parenting: Status and social conditions of parenting* (Vol. 3, pp. 113–150). Mahwah, NJ: Lawrence Erlbaum Associates.

Brooks-Gunn, J., & Duncan, G.J. (1997). The effects of poverty on children. *The Future of Children: Children and Poverty, 7*(2), 55–71.

Brooks-Gunn, J., Duncan, G.J., & Aber, J.L. (Eds.). (1997). *Neighborhood poverty: Vol. 1. Context and consequences for children.* New York: Russell Sage Foundation.

Brooks-Gunn, J., & Furstenberg, F.F., Jr. (1987). Continuity and change in the context of poverty: Adolescent mothers and their children. In J.J. Gallagher & C.T. Ramey (Eds.), *The malleability of children* (pp. 171–188). New York: Plenum.

Brown, A.L., & Campione, J.C. (1994). Guided discovery in a community of learners. In K. McGill (Ed.), *Classroom lessons: Integrating cognitive theory and classroom practice.* Cambridge, MA: MIT Press/Bradford Books.

Brown, D. (1999a). *Proven strategies for improving learning & achievement.* Greensboro, NC: CAPS Publications.

Brown, E.L. (1999b). Review of Haberman, Martin. (1995). *Star teachers of children in poverty.* Bloomington, IN: Kappa Delta Pi. Educational Review. Retrieved May 13, 2007, from http://edrev.asu.edu/reviews/rev64.htm

Brown, L., & Pollit, E. (1996). Malnutrition, poverty and intellectual development. *Scientific American, 274*(2), 38–43.

Brown-Chidsey, R. (2005). Academic skills are basic (to) children's personal wellness. *Trainer's Forum, 25*(1), 4–8.

Brown-Chidsey, R., & Steege, M.W. (2005). *Response to intervention: Principles and strategies for effective practices.* New York: The Guilford Press.

Budoff, M. (1987). Measures for assessing learning potential. In C.S. Lidz (Ed.), *Dynamic assessment: An interactive approach to evaluating learning potential* (pp. 173–195). New York: The Guilford Press.

Burroughs, R. (1993, July). The uses of literature. *The Executive Educator, 15*(7), 27–29.

Burton, L.M., Obeidallah, D.A., & Allison, K. (1996). Ethnographic insights on social context and adolescent development among inner-city African-American teens. In R. Jessor & A. Colby (Eds.), *Ethnography and human development: Context and meaning in social inquiry* (pp. 395–418). Chicago: University of Chicago Press.

Butcher, J.N., Dalhstrom, W.G., Graham, J.R., Tellegen, A., & Kaemmer, B. (1989). *MMPI–2: Manual for administration and scoring.* Minneapolis: University of Minnesota Press.

Butler, K.M., Husson, R.N., Balis, F.M., Browers, P., Eddy, J., el-Amin, D., & Guess, J. (1991). Dideoxyinosine in children with symptomatic human immunodeficiency virus. *New England Journal of Medicine, 324,* 137–144.

Canter, A. (2004, December). A problem-solving model for improving achievement. *Principal Leadership Magazine, 5*(4), 11–15.

Carbo, M. (1987, October). Matching reading styles: Correcting ineffective instruction. *Educational Leadership, 45*(2), 40–47.

Carey, K. (2005). *The funding gap 2004: Many states still shortchange low-income and minority students.* Washington, DC: The Education Trust.

Carnine, D. (1990, January). New research on the brain: Implications for instruction. *Phi Delta Kappan, 71*(5), 372–377.

Carnine, D. (1994). Diverse learners and prevailing, emerging and research-based educational approaches and their tools. *School Psychology Review, 23,* 341–350.

Carnine, D.W., Silbert, J., Kame'enui, E.J., & Tarver, S.G. (Eds.). (2004). Direct Instruction Reading (4th ed.). Upper Saddle River, NJ: Pearson.

Carolina Abecedarian Project. (1999). *Early learning, later success: The Abecedarian Study.* Retrieved December 1, 2006, from http://www.fpg.unc.edu/~abc/

Carr, K.S. (1988, Winter). How can we teach critical thinking? *Childhood Education, 65*(2), 69–73.

Carroll, J. (1993). *Human cognitive abilities: A survey of factor-analytic studies.* New York: Cambridge University Press.

Carter, T.S., & Dean, E.O. (2006). Mathematics intervention for grades 5–11: Teaching mathematics, reading, or both. *Reading Psychology, 27,* 127–146.

Cartledge, G., & Lo, Y. (2006). *Teaching urban learners.* Champaign, IL: Research Press.

Cartledge, G., & Milburn, J.F. (1996). A model for teaching social skills. In G. Cartledge (Ed.), *Cultural diversity and social skills instruction* (pp. 45–85), Champaign, IL: Research Press.

Caspi, A., Wright, B.E., Moffit, T.E., & Silva, P.A. (1998). Childhood predictors of unemployment in early adulthood. *American Sociological Review, 63*(3), 424–451.

Cauce, A.M., Paradise, M., Domenech-Rodriguez, M., Cochran, B.N., Shea, J.M., Srebnik, D., & Baydar, N. (2002). Cultural and contextual influences in mental health help seeking: A focus on ethnic minority youth. *Journal of Consulting and Clinical Psychology, 70*(1), 44–55.

Cauthen, N., & Lu, H. (2003). *Living at the edge: Employment alone is not enough for American's low-income children and families.* New York: National Center for Children in Poverty.

Center on Addiction and Substance Abuse. (1996, June 5). *CASA releases report on substance abuse and the American woman.* New York: Columbia University. Retrieved on April 17, 2007, from http://permanent.access.gpo.gov/lps9890/lps9890/www.casacolumbia.org/ newsletter1457/newsletter_list.htm-section = News%20Releases

Center for Educational Policy. (2004, January). *From the capital to the classroom: Year Four of the No Child Left Behind Act.* Retrieved May 11, 2007, from http:// www.civilrights.org/library/remote_page.jsp?itemID:28322565

Center for Research on Effective Schooling for Disadvantaged Students. (1990, November). *One-to-one tutoring: Procedures for early reading success.* Baltimore: Johns Hopkins University Press.

Center for School Improvement and the Chicago Panel on School Policy. (1996). *Pervasive student mobility: A moving target for school improvement.* Chicago: Center for School Improvement and the Chicago Panel on School Policy.

Centers for Disease Control and Prevention. (1995). Sociodemographic and behavioral characteristics associated with alcohol consumption during pregnancy: United States, 1988. *Journal of the American Medical Association, 273*, 1406.

Centers for Disease Control and Prevention. (1997, November). *Screening young children for lead poisoning: Guidance for state and local public health officials.* Washington, DC: U.S. Department of Health and Human Services, Public Health Service.

Centers for Disease Control and Prevention. (2000). Blood lead levels in young children: United States and selected states, 1996–1999. *Morbidity and Mortality Weekly Report, 49*, 1133–1137.

Centers for Disease Control and Prevention. (2006). *Fetal alcohol spectrum disorder.* Retrieved August, 3, 2006, from http://www.cdc.gov/ncbddd/fas/fassurv.htm

Chen, C., Lee, S., & Stevenson, H.W. (1996). Long-term prediction of academic achievement of American, Chinese, and Japanese adolescents. *Journal of Educational Psychology, 18*, 750–759.

Chiodo, L.M., Jacobson, S.W., & Jacobson, J.L. (2004, May-June). Neurodevelopmental effects of postnatal lead exposure at very low levels. *Neurotoxicology and Teratology, 26*(3), 359–371.

Chomitz, V.R., Cheung, L.W.Y., & Lieberman, E. (1995). The role of lifestyle in preventing low birth weight, *The Future of Children, 5*(1). Retrieved July 17, 2006, from http:// www.futureofchildren.org/information2826_show.htm?doc_id = 79889

Christenson, S.L., & Sheridan, S.M. (2001). *Schools and families.* New York: The Guilford Press.

Cicchetti, D., & Rogosch, F.A. (1997). The role of self-organization in the promotion of resilience in maltreated children. *Development and Psychopathology, 9*, 797–815.

Citro, C.F., & Michael, R.T. (1995). *Measuring poverty: A new approach.* Washington, DC: National Academies Press.

Clark, R.M. (1990). Why disadvantaged students succeed: What happened outside school is critical. *Public Welfare*, 17–23.

Clark, R.M. (1993). Homework-focused parenting practices that positively affect student achievement. In N.F. Chavkin (Ed.), *Families and schools in a pluralistic society* (pp. 85–105). Albany: State University of New York Press.

Coates, K., & Silburn, R. (1970). *Poverty: The forgotten Englishmen*. Harmondsworth: Penguin.

Cohen, M.A. (1998). The monetary value of saving a high-risk youth. *Journal of Quantitative Criminology, 14*, 5–33.

Coie, J.D., & Jacobs, M.R. (1993). The role of social context in the prevention of conduct disorder. *Development & Psychopathology, 5*, 263–275.

Colombo, M., de la Parra, A., & Lopez, I. (1992). Intellectual and physical outcome of children undernourished in early life is influenced by later environmental conditions. *Developmental Medicine and Child Neurology, 6*, 7–14.

Comer, J.P. (1988). Educating poor minority children. *Scientific American, 259*(5), 2–8.

Comer, J.P. (1995). *School power: Implications of an intervention project*. New York: Free Press.

Comer, J.P. (1999). *Child by child: The Comer process for change in education*. New York: Teachers College Press.

Comer, J.P., & Haynes, N.M. (1991). Parent involvement in schools: An ecological approach. *Elementary School Journal, 91*(3), 271–278.

Comer, J.P., & Haynes, N.M. (1992). *Summary of School Development Program (SDP) effects*. Unpublished paper. New Haven, CT: Yale Child Study Center.

Comer, J.P., Haynes, N.M., Joyner, E.T., & Ben-Avie, M. (1996). *Rallying the whole village: The Comer process for reforming education*. New York: Teachers College Press.

Comuntzis-Page, G. (1996). Critical issues: Creating the school climate and structures to support parent and family involvement. Center on School, Family, and Community Partnerships, Johns Hopkins University, Baltimore. Retrieved November 22, 2006, from http://www.ncrel.org/sdrs/areas/issues/envrnmnt/famncomm/pa300.htm

Consortium on Chicago School Research. (1994). *Charting reform: The students speak*. Chicago: Author.

Cook, T.D., Murphy, R.F., & Hunt, H.D. (2000). Comer's School Development Program in Chicago: A theory-based evaluation. *American Educational Research Journal, 37*(2), 535–597.

Cornelius, M.D., Leech, S.L., Goldschmidt, L., & Day, N.L. (2000). Prenatal tobacco exposure: Is it a risk factor for early tobacco experimentation? *Nicotine & Tobacco Research, 2*, 45–52.

Coscia, J.M., Douglas, M., Succop, P.A., & Dietrich, K.M. (2003, March). Cognitive development of lead exposed children from ages 6 to 15 years: An application of growth curve analysis. *Child Neuropsychology, 9*(1), 10–21.

Costantino, G., Flanagan, R., & Malgady, R.G. (2001). Narrative assessments: TAT, CAT, and TEMAS. In L. Suzuki, J.G. Ponterotto, & P.J. Meller (Eds.), *Handbook of multicultural assessment* (2nd ed., pp. 217–236). San Francisco: Jossey-Bass.

Costantino, G., Malgady, R.G., Colon-Malgady, G., & Bailey, J. (1992). Clinical utility of the TEMAS with nonminority children. *Journal of Personality Assessment, 59*(3), 433–438.

Costantino, G., Malgady, R.G., & Rogler, L.H. (1988). *Tell-me-a-story*. Los Angeles: Western Psychological Services.

Cotton, K. (1991). *Computer-assisted instruction*. Retrieved December 10, 2006, from http://www.nwrel.org/scpd/sirs/5/cu10.html

Coulter, P. (1993, September). The Comer School Development Program. *Education*

Research Consumer Guide, No. 6. Office of Educational Research and Improvement (OERI) of the U.S. Department of Education, ED/OERI 92–138.

Crawford-Brown, C., & Rattray, J.M. (2001). Parent–child relationships in Caribbean families. In N. Boyd Webb & D. Lum (Eds.), *Culturally diverse parent–child and families relationships* (pp. 107–130). New York: Columbia University Press.

Crespi, T.D., & Cooke, D.T. (2003, Summer). Specialization in neuropsychology: Contemporary concerns and considerations for school psychology. *The School Psychologist,* 97–100.

Crosby, W.M. (1991). Studies in fetal malnutrition. *American Journal of Diseases of Childhood, 145,* 871–876.

Cummings, E.M., Davies, P.T., & Campbell, S.B. (2000). *Developmental psychopathology and family process.* New York: The Guilford Press.

Cummins, J. (1983). Bilingualism and special education: Program and pedagogical issues. *Learning Disability Quarterly, 6,* 373–386.

Cummins, J.C. (1984). *Bilingual and special education: Issues in assessment and pedagogy.* Austin, TX: PRO-ED.

Curley, A.M. (2005, June). Theories of urban poverty and implications for public housing policy. *Journal of Sociology & Social Welfare, 32*(2), 97–119.

Cutrona, C.E., Russell, D.W., Brown, P.A., Clark, L.A., Hessling, R.M., & Gardner, K.A. (2005). Neighborhood context, personality, and stressful life events as predictors of depression among African American women. *Journal of Abnormal Psychology, 114*(1), 3–15.

Dalaker, J. (2001). *Poverty in the United States: 2000. Current population reports: Consumer income.* Washington, DC: U.S. Census Bureau, U.S. Department of Commerce

D'Amato, R.C., Crepeau-Hobson F., Huang, L.V., & Geil, M. (2005, June). Ecological neuropsychology: An alternative to the deficit model for conceptualizing and serving students with learning disabilities. *Neuropsychology Review, 15*(2), 97–103.

D'Ambrosio, B., Johnson, H., & Hobbs, L. (1995). Strategies for increasing achievement in mathematics. In Association for Supervision and Curriculum Development (Ed.), *Educating everybody's children* (pp. 121–137). Alexandria, VA: Association for Supervision and Curriculum Development.

Dana, R.H. (1993). *Multicultural assessment perspectives for professional psychology.* Boston: Allyn & Bacon.

Darling-Hammond, L. (2004). From "separate but equal" to "No Child Left Behind": The collision of new standards and old inequalities. In D. Meier & G. Wood (Eds.), *Many children left behind* (pp. 3–32), Boston: Beacon Press.

Darling-Hammond, L., & Post, L. (2000). Inequality in teaching and schooling: Supporting high-quality teaching and leadership in low-income schools. In R.D. Kahlenberg (Ed.), *A notion at risk: Preserving public education as an engine for social mobility* (pp. 127–167). New York: The Century Foundation Press.

Davis, M.K. (2001). Breastfeeding and chronic disease in childhood and adolescence. *Pediatric Clinics of North America, 48*(1), 125–141.

Dawson, G., Frey, K., Pangiotides, H., Osterling, J., & Hessl, D. (1997). Infants of depressed mothers exhibit atypical frontal brain activity: A replication and extension of previous findings. *Journal of Child Psychology and Psychiatry and Allied Disciplines, 38,* 179–186.

Dawson, P., & Guare, R. (2004). *Executive skills in children and adolescents.* New York: The Guilford Press.

Dearing, E., McCartney, K., & Taylor, B.A. (2006). Within-child associations between family income and externalizing and internalizing problems. *Developmental Psychology, 42*(2), 237–252.

Deci, E.L., & Flaste, R. (1995). *Why we do what we do: Understanding self-motivation.* New York: Penguin Books.

Deci, E.L., Hodges, R., Pierson, L., & Tomassone, J. (1992). Autonomy and competence as motivational factors in students with learning disabilities and emotional handicaps. *Journal of Learning Disabilities, 25,* 457–471.

de Cubas, M. M., & Field, T. (1993). Children of methadone-dependent women: Developmental outcomes. *American Journal of Orthopsychiatry, 63,* 266–276.

De Fina, P.A. (2004, August). *An integrated developmental neuro-educational model for diagnosis and intervention/prevention in schools.* Presented at Neuro-Educational Training Associates School Neuropsychology Training Program. Elmsford, New York.

Delisio, E. (2005). *Improving school culture.* Retrieved November 22, 2006, from http://www.education-world.com/a_admin/admin/admin407.shtml

Delpit, L. (1995). *Other people's children: Cultural conflict in the classroom.* New York: New Press.

Deno, S. (2005). Problem-solving assessment. In R. Brown-Chidney (Ed.), *Assessment for intervention: A problem-solving approach* (pp. 10–42). New York: Guilford Press.

Diamond, M. (1988). *Enriching heredity: The impact of the environment on the anatomy of the brain.* New York: Free Press.

Dillon, J.T. (1984). Research on questioning and discussion. *Educational Leadership, 42*(3), 50–56.

Dodge, K.A., & Pettit, G.S. (2004). A biopsychosocial model of the development of chronic conduct problems in adolescence. *Developmental Psychology, 39,* 349–371.

Doll, B., Zucker, S., & Brehm, K. (2004). *Resilient classrooms.* New York: Guilford Press.

Dominguez, S., & Watkins, C. (2003). Creating networks for survival and mobility: Social capital among African-American and Latin-American low-income mothers. *Social Problems, 50*(1), 111–135.

Donovan, M.S., & Cross, C.T. (Eds.) (2002). *Minority students in special education and gifted education.* Washington, DC: National Academy Press.

Dore, M.M. (1999). Emotionally and behaviorally disturbed children in the child welfare system: Points of preventive intervention. *Children & Youth Services Review, 21*(1), 7–29.

Downer, J., & Pianta, D. (2006). Academic and cognitive functioning in first grade: Association with earlier home and child care predictors and with concurrent home and classroom experience. *School Psychology Review, 35*(1), National Association of School Psychologists.

Drummond, T. (1993). *The Student Risk Screening Scale (SRSS).* Grants Pass, OR: Josephine County Mental Health Program.

Dumas, J.E., & Wekerle, C. (1995). Maternal report of child behavior problems and personal distress as predictors of dysfunctional parenting. *Development & Psychopathology, 7,* 465–479.

Duncan, G.J. (1994). Families and neighbors as sources of disadvantage in the schooling decisions of white and black adolescents. *American Journal of Education, 103,* 20–53.

Dunn, R., & Dunn, K. (1992). *Teaching secondary students through their individual learning styles: Practical approaches for grades 7–12.* Boston: Allyn & Bacon.

Edelbrock, C.S., & Costello, A.J. (1988). Convergence between statistically derived behavior problem syndromes and child psychiatric diagnoses. *Journal of Abnormal Child Psychology, 16,* 219–231.

Ehri, L.C. (1998). Grapheme-phoneme knowledge is essential for learning to read words in English. In J.L. Metsala & L.C. Ehri (Eds.), *Word recognition in beginning literacy* (pp. 3–40). Mahwah, NJ: Lawrence Erlbaum Associates.

Elbert, T., Heim, S., & Rockstroh, B. (2001). Neural plasticity and development. In C.A.

Nelson & M. Luciana (Eds.), *Handbook of developmental cognitive neuroscience* (pp. 191–204). Cambridge, MA: The MIT Press.

Elliot, S.N., & Fuchs, L.S. (1997). The utility of curriculum-based measurement and performance assessment as alternatives to traditional intelligence tests. *School Psychology Review, 26,* 224–233.

Elliot, T., & Ritzler, B. (1998). *Comparisons between the TEMAS and the Rorschach Comprehensive System: A multicultural validation.* Unpublished doctoral dissertation, Long Island University.

Ellis, M.R., & Kane, K.Y. (2000). Lightening the lead load in children. *American Family Physician, 62*(3), 545–554, 559–560.

Englert, C.S. (1992). Writing instruction from a sociocultural perspective: The holistic, dialogic, and social enterprise of writing. *Journal of Learning Disabilities, 25,* 153–172.

Entwisle, D.R., & Alexander, K.L. (2000). Early schooling and social stratification. In R.C. Pianta & M.J. Cox (Eds.), *The transition to kindergarten* (pp. 13–38). Baltimore: Paul H. Brookes Publishing Co.

Entwisle, D., Alexander, K., & Olson, L. (1997). *Children, schools, and inequality.* Boulder, CO: Westview Press.

Epstein, J.L. (1986). Parents' reactions to teacher practices of parent involvement. *Elementary School Journal, 86,* 277–294.

Epstein, J.L. (1995). School/family/community partnerships: Caring for the children we share. *Phi Delta Kappan, 76*(9), 701–712.

Erchul, W.P., Covington, C.G., Hughes, J.N., & Meyers, J. (1995). Further explorations of request-centered relational communication within school consultation. *School Psychology Review, 24,* 621–632.

Escalona, S.K. (1982). Babies at double hazard: Early development of infants biologic and social risk. *Pediatrics, 70,* 670–676.

Espinosa, L.M. (2002, November). High-quality preschool: Why we need it and what it looks like. *Preschool Policy Matters, Issue 1.* New Brunswick, NJ: National Institute for Early Education Research, The State University of New Jersey, Rutgers.

Esposito, C. (1999). Learning in urban blight: School climate and its effect on the school performance of urban, minority, low-income children. *School Psychology Review, 28*(3), 365–377.

Evans, G.W. (2004). The environment of childhood poverty. *American Psychologist, 59,* 77–92.

Fantuzzo, J., McWayne, C., & Bulotsky, R. (2003). Forging, strategic partnership to advance mental health science and practice for vulnerable children. *School Psychology Review, 32*(1), 17–37.

Farber, A.F., Yanni, C.C., & Batshaw, M.L. (1997). Nutrition: Good and bad. In M.L. Batshaw (Ed.), *Children with disabilities.* (4th ed., pp. 183–210). Baltimore: Paul H. Brookes Publishing Co.

Farkas, S., Johnson, J., Duffett, A., Syat, B., & Vine, J. (2003). *Rolling up their sleeves: Superintendent and principals talk about what's needed to fix public schools.* Washington, DC: Public Agenda.

Farley, R. (1997). Racial trends and differences in the United States 30 years after the civil rights decade. *Social Science Research, 26,* 235–262.

Federal Interagency Forum on Child and Family Statistics. (2003). *America's children: Key national indicators of well-being, 2003.* Washington, DC: U.S. Government Printing Office.

Felner, R.D. (2006). Poverty in childhood and adolescence. In S. Goldstein & R.B. Brooks (Eds.), *Handbook of resilience in children* (pp. 125–147). New York: Springer.

Ferri, B.A., & Connor, D.J. (2005). Tools of exclusion: Race, disability, and (re)segregated education. *Teachers College Records, 107*(3), 453–474.

Feuerstein, R., Rand, Y., & Hoffman, M.B. (1979). *The dynamic assessment of retarded*

performers: The Learning Potential Assessment Device: Theory, instrument and techniques.
Baltimore: University Park Press.

Fewtrell, M.S. (2004). The long-term benefits of having been breast-fed. *Current Paediatrics, 14,* 97–103.

Fisher, G. (1992, Winter). The development and history of the poverty threshold. *Social Security Bulletin, 55*(4), pp. 3–14.

Fitzpatrick, K.M. (1993). Exposure to violence and presence of depression among low-income African-American youth. *Journal of Consulting and Clinical Psychology, 61,* 528–531.

Flanagan, D.P., & Ortiz, S.O. (2001). *Essentials of cross-battery assessment.* New York: Wiley.

Fletcher-Vincent, S., Reece, E.R., & Malveaux, F.J. (1994). Reactivity to cockroach and other allergens in an inner city population with rhinitis and asthma. *Journal of Allergy Clinic Immunology, 93,* 174.

Fogarty, R. (1997). *Brain compatible classrooms.* Arlington Heights, IL: Skylight Training and Publishing.

Forness, S.R., Kavale, K.A., & Lopez, M. (1993). Conduct disorders in the schools: Special education eligibility and comorbidity. *Journal of Emotional and Behavioral Disorders, 1,* 101–108.

Foster, R.P. (2001). When immigration is trauma: Guidelines for the individual and family clinician. *American Journal of Orthopsychiatry, 71*(2), 153–169.

Fowler, M.G. (1994). Pediatric HIV infection: Neurological and neuropsychologic findings. *Acta Paediatrics,* (Suppl. 400), 59–62.

Freeman, R. (1996). Why do so many young American men commit crimes and what might we do about it? *Journal of Economic Perspectives, 10*(1), 25–42.

Frey, K.S., Hirschstein, M.K., & Guzzo, B.A. (2000). Second step: Preventing aggression by promoting social competence. *Journal of Emotional and Behavioral Disorders, 8,* 102–112.

Frick, P.J., Silverthorn, P., & Evans, C.S. (1994). Assessment of childhood anxiety using structured interviews: Patterns of agreement among informants and association with maternal anxiety. *Psychological Assessment, 6,* 372–379.

Fry, R. (2003). *Hispanic youth dropping out of U.S. schools: Measuring the challenge.* Retrieved May 11, 2007, from http://wwwpewtrusts.com/pdf/vf_pew_hispanic_dropoout.pdf

Fuchs, D., Mock, D., Morgan, P.L., & Young, C.L. (2003). Responsiveness-to-intervention: Definitions, evidence, and implications for the learning disabilities construct. *Learning Disabilities Research and Practice, 18,* 157–171.

Fuchs, L.S., & Vaughn, S.R. (2005). Response to intervention as a framework for the identification of learning disabilities. *Trainer's Forum, 25*(1), 12–19.

Fujiura, G.T., & Yamaki, K. (2000). Trends in demography of childhood poverty and disability. *Exceptional Children, 66,* 187–199.

Furstenberg, F., Brooks-Gunn, J., & Morgan, S.P. (1987). *Adolescent mothers in later life.* New York: Cambridge.

Galler, J.R., Harrison, R.H., Ramsey, F., Forde, V., & Butler, S.C. (2000). Maternal depressive symptoms affect infant cognitive development Barbados. *Journal of Child Psychology and Psychiatry and Allied Disciplines, 41,* 747–757.

Gans, H.J. (1995). *The war against the poor: The underclass and antipoverty policy.* New York: BasicBooks.

Garb, H.N., Lilienfeld, S.O., Wood, J.M., & Nezworski, M.T. (2002). Effective use of projective techniques in clinical practice: Let the data help with selection and interpretation. *Professional Psychology: Research and Practice, 33*(5), 454–463.

Garbarino, J. (1995). The American war zone: What children can tell us about living with violence. *Developmental and Behavioral Pediatrics, 16,* 431–434.

Garcia, G.E. (2000). Bilingual children's reading. In M.L. Kamil, P.B. Mosenthal, P.D. Pearson, & R. Barr (Eds.), *Handbook of reading research* (Vol. 3, pp. 813–834). Mahwah, N.J.: Lawrence Erlbaum Associates.

Garcia-Vazquez, E., & Ehly, S. (1995). Best practice in facilitating peer tutoring programs. In A. Thomas & J. Grimes (Eds.), *Best practice in school psychology–III* (pp. 403–411). Washington, DC: National Association of School Psychologists.

Gardner, E. (1975). Fundamentals of neurology (6th ed.). Philadelphia: W.B. Saunders.

Garmezy, N. (1974). The study of competence in children at risk for severe psychopathology. In E.J. Anthony & C. Koupernik (Eds.). *The child in his family: Vol. 3. Children as psychiatric risk* (pp. 77–97). New York: Wiley.

Gauvain, M. (1995). Thinking in niches: Sociocultural influences on cognitive development. *Human Development, 38,* 25–45.

Geller, B., Fox, L.W., & Fletcher, M. (1993). Effect of tricyclic antidepressants on switching to mania and on the onset of bipolarity in depressed 6- to 12-year-olds. *Journal of the American Academy of Child and Adolescent Psychiatry, 32,* 43–50.

Gerard, A.B. (1994). *Parent–Child Relationship Inventory.* Los Angeles: Western Psychological Services.

Gettinger, M. (1986). Issues and trends in academic engaged time of students. *Special Services in the Schools, 2,* 1–17.

Gibbs, J.T., & Huang, L.N. (1998). *Children of color.* San Francisco: Jossey-Bass.

Gilbert, D.L. (2003). *The American class structure in an age of growing inequality* (6th ed.). Belmont, CA: Wadsworth Publishing.

Giscombé, C.L., & Lobel, M. (2005). Explaining disproportionately high rates of adverse birth outcomes among African Americans: The impact of stress, racism, and related factors in pregnancy. *Psychological Bulletin, 131*(5), 662–683.

Goldstein, S., & Brooks, R.B. (2006a). *Resilience in children.* New York: Springer Science.

Goldstein, S., & Brooks, R.B. (2006b). Why study resilience? In S. Goldstein & R.B.Brooks (Eds.), *Resilience in children* (pp. 3–15). New York: Springer Science.

Good, R., & Prakash, M.S. (2000). Global education. In D. Gabbart (Ed.), *Knowledge and power in the global economy: Politics and the rhetoric of school reform* (pp. 271–277). Mahwah, NJ: Lawrence Erlbaum Associates.

Goodman, S.H., & Gotlib, I.H. (1999). Risk for psychopathology in the children of depressed mothers: A developmental model for understanding mechanism of transmission. *Psychological Review, 106,* 458–490.

Gopaul-McNicol, S., & Thomas-Presswood, T. (1998). *Working with linguistically and culturally different children: Innovative clinical and educational approaches.* Boston: Allyn & Bacon.

Gormley, W.T., Gayer, T., Phillips, D., & Dawson, B. (2005). The effects of universal pre-k on cognitive development. *Developmental Psychology, 41*(6), 872–884.

Gorski, P.C. (2005, September). Savage unrealities: Uncovering classism in Ruby Payne's framework. Retrieved October 19, 2006, from http://www.EdChange.org

Gottfredson, G.D., Gottfredson, D.C., & Czeh, E.R. (2000). *National study of delinquency prevention in schools.* Ellicott City, MD: Gottfredson Associates.

Gottschalk, P., McLanahan, S., & Sandefur, G. (1994). The dynamics and intergenerational transmission of poverty and welfare participation. In G.D. Sandefur, S.H. Danziger, & D.H. Weinberg (Eds.), *Confronting poverty: Prescriptions for change* (pp. 378–389). Cambridge, MA: Harvard University Press.

Graff, J. (2003). *Poverty and development.* Cape Town: Oxford University Press Southern Africa.

Graham, E.M., & Morgan, M. (1997). Growth before birth. In M.L. Batshaw (Ed.), *Children with disabilities* (4th ed., p. 53–69). Baltimore: Paul H. Brookes Publishing Co.

Granovetter, M. (1974). *Getting a job: A study of contacts and careers.* Cambridge, MA: Harvard University Press.

Greenberg, M., & Rahmanou, H. (2004). Looking to the future: A commentary on children of immigrant families. In M.K. Shields (Ed.), *Children of immigrant families: The future of children, 14*(2), pp. 139–145. Retrieved May 29, 2007, from www.futureofchildren.org/information2826/information_show.htm?doc_id=240619

Greenough, W.T., Black, J.E., & Wallace, C. (1987). Experience and brain development. *Child Development, 58*, 539–559.

Greenough, W.T., & Juraska, J.M. (1986). *Developmental neuropsychobiology.* Orlando, FL: Academic Press.

Gresham, F.M., & Elliot, S. (1990). *Social Skills Rating System.* Circles Pines, MN: American Guidance Service.

Gresham, F.M., Watson, T.S., & Skinner, C.H. (2001). Functional behavioral assessment: Principles, procedures, and future directions. *School Psychology Review, 30*(2), 156–172.

Grubman, S., Gross, E., Lerner-Weiss, X., Hernandez, M., McSherry, G.D., Hoyt, L.G., et al. (1995). Older children and adolescents living with perinatally acquired human immunodeficiency virus infection. *Pediatrics, 95*, 657–663.

Guidubaldi, J., & Cleminshaw, H.K. (1994). *Parenting Satisfaction Scale.* San Antonio, TX: The Psychological Corporation.

Gunnar, M.R. (2001). Effects of early deprivation: Findings from orphanage-reared infants and children. In C.A. Nelson & M. Luciana (Eds.), *Handbook of developmental cognitive neuroscience* (pp. 617–629). Cambridge, MA: The MIT Press.

Gutman, L.M., & McLoyd, V.C. (2000). Parents' management of their children's education within the home, at school, and in the community: An examination of African-American families living in poverty. *The Urban Review, 32*(1), 1–24.

Haberman, M. (1997). Unemployment training: The ideology of nonwork learned in urban schools. *Phi Delta Kappan, 78*(7), 499–503.

Haberman, M. (1999). *Star principal serving children in poverty.* Indianapolis, IN: Kappa Delta Pi.

Haberman, M. (2004, May). Can star teachers create learning communities? *Educational Leadership, 61*(8), 52–56.

Haberman, M. (2005). *Star teachers.* Houston, TX: The Haberman Educational Foundation.

Haberman, M., & Dill, V.S. (1995). Commitment to violence among teenagers in poverty. *Kappa Delta Pi Records, 31*(4), 148–156.

Hack, M., Klein, N.K., & Taylor, H.G (1995). Long-term developmental outcomes of low birth weight infants. *The Future of Children, 5*(1), 176–196.

Hagenaars, A., & De Vos, K. (1988). The definition and measurement of poverty. *The Journal of Human Resources, 23*(2), 211–221.

Hale, J.B., & Fiorello, C.A. (2004). *School neuropsychology: A practitioner's handbook.* New York: Guilford Press.

Hall, S.H., & Henderson, A. (1990, Summer). Restructuring schools through parent involvement. *Network for Public Schools, 15*(6), 1–8.

Hallenbeck, M.J. (1996). The cognitive strategy in writing: Welcome relief for adolescents with learning disabilities. *Learning Disabilities Research & Practice, 11*, 107–119.

Hallinger, P., Bickman, L., & Davis, K. (1996). School context, principal leadership, and student reading achievement. *The Elementary School Journal, 96*, 527–549.

Hamilton, B.E., Ventura, S.J., Martin, J.A., & Sutton, P.D. (2005). *Preliminary births for 2004: Health E-stats.* Hyatsville, MD: National Center for Health Statistics.

Hampton, S. (1995). Strategies for increasing achievement in writing. In Association for Supervision and Curriculum Development (Ed.), *Educating everybody's children* (pp. 99–120). Alexandria, VA: Association for Supervision and Curriculum Development.

Hansen, D.A. (1986). Family-school articulations: The effects of interaction rule mismatch. *American Educational Research Journal, 23*(4), 643–659.

Hanson, M.J., & Lynch, E.W. (1992). Family diversity: Implications for policy and practice. *Topics in Early Childhood Special Education, 12,* 283–306.

Hanson, M.J., & Lynch, E.W. (2004). *Understanding families: Approaches to diversity, disability, and risk.* Baltimore: Paul H. Brookes Publishing Co.

Harrington, M. (1962). The other America: Poverty in the U.S. New York: Macmillan.

Harris, T., & Hodges, R. (Eds.). (1995). *The literacy dictionary.* Newark, DE: International Reading Association.

Harry, B., Kalyanpur, M., & Day, M. (1999). *Building cultural reciprocity with families: Case studies in special education.* Baltimore: Paul H. Brookes Publishing Co.

Harvard Graduate School of Education. (1987). Big kids teach little kids: What we know about cross-age tutoring. *Harvard Education Letter, 3*(2), 1–4.

Hauser-Cram, P., Sirin, S.R., & Stipek, D. (2003). When teachers' and parents' values differ: Teachers' ratings of academic competence in children from low-income families. *Journal of Educational Psychology, 95*(4), 813–820.

Hausfather, A., Toharia, A., LaRoche, C., & Engelsmann, F. (1997). Effects of age of entry, day-care quality, and family characteristics on preschool behavior. *Journal of Child Psychology and Psychiatry, 38,* 441–448.

Hay, D.F., Angold, A., Pawlby, S., Harold, G.T., & Sharp, D. (2003). Pathways to violence in the children of mothers who are depressed postpartum. *Developmental Psychology, 39*(6), 1083–1094.

Hay, D.F, Pawlby, S., Sharp, D., Asten, P., Mills, A., & Kumar, R. (2001, October). Intellectual problems shown by 11-year-old children whose mothers had postnatal depression. *Journal of Child Psychology and Psychiatry, 42*(7), 871–889.

Haynes, N., & Comer, J. (1990). The effects of a school development program on self-concept. *Yale Journal of Biological Medicine, 63*(4), 275–283.

Helzer, J.E. (1988). Schizophrenia: Epidemiology. In R. Michels, J.O. Cavenar, A.M. Cooper, S.B. Guze, L.L. Judd, G.L. Klerman, & A.J. Solnit (Eds.), *Psychiatry.* New York: Lippincott.

Henslin, J.M. (2006). *Essentials of sociology: A down-to-earth approach* (6th ed.). Boston: Allyn & Bacon.

Hetherington, E.M. (1997). Teenaged childbearing and divorce. In S.S Luthar, J.A. Burack, D. Cicchetti, & J.R. Weisz (Eds.), *Developmental psychopathology: Perspectives on adjustment, risk, and disorder* (pp. 350–373). New York: Cambridge.

Hetherington, E.M., & Martin, B. (1986). Family factors and psychopathology in children. In H.C. Quay & J.S. Werry (Eds.), *Psychopathological disorders of childhood* (3rd ed., pp. 332–390). New York: John Wiley & Sons.

Hill, J.B., & Haffner, W.H.J. (2002). Growth before birth, In M.L. Batshaw (Ed.), *Children with disabilities* (5th ed., pp. 43–54). Baltimore: Paul H. Brookes Publishing Co.

Hinkle, J.S., & Wells, M.E. (1995). *Family counseling in the school.* Greensboro, NC: ERIC/CASS Publications.

Hodges, H. (1994, January). A consumer's guide to learning styles programs: An expert's advice on selecting and implementing various models in the classroom. *The School Administrator, 51*(1), 14–18.

Hollins, E.R. (1993, Spring). Assessing teacher competence for diverse populations. *Theory Into Practice, 32*(1), 93–99.

Holman, A.M. (1983). *Family assessment: Tools for understanding and intervention.* Thousand Oaks, CA: Sage Publications.

Hooks, B. (2000). *Where we stand: Class matters.* New York: Routledge.

Hopfenberg, W.S., Levin, H.M., Meister, G., & Rogers, J. (1990, August). *Towards accelerated middle schools for at-risk youth.* Stanford, CA: Stanford University, Accelerated School Project.

Horner, R.H., Sugai, G., Lewis-Palmer, T., & Todd, A. (2001). Teaching school-wide behavioral expectations. *Report on Emotional and Behavioral Disorders in Youth, 1*(4), 77–80.

Horton, H.D., & Allen, B.L. (1998). Race, family, structure and rural poverty: An assessment of population and structural change. *Journal of Comparative Family Studies, 29*, 397–406.

Hubel, D.H., & Wiesel, T.N. (1963). Receptive field of cells in striate cortex of very young, visually inexperienced kittens. *Journal of Neurophysiology, 26*, 994–1002.

Human, J., & Wasem, C. (1991). Rural mental health in America. *American Psychologist, 46*(3), 232–239.

Huston, A.C., Duncan, G.J., McLoyd, V.C., Crosby, D.A., Ripke, M.N., Weisner, T.S., et al. (2005). Impacts on children of a policy to promote employment and reduce poverty for low-income parents: New hope after 5 years. *Developmental Psychology, 41*(6), 902–918.

Huston, A.C., McLoyd, V.C., & Garcia Coll, C. (1994). Children and poverty: Issues in contemporary research. *Child Development, 65*, 275–282.

Idol, L., Nevin, A., & Paolucci-Whitcomb, P. (1999). *Models of curriculum-based assessment* (3rd ed.). Austin, TX: PRO-ED.

Individuals with Disabilities Education Act (IDEA) Amendments of 1997, 20 U.S.C. §§ 1400 *et seq.*

Individuals with Disabilities Education Improvement Act (IDEA) of 2004, 20 U.S.C. §§ 1400 *et seq.*

Ispa, J., Thornburg, K., & Fine, M. (2006). *Keepin' on: The everyday struggles of young families in poverty.* Baltimore: Paul H. Brookes Publishing Co.

Jacobson, M. (1991). *Developmental neurobiology* (3rd ed.). New York: Plenum Press.

Jimerson, S.R. (1999). On the failure of failure: Examining the association between early grade retention and education and employment outcome during late adolescence. *Journal of School Psychology, 37*, 243–272.

Jimerson, S.R. (2001). Meta-analysis of grade retention research: Implications for practice in the 21st century. *School Psychology Review, 30*, 312–330.

Johnson, J.P., Schwartz, R.A., Livingston, M., & Slate, J.R. (2000). What makes a good elementary school? A critical examination. *Journal of Educational Research, 93*, 339–348.

Jordan, C., Tharp, R., & Baird-Vogt, L. (1992). Just open the door: Cultural compatibility and classroom rapport. In M. Saravia-Shore & S.F. Arvizu (Eds.), *Cross-cultural literacy: Ethnographies of communication in multiethnic classrooms* (pp. 3–18). New York: Garland.

Juel, C. (1988). Learning to read and write: A longitudinal study of 54 children from first to fourth grades. *Journal of Educational Psychology, 80*(4), 437–447.

Kamil, M.L. (2004). Vocabulary and comprehension instruction: Summary and implications of the National Reading Panel findings. In P. McCardle & V. Chhabra (Eds.), *The voice of evidence in reading research* (pp. 213–234). Baltimore: Paul H. Brookes Publishing Co.

Kamphaus, R.W., & Frick, P.J. (2004). *Clinical assessment of child and adolescent personality and behavior* (3rd ed.). Boston: Allyn & Bacon.

Kamphaus, R.W., Petoskey, M.D., & Rowe, E.W. (2000). Current trends in psychological testing in children. *Professional Psychology: Research and Practice, 31*(2), 155–164.

Kane, S. & Kirby, M. (2003). *Wealth, poverty, and welfare.* New York: Palgrave Macmillan.

Karoly, L.A., Greenwood, P.W., Everingham, S.S., Hoube, J., Kilburn, M., Rydell, R., et al. (1998). *Investing in our children: What we know and don't know about the cost and benefits of early childhood interventions.* Santa Ana, CA: RAND.

Kattan, M., Stearns, S.C., Crain, E.F., Stout, J.W., Gergen, P.J., Evans, R., et al. (2005). Cost-effectiveness of a home-based environmental intervention for inner-city children with asthma. *Journal of Allergy and Clinical Immunology, 116*(5), 1058–1063.

Katz, L. (1999). *Curriculum disputes in early childhood education.* Retrieved November 12, 2006, from http://ccep.crc.uiuc.edu/eecearchive/digests/1999/katz99b.pdf

Katz, M. (1997). *On playing a poor hand well: Insights from the lives of those who have overcome childhood risks and adversities.* New York: Norton.

Kaufman, A.S., & Kaufman, N.L. (2004). *Kaufman Assessment Battery for Children* (2nd ed.). Circle Pines, MN: American Guidance System.

Kaufman, J.M. (1997). *Characteristics of children's behavior disorders* (4th ed.). Columbus, OH: Charles E. Merrill.

Kaufman, P., Alt, M.N., & Chapman, C.D. (2001). *Dropout rates in the United States: 2000.* Washington, DC: U.S. Department of Education, National Center for Education Statistics. Available at http://nces.ed.gov/pubs2002/droppub_2001/

Kazdin, A.E. (1997). Conduct disorder across the life-span. In S. Luthar, J.A. Burack, D. Cicchetti, & J.R. Weisz (Eds.), *Developmental psychopathology: Perspectives on adjustment, risk, and disorder* (pp. 248–272). New York: Cambridge University Press.

Kellaghan, T., Sloane, K., Alvarez, B., & Bloom, B.S. (1993). *The home environment and school learning: Promoting parental involvement in the education of children.* San Francisco: Jossey-Bass.

Kelley, M.L., Power, T.G., & Wimbush, D.D. (1992). Determinants of disciplinary practices in low-income black mothers. *Child Development, 63*, 573–582.

Kerker, B.D., & Dore, M.M. (2006). Mental health needs and treatment of foster youth: Barriers and opportunities. *American Journal of Orthopsychiatry, 76*(1), 138–147.

Kinder, C. (1993). *Preventing lead poisoning in children.* Retrieved July 27, 2006, from http://www.yale.edu/ynhti/curriculum/units/1993/5/93.05.06.x.html

Kline, L.W. (1995). A baker's dozen: Effective instructional strategies. In Association for Supervision and Curriculum Development (Ed.), *Educating everybody's children* (pp. 21–43). Alexandria, VA: Association for Supervision and Curriculum Development.

Kloosterman, P., & Lester, F.K. (2004). *Results and interpretations of the 1990 through 2000 mathematics assessments of the National Assessment of Educational Progress.* Reston, VA: National Council of Teachers of Mathematics.

Knapp, M., & Shields, P.M. (1990, June). Reconceiving academic instruction for the children of poverty. *Phi Delta Kappan, 71*(10), 753–758.

Knyder-Coe, S. (1991). *Homeless children and youth.* New Brunswick, NJ: Transactional.

Kolb, B., & Fantie, B. (1989). Development of the child's brain and behavior. In C.R. Reynolds & E.F. Janzen (Eds.), *Handbook of clinical child neuropsychology* (pp. 17–40). New York: Plenum Press.

Kolb, B., & Whishaw, Q. (2003). *Fundamentals of human neuropsychology* (5th ed.). New York: Worth Publishers.

Kopp, C.B., & Krakow, J.B. (1983). The developmentalist and the study of biological risk: A view of the past with an eye toward the future. *Child Development, 54*(5), 1086–1108.

Kotulak, R. (1997). *Inside the brain.* Kansas City, MO: Andrews McMeel Publishing.

Kovacs, M. (1992). *The Children's Depression Inventory manual.* New York: Multi-Health Systems.

Kozol, J. (1992). *Savage inequalities: Children in America's schools.* New York: HarperCollins.

Kramer, S., Chalmers, B., Hodnett, E.D., Sevkovskaya, Z., Dzikovich, I., Shapiro, S., et al. (2001). Promotion of breastfeeding intervention trial (PROBIT): A randomized trial in the Republic of Belarus. *Journal of the American Medical Association, 285*(4), 413–420.

Kratochwill, T.R., Elliot, S.R., & Busse, R.T. (1995). Behavioral consultation: A five-year evaluation of consultant and client outcomes. *School Psychology Quarterly, 10*, 87–117.

Kreider, R.M., & Fields, J. (2005). *Living arrangements of children, 2001 current political reports* (pp. 70–104). Washington, DC: U.S. Census Bureau.

Krovetz, M.L. (1999). *Fostering resiliency: Expecting all students to use their minds and hearts well.* Thousand Oaks, CA: Corwin Press.

Lang, C. (1992). *Head Start: New challenges, new chances.* Newton, MA: Education Development Center.

Lareau, A. (1987). Social class differences in family–school relationships: The importance of cultural capital. *Sociology of Education, 60,* 73–85.

LaRue, A. (1992). *Aging and neuropsychological assessment.* New York: Plenum.

Lazarus, B.D. (1993). Self-management and achievement of students with behavior disorders. *Psychology in the Schools, 30*(1), 67–74.

LeBlanc, M. (1998). Screening of serious and violent juvenile offenders. In R. Loeber & D. Farrington (Eds.), *Serious and violent juvenile offenders* (pp. 167–193). Thousand Oaks, CA: Sage Publications.

Lee, V.E., & Burkam, D.T. (2002*). Inequality at the starting gate: Social background differences in achievement as children begin school.* Washington, DC: Economic Policy Institute.

Leo-Rhynie, E. (1993). *The Jamaican family: Continuity and change* (Grace Kennedy Foundation lecture). Kingston, Jamaica: Grace Kennedy Foundation.

Leslie, L.K., Landsverk, J., Ezzet-Loftstrom, R., Tschann, J.M., Slymen, D.J., & Garland, A.F. (2000). Children in foster care: Factors influencing outpatient mental health service use. *Child Abuse & Neglect, 24,* 465–476.

Leventhal, T., Fauth, R.C., & Brooks-Gunn, J. (2005). Neighborhood poverty and public policy: A 5-year follow-up of children's educational outcomes in the New York City moving to opportunity demonstration. *Developmental Psychology, 41*(6), 933–952.

Levin, H.M., & Hopfenberg, W.S. (1991, January). Don't remediate: Accelerate! *Principal, 70*(3), 11–13.

Levine, A. (2005). *Educating school leaders.* Washington, DC: The Education School Project.

Levine, A. (2006). *Educating school teachers.* Washington, DC: The Education School Project.

Lewis, O. (1966). The culture of poverty. *Scientific American, 215*(4), 19–25.

Lewis, T.J., & Sugai, G. (1999). Effective behavior support: A systems approach to proactive schoolwide management. *Focus on Exceptional Children, 31,* 1–24.

Lezak, M.D., Howieson, D.B., & Loring, D.W. (2004). *Neuropsychological Assessment* (4th ed.). New York: Oxford University Press.

Lidz, C.S. (1991). *Practitioner's guide to dynamic assessment.* New York: Guilford Press.

Lidz, C.S. (2003). *Early childhood assessment.* Mahwah, NJ: John Wiley & Sons.

Lidz, C.S., & Macrineb, S.L. (2001). An alternative approach to the identification of gifted culturally and linguistically diverse learners: The contribution of dynamic assessment. *School Psychology International, 22*(1), 74–96.

Lieberman, D. (1999, July). Internet gap widening. *USA Today,* 1A.

Lilienfeld, S.O., Wood, J.M., & Garb, H.N. (2000). The scientific status of projective techniques. *Psychological Science in the Public Interest, 1*(2), 27–66.

Linden, D.W., Paroli, E.T., & Doron, M.W. (2000). *Preemies.* New York: Pocket Books.

Liptak, G. (2002). Neural tube defects. In M. Batshaw (Ed.), *Children with disabilities* (5th ed., pp. 467–492). Baltimore: Paul H. Brooks Publishing Co.

Littky, D. (2004). *The big picture.* Alexandria, VA: Association for Supervision and Curriculum Development.

Lochman, J.E., Burch, P.R., Curry, J.F., & Lampron, L.B. (1984). Treatment and generalization effects of cognitive-behavioral and goal setting interventions with aggressive boys. *Journal of Consulting and Clinical Psychology, 52,* 915–916.

Lochman, J.E., Coie, J.D., Underwood, M.K., & Terry, R. (1993). Effectiveness of a social relations intervention program for aggressive and nonagressive rejected children. *Journal of Consulting and Clinical Psychology, 61*(6), 1053–1058.

Lonner, W.J. (1985, October). Issues in testing and assessment in cross-cultural counseling. *Counseling Psychologist, 13*(4), 599–614.

Losen, D.J., & Orfield, G. (2002). Introduction: Racial inequity in special education. In D.J. Losen & G. Orfield (Eds.), *Racial inequity in special education* (pp. xv–xxxvii). Cambridge, MA: Harvard Education Press.

Lurie, N., Bauer, E.J., & Brady, C. (2001, January). Asthma outcomes at an inner-city school-based health center. *The Journal of School Health, 71*(1), 9–16.

Luster, T., & McAdoo, H.P. (1994). Factors related to the achievement and adjustment of young African American children. *Child Development, 65,* 1080–1094.

Luthar, S.S. (1997). Sociodemographic disadvantage and psychosocial adjustment: Perspectives from developmental psychopathology. In S.S. Luthar, J.A. Burack, D. Cicchetti, & J.R. Weisz (Eds.), *Developmental psychopathology Perspectives on adjustment, risk, and disorder* (pp. 459–485). New York: Cambridge.

Luthar, S.S. (1999). *Poverty and children's adjustment* (Vol. 41). Thousand Oaks, CA: Sage Publications.

Lynch, E.W. (2004). Developing cross-cultural competence. In E.W. Lynch & M.J. Hanson (Eds.), *Developing cross-cultural competence: A guide for working with children and their families* (3rd ed., pp. 41–77). Baltimore: Paul H. Brookes Publishing Co.

Lyon, G.R., Fletcher, J.M., Shaywitz, S.E., Shaywitz, B.A., Torgesen, J.K., Wood, F.B., et al. (2001). Re-thinking learning disabilities. In C.E. Finn, A.J. Rotherham, & C.R. Hokanson, Jr. (Eds.), *Rethinking special education for a new century* (pp. 259–287). Washington, DC: Thomas B. Fordham Foundation and the Progressive Policy Institute.

Madden, N.A., Slavin, R.E., Karweit, N.L., Dolan, L., & Wasik, B.A., (1992, March). *Success for all: Longitudinal effects of a restructuring program for inner-city elementary schools.* Baltimore: Johns Hopkins University, Center for Research on Effective Schooling for Disadvantaged Students.

Malveaux, F.J., & Fletcher-Vincent, A. (1995). Environmental risk factors of childhood asthma in urban centers. *Environmental Health Perspectives, 103*(3), 59–62.

Margolis, H., & Brannigan, G.G. (1990). Strategies for resolving parent–school conflict. *Reading, Writing, and Learning Disabilities, 6,* 1–23.

Marild, S., Hansson, S., Jodal, U., Oden, A., & Svedberg, K. (2004). Protective effect of breastfeeding against urinary tract infection, *Acta Paediatrica Scandinavica, 93*(2), 164–168.

Marston, D. (2002). A functional and intervention-based assessment approach to establishing discrepancy for students with learning disabilities. In R. Bradley, L. Donaldson, & D. Hallahan (Eds.), *Identification of learning disabilities* (pp. 437–447). Mahwah, NJ: Lawrence Erlbaum Associates.

Martin, J.A., Hamilton, B.E., Ventura, S.J., Menacker, F., Park, M., & Sutton, P. (2002).Births: Final data for 2002. *National Vital Statistics Report, 51*(2), 1–102.

Mash, E.J., & Terdal, L.G. (1997). Assessment of child and family disturbance: A behavioral-systems approach. In E.J. Mash & L.G. Terdal (Eds.), *Assessment of childhood disorders* (3rd ed., pp. 3–68). New York: Guilford Press.

Massey, D.S., & Denton, N.R. (1993). *American apartheid: Segregation and the making of the underclass.* Cambridge, MA: Harvard University Press.

Massey, D.S., & Shibuya, K. (1995). Unraveling the tangle of pathology: The effect of spatially concentrated joblessness on the well-being of African Americans. *Social Science Research, 24,* 352–366.

Masten, A.S. (1992). Homeless children in the United States: Mark of a nation. *Current Directions in Psychological Science, 1*(2), 41–44.

Masten, A.S. (2001). Ordinary magic: Resilience processes in development. *American Psychologist, 56*(3), 227–238.

Mastropieri, M.A., Leinart, A., & Scruggs, T.E. (1999). Strategies to increase reading fluency. *Intervention in School and Clinic, 34,* 278–283.

Mather, N., & Goldstein, S. (2001). *Learning disabilities and challenging behaviors: A guide to intervention and classroom management.* Baltimore: Paul H. Brookes Publishing Co.

Mather, N., & Wendling, B.J. (2005). Linking cognitive assessment results to academic interventions for students with learning disabilities. In D.P. Flanagan & P.L. Harrison (Eds.), *Contemporary intellectual assessment* (pp. 545–556). New York: Guilford Press.

Mayes, L.C., & Bornstein, M.H. (1997). The development of children exposed to cocaine. In S.S. Luthar, J. Burack, D. Cicchetti, & J.R. Weisz (Eds.), *Developmental psychopathology: Perspectives on adjustment, risk, and disorder* (pp. 166–188). New York: Cambridge.

Maynard, R.A. (1996). *Kids having kids: A Robin Hood Foundation special report on the cost of adolescent childbearing.* New York: The Robin Hood Foundation.

McAfee, O., & Leong, D.J. (2002). *Assessing and guiding young children's development and learning* (3rd ed.). Boston: Allyn & Bacon.

McCallum, S.R. (2003). Context for nonverbal assessment of intelligence and related abilities. In R.S. McCallum (Ed.), *Handbook of nonverbal assessment* (pp. 3–21). New York: Kluwer Academic/Plenum Publishers.

McCarthy, J., & Still, S. (1993). Hollibrook Accelerated Elementary School. In J. Murphy & P. Hallinger (Eds.), *Restructuring schooling: Learning from ongoing efforts* (pp. 63–83). Newbury Park, CA: Corwin.

McEvoy, A., & Welker, R. (2000). Antisocial behavior, academic failure, and school climate: A critical review. In H. Walker & M. Emstein (Eds.), *Making schools safer and violence free: Critical issues, solutions, and recommended practices* (pp. 130–140). Austin, TX: PRO-ED.

McEwen, B.S. (1995). *Stressful experiences, brain, and emotions: Behavioral and neuroendocrine correlates. The cognitive neurosciences.* Cambridge, MA: The MIT Press.

McFarland, R. (1986). *Coping through assertiveness.* New York: Rosen.

McGoldrick, M., Giordano, J., & Garcia-Preto, N. (2005). *Ethnicity and family therapy* (3rd ed.). New York: Guilford Press.

McKenna, M.C., & Stahl, S.A. (2003). *Assessment for reading instruction.* New York: Guilford Press.

McLoyd, V.C. (1998). Socioeconomic disadvantage and child development. *American Psychologist, 53,* 185–204.

McLoyd, V.C., & Wilson, L. (1994). The strain of living poor: Parenting, social support, and child mental health. In A.C. Huston (Ed.), *Children in poverty* (pp. 105–135). New York: Cambridge.

McNeil, L., & Valenzuela, A. (2001). The harmful impact of the TAAS system of testing in Texas: Beneath the accountability rhetoric. In G. Orfield & M.L. Kornhaber (Eds.), *Raising standards or raising barriers? Inequity and high-stakes testing in public education* (pp. 1–18). New York: The Century Foundation Press.

McPartland, J.M., & Slavin, R.E. (1990). *Policy perspectives: Increasing achievement of at-risk students at each grade level.* Washington, DC: U.S. Department of Education.

Meyer, M.S., & Felton, R.H. (1999). Repeated reading to enhance fluency: Old approaches and new directions. *Annals of Dyslexia, 49,* 283–306.

Miller, P., Mulvey, C., & Martin, N. (1995). What do twin studies reveal about economic returns to education? A comparison of Australian and U.S. findings. *The American Economic Review, 85*(3), 586–599.

Millsap, M.A., Chase, A., Obdeidallah, D., Perez-Smith, A., Brigham, N., & Johnston, K. (2000). *Evaluation of Detroit's Comer Schools and Families Initiative: Final report.* Cambridge, MA: Abt Associates.

Milne, A.M. (1989). Family structure and the achievement of children. In W.J. Weston (Ed.), *Education and the American family* (pp. 32–65). New York: New York University Press.

Milunsky, A., Jick, H., Jick, S.S., Bruell, C.L., MacLaughlin, D.S., Rothman, K.J., et al. (1989). Multivitamin/folic acid supplementation in early pregnancy reduces the prevalence of neural tube defects. *Journal of the American Medical Association, 262*(20), 2847–2852.

Mioduser, D.D., Tur-Kaspa, H.H., & Leitner, I.I. (2000). The learning value of computer-based instruction of early reading skills. *Journal of Computer Assisted Learning, 6*(1), 54–63.

Moll, L.C., Diaz, S., Estrada, E., & Lopes, L.M. (1992). Making contexts: The social construction of lessons in two languages. In M. Saravia-Shore & S.F. Arvizu (Eds.), *Cross-cultural literacy: Ethnographies of communication in multiethnic classrooms* (pp. 339–366). New York: Garland.

Moore, K.L., & Persaud, T.V.N. (1993). *Before we are born: Essentials of embryology and birth defects.* Philadelphia: Elsevier.

Moos, R.H. (1979). *Evaluating educational environments: Procedures, measures, findings, and policy implications.* San Francisco: Jossey-Bass.

Morgan, C.D., & Murray, H.A. (1935). A method of investigating fantasies: The Thematic Apperception Test. *Archives of Neurology and Psychiatry, 34,* 289–306.

Moriarty, M.L., & Fine, M.J. (2001). Educating parents to be advocates for their children. In M.J. Fine & S.W. Lee (Eds.), *Handbook of diversity in parent education* (pp. 315–336). San Diego: Academic Press.

Morrissey, E.S. (1990, June-September). Poverty among rural workers. *Rural Development Perspectives,* 37–42.

Motta, R.W., Little, S.G., & Tobin, M.I. (1993). The use and abuse of human figure drawings. *School Psychology Quarterly, 8,* 162–169.

Moynihan, D.P. (1965). *The negro family: The case for national action.* Washington, DC: Office of Policy Planning and Research, U.S. Department of Labor.

Mulinare, J., Cordero, J.F., Erickson, J.D., & Berry, R.J. (1988). Periconceptional use of multivitamins and the occurrence of neural tube defects. *Journal of the American Medical Association, 260*(21), 341–345.

Mullis, I.V.S., Dossey, J.A., Owen, E.H., & Phillips, G.W. (1991, June). *The state of mathematics achievement: NAEP's 1990 assessment of the nation and the trial assessment of the states.* Princeton, NJ: Educational Testing Service and National Assessment of Education Progress.

Muñoz-Sandoval, A.F., Woodcock, R.W., McGrew, K.S., & Mather, N. (2005). *Bacteria III Woodcock-Munoz Pruebas de Habilidades Cognicitivas.* Itasca, IL: Riverside Publishing.

Murray, J.D., & Keller, P.A. (1991, March). Psychology and rural America: Current status and future directions. *American Psychologist, 46*(3), 220–231.

Naglieri, J.A., & Das, J.P. (1997). *Cognitive Assessment System.* Itasca, IL: Riverside.

Naglieri, J.A., & Das, J.P. (2005). Planning, attention, simultaneous, successive (PASS) theory: A revision of the concept of intelligence. In D.P. Flanagan & P.L. Harrison (Eds.), *Contemporary intellectual assessment: Theories, tests and issues* (2nd ed., pp. 120–135). New York: Guilford Press.

Naglieri, J.A., McNeish, T.J., & Bardos, A.N. (1991). *Draw-A-Person: Screening procedure for emotional disturbance.* Austin, TX: PRO-ED.

Nath, L.R., & Ross, S.M. (2001). The influence of a peer-tutoring training model for implementing cooperative groupings with elementary students. *Educational Technology, Research and Development, 49*(2), 41–56.

National Alliance of Black School Educators (NABSE) & ILIAD Project. (2002). *Addressing over-representation of African American students in special education: The pre referral intervention process. An administrator's guide.* Arlington, VA: Council for Exceptional Children, and Washington, DC: National Alliance of Black School Educators.

National Association of Community Health Centers and National Rural Health Association. (1988). Health care in rural America: The crisis unfolds. In *Report of The Joint Task Force of the National Association of Community Health Centers, Inc., and the National Rural Health Association.* Washington, DC: Author.

National Association of School Psychologists. (2000). *Standards for training and field placement programs in school psychology.* Bethesda, MD: Author.

National Center for Children Exposed to Violence. (2003). *Domestic violence.* New Haven, CT: Yale University Child Study Center. Retrieved August 31, 2007, from http://www.cccev.org/violence/domestic.html

National Center for Children in Poverty. (2003). *Low income children in the United States: A brief demographic profile.* Retrieved May 11, 2007, from http://cpmcnet.columbia.edu/dept/nccp/ecp302.html

National Center for Children in Poverty (2006, September). *Basic facts about low-income children: Birth to age 18.* Retrieved August 30, 2007, from www.nccp.org

National Center for Educational Statistics. (2004). *Issues brief: Educational attainment of high school drop outs eight years later, NCES 2005-026.* Washington, DC: U.S. Department of Education Services. Institute of Education Sciences. Available at http://nces.ed.gov/pubs2005/2005026.pdf

National Center for Health Statistics (NCHS). (2003). *Technical appendix: Vital statistics of the United States-2003.* Washington, DC: U.S. Department of Health and Human Services, Centers for Disease Control and Prevention, National Center for Health Statistics.

National Council of Teachers of Mathematics. (1989). *Curriculum and evaluation standards for school mathematics.* Reston, VA: Author.

National Institute of Child Health and Human Development. (2000). Characteristics and quality of child care for toddlers and preschoolers. *Applied Developmental Science, 4*(3), 116–135.

National Institute on Drug Abuse. (1995, January/February). *Drug use during pregnancy.* Washington, DC: Author.

National Institute on Drug Abuse. (2002). *Research report series methamphetamine abuse addiction.* Washington, DC: Author.

National Institute of Environmental Health Sciences. (2005). *Lead and your health.* Research Triangle Park, NC: National Institute of Health. Retrieved April 17, 2007, from http://w2ww.niehs.nih.gov

National Institutes of Health (NIH). (2000). *Emergent literacy workshop: Current status and research directions.* Washington, DC: Author.

National Institutes of Health (NIH). (2006). *Asthma.* Retrieved August, 1, 2006, from http://www.nhlbi.nih.gov/health/dci/Diseases/Asthma/Asthma_WhatIs.html

National Reading Panel. (2000). *Report of the subgroups: National reading panel.* Washington, DC: National Institute of Child Health and Development.

National Research Council (NRC). (2002). *Minority students in special and gifted education* Washington, DC: National Academies Press.

Nelson, J.R. (2000). Designing schools to meet the needs of students who exhibit disruptive behavior. In H. Walker & M. Epstein (Eds.), *Making schools safer and violence free: Critical issues, solutions, and recommended practices* (pp. 50–57). Austin, TX: PRO-ED.

Nelson, J.R., Covin, G., & Smith, D. (1996). The effects of setting clear limits on the social behaviors of students in the common areas of the school. *Journal for At-Risk Issues, 3,* 10–19.

Neuman, S.B., & Celano, D. (2001). Access to print in low-income and middle-income communities: An ecological study of four neighborhoods. *Reading Research Quarterly, 36*, 8–26.

Nieto, S. (2000). *Affirming diversity: The sociopolitical context of multicultural education* (3rd ed.). New York: Longman.

No Child Left Behind Act of 2001, 115 Stat. 1425, 20 U.S.C. §§ 6301 *et seq.*

Noblit, G.W., Malloy, W.W., & Malloy, C.E. (2001). *The kids got smarter: Case studies of successful Comer schools.* Cresskill, NJ: Hampton Press.

Noll, M.B., Kamps, D., & Seaborn, C.F. (1993). Prereferral intervention for students with emotional or behavioral risks: Use of a behavioral consultation model. *Journal of Emotional and Behavioral Disorders, 1*, 203–214.

Oberg, C.N., Bertrand, J., & Muret-Wagstaff, S. (1999). Psychosocial effects of environmental factors. In V.L. Schwean & D.H. Saklofske (Eds.), *Handbook of psychosocial characteristics of exceptional children* (pp. 95–110). New York: Kluwer Academic/ Plenum.

Ochoa, S.H., Rivera, B.D., & Ford, L. (1997). An investigation of school psychology training pertaining to bilingual psycho-educational assessment of primarily Hispanic students: Twenty-five years after Diana v. California. *Journal of School Psychology, 35*(4), 329–349.

Office of Special Education Programs (2000, December). *Prenatal exposure to alcohol and nicotine: Implications for special education.* Twenty-second annual report to Congress on the implementation of the Individuals with Disabilities Education Act (pp. 1–15 through 1–34). Washington, DC: U.S. Department of Education.

Offord, D.R., Boyle, M.H., Racine, Y.A., & Fleming, J.E. (1992). Outcome, prognosis, and risk in a longitudinal follow-up study. *Journal of the American Academy of Child & Adolescent Psychiatry, 31*, 916–923.

O'Hare, W.P. (1996, October). U.S. poverty myths explored: Many poor work year-round, few still poor after five years. *Population Today: News, Numbers, and Analysis, 24*(10), 1–2.

Oliveti, J.F., Keresmar, C.M., & Redline, S. (1996). Pre- and perinatal risk factors for asthma in inner city African-American children. *American Journal of Epidemiology, 143*, 570–577.

Olweus, D. (1993). *Bullying at school.* Cambridge, MA: Blackwell.

Orpinas, P., Horne, A.M., & Staniszewski, D. (2003). Mini-series: Bullying prevention and intervention: Integrating research and evaluation findings. School bullying: Changing the problem by changing the school. *School Psychology Review, 32*(3), 431–445.

Ortiz, S.O., & Dynda, A.M. (2005). Use of intelligence tests with culturally and linguistically diverse populations. In D.P. Flanagan & P.L. Harrison (Eds.), *Contemporary intellectual assessment* (pp. 545–556). New York: Guilford Press.

Ortiz, S.O., & Ochoa, S.H. (2005). Advances in cognitive assessment of culturally and linguistically diverse individuals (2nd ed.). In D.P. Flanagan & P.I. Harrison (Eds.), *Contemporary intellectual assessment* (pp. 234–250). New York: Guilford Press.

Oswald, D.P., Coutinho, M.J., & Best, A.M. (2002). Community and school predictors of overrepresentation of minority children in special education. In D.J. Losen & G. Orfield (Eds.), *Racial inequity in special education* (pp. 1–14). Cambridge, MA: Harvard Education Press.

Pace, T.M., Robbins, R.R., Choney, S.K., Hill, J.S., Lacey, K., & Blair, G. (2006). A cultural-contextual perspective on the validity of the MMPI-2 with American Indians. *Cultural Diversity and Ethnic Minority Psychology, 12*(2), 320–333.

Padilla, A. (2001). Issues in culturally appropriate assessment. In L.A. Suzuki, J.G. Ponterotto, & P.J. Meller (Eds.), *Handbook of multicultural assessment* (2nd ed., pp. 5–27). San Francisco: Jossey-Bass.

Parke, R., & Buriel, R. (1998). Socialization in the family: Ethnic and ecological perspectives. In W. Damon (Series Ed.) & N. Eisenberg (Vol. Ed.), *Handbook of child psychology:*

Social, emotional, and personality development (Vol. 3, 5th ed., pp. 463–552). New York: John Wiley & Sons.

Parker, S., Greer, S., & Zuckerman, B. (1988). Double jeopardy: The impact of poverty on early child development. *Pediatric Clinics of North America, 35,* 1227–1240.

Parrish, T. (2002). Racial disparities in the identification, funding, and provision of special education. In D.J. Losen & G. Orfield (Eds.), *Racial inequity in special education* (pp. 15–37). Cambridge, MA: Harvard Education Press.

Patrick, H., Hicks, L., & Ryan, A.M. (1997). Relations of perceived social efficacy and social goal pursuit to self-efficacy for academic work. *Journal of Early Adolescence, 17,* 109–128.

Payne, R. (2005). *A framework for understanding poverty* (4th ed.). Highland, TX: Aha! Process Inc.

Peisner-Feinberg, E., & Burchinal, M. (1997). Relations between preschool children's child care experiences and concurrent development: The cost, quality, and outcome study. *Merrill-Palmer Quarterly, 43*(3), 451–477.

Peña, E.D., Iglesias, A., & Lidz, C.S. (2001). Reducing test bias through dynamic assessment of children's word learning ability. *American Journal of Speech-Language Pathology, 10,* 138–154.

Perie, M., Grigg, W., & Dion, G. (2005). *The nation's report card: Mathematics 2005* (NCES 2006-453) U.S. Department of Education. Washington, DC: U.S. Government Printing Office.

Perry, B.D. (1994). Neurobiological sequelae of childhood trauma: PTSD in children. In M. Murburg (Ed.), *Catecholamine function in post traumatic stress disorder: Emerging concept* (pp. 233–255). Washington, DC: American Psychiatric Press.

Perry, B.D. (1997). Incubated in terror: Neurodevelopmental factors in the "cycle of violence." In J. Osofsky (Ed.), *Children, youth and violence: Searching for solutions* (pp. 124–148). New York: Guilford Press.

Peterson, R.L., & Ishii-Jordan, S. (1994). Multicultural education and the education of students with behavioral disorders. In R.L. Peterson & S. Ishii-Jordan (Eds.), *Multicultural issues in the education of students with behavioral disorders* (pp. 3–26). Cambridge, MA: Brookline Books.

Piaget, J. (1971). *The construction of reality in the child.* New York: Ballantine.

Piaget, J., & Inhelder, B. (1969). *The psychology of the child* (H. Weaver, Trans.). London: Routledge & Kegan Paul.

Pianta, R., & Walsh, D.B. (1996). *High-risk children in schools: Constructing sustaining relationships.* New York: Routledge.

Picciano, A.G., (2006). *Data-driven decision making for effective school leadership.* Upper Saddle River, NJ: Pearson.

Pilowsky, D. (1995). Psychopathology among children placed in family foster care. *Psychiatric Services, 46,* 906–910.

Pintrich, P.R., & Blumenfeld, P.C. (1985). Classroom experience and children's self-perception of ability, effort, and conduct. *Journal of Educational Psychology, 77*(6), 646–657.

Pirkle, J.L., Brody, D.J., Gunter, E.W., Kramer, R.A., Paschal, D.C., Flegal, K.M., & Matte, T.D. (1994). The decline in blood lead levels in the United States: The National Health and Nutrition Examination Surveys (NHANES). *Journal of the American Medical Association, 272,* 284–291.

Pliszka, S.R. (2003). *Neuroscience for the mental health clinician.* New York: The Guilford Press.

Pottinger, A.M. (2005). Children's experience of loss by parental migration in inner-city Jamaica. *American Journal of Orthopsychiatry, 75*(4), 485–496.

Pugh, L.C., Milligan, R.A., Frick, K.D., Spatz, D., & Bronner, Y. (2002). Breastfeeding duration, costs, and benefits of a support program for low-income breastfeeding women. *Birth, 29*(2), 95–100.

Purkey, W.W., & Schmidt, J.J. (1996). *Invitational counseling.* Pacific Grove, CA: Brooks/ Cole Thomson Learning.

Putnam, R. (2000). *Bowling alone.* New York: Simon & Schuster.

Quirk, K. (2005). *Haberman's career dedicated to quality public school education.* Milwaukee: University of Wisconsin-Milwaukee.

Ramsey, C.D., Celedon, J.C., Sredl, D.L., Weiss, S.T., & Cloutier, M.M. (2005, March). Predictors of disease severity in children with asthma in Hartford, Connecticut. *Pediatric Pulmonology, 39*(3), 268–275.

Rank, M.R. (2004). *One nation, underpriviledged: Why American poverty affects all.* New York: Oxford University Press.

Red Horse, Y. (1982). A cultural network model: Perspectives for adolescent services and paraprofessional training. In S.M. Manson (Ed.), *New directions in prevention among American Indian and Alaska Native communities* (pp. 36–54). Portland: Oregon Health Science University.

Reinis, S., & Goldman, J.M. (1980). *The development of the brain: Biological and functional perspectives.* Springfield, IL: Charles C. Thomas.

Renfrew, M., Dyson, L., Wallace, L., D'Souza, L., McCormick, F., & Spiby, H. (2005, April). The effectiveness of public health intervention to promote the duration of breastfeeding. London: National Institute for Health and Clinical Excellence (NICE). Retrieved on May 5, 2007, from www.nice.or.uk

Reschly, D., & Tilly, W.D. III (1999). Reform trends and system design alternatives. In D. Reschly, W.D. Tilly III, & J. Grimes (Eds.), *Special education in transition: Functional assessment and noncategorical programming* (pp. 19–48). Longmont, CO: Sopris West.

Reynolds, A.J. (1994). Effects of a preschool plus follow-on intervention for children at risk. *Developmental Psychology, 30*(6), 787–804.

Reynolds, A.J. (2001, February 9). *Chicago child parent centers linked to juvenile crime prevention.* Speech given at Fight Crime: Invest in Kids press conference. Washington, D.C.

Reynolds, A.J., Temple, J.A., Robertson, D.L., & Mann, E.A. (2001, May). Long-term effects of an early childhood intervention on educational achievement and juvenile arrest: A 15-year follow-up of low-income children in public schools, *Journal of the American Medical Association, 285*(18), 2339–2346.

Reynolds, C., & Kamphaus, R. (2004). *Behavior Assessment Scale for Children* (2nd ed.). Circle Pines, MN: American Guidance Service.

Rhodes, R.L., Ochoa, S.H., & Ortiz, S.O. (2005). *Assessing culturally and linguistically diverse students.* New York: Guilford Press.

Ripple, C.H., & Zigler, E. (2003). Research, policy, and the federal role in prevention initiatives for children. *American Psychologist, 58*(6/7), 482–490.

Roberts, G.E., & Gruber, C. (2005). *Robert-2 Manual.* Los Angeles: Western Psychological Services.

Roberts, M.C., Jacobs, A.K., Puddy, R.W., Nyre, J.E., & Vernberg, E.M. (2003). Treating children with serious emotional disturbances in schools and community: The intensive mental health program. *Professional Psychology: Research and Practice, 34*(5), 519–526.

Rodriguez, E.M., Mofenson, L.M., Chang, B.H., Rich, K.C., Fowler, M.G., Smeriglio, V., et al. (1996). Association of maternal drug use during pregnancy with maternal HIV culture positivity and perinatal HIV transmission. *AIDS, 10*(3), 273–282.

Rogers, M.F., Caldwell, M.B., Gwinn, M.L., & Simonds, R.L. (1994). Epidemiology of pediatric human immunodeficiency virus infection in the United States. *Acta Paediatrics,* (Suppl. 400), 5–7.

Rorschach, H. (1942). *Psychodiagnostics* (5th ed.). Bern, Switzerland: Hans Huber.

Rosado, J.W. (1986, June). Towards an interfacing of Hispanic cultural variables with school psychology service delivery systems. *Professional Psychology: Research and Practice, 17*(3), 191–199.

Rose, C. (1985). *Empowering the spectrum of your mind.* Flushing, NY: Spectrum Educational Services.

Roseberry-McKibbin, C. (2002). *Multicultural students with special language needs* (2nd ed.). Oceanside, CA: Academic Communication Associates.

Rosen, J.F. (1995). Adverse health effects of lead at low exposure levels: Trends in the management of childhood lead poisoning. *Toxicology, 77,* 7–11.

Rosman, E., Kass, D., & Kirsch, J. (2006). *High-quality preschool: The key to crime prevention and school success in Iowa.* Washington, DC: Fight Crime: Invest in Kids.

Ross, C.E. (2000). Neighborhood disadvantage and adult depression. *Journal of Health and Social Behavior, 41,* 177–187.

Ross, S.M., Wang, L.W., Alberg, M., Sanders, W.L., Wright, S.P., & Stringfield, S. (2001, April). *Fourth-year achievement results on the Tennessee Value-Added Assessment System for restructuring schools in Memphis.* Paper presented at the annual meeting of the American Educational Research Association, Seattle.

Ross, S.M., Wang, L.W., Sanders, W.L., Wright, S.P., & Stringfield, S. (1999). *Two- and three-year achievement results on the Tennessee Value-Added Assessment System for restructuring schools in Memphis.* Memphis: Center for Research in Educational Policy.

Rumberger, R.W. (1995). Dropping out of middle school: A multilevel analysis of students and schools. *American Educational Research Journal, 32*(3), 583–625.

Rustein, R.M., Conlon, C.J., & Batshaw, M.L. (1997). In M.L. Batshaw (Ed.), *Children with disabilities* (4th ed., pp. 163–182). Baltimore: Paul H. Brookes Publishing Co.

Rutter, M. (1979). Protective factors in children's responses to stress and disadvantage. In M.W. Kent & J.E. Rolf (Eds.), *Primary prevention in psychopathology* (pp. 49–74). Hanover, NH: University Press of New England.

Rutter, M. (1990). Psychosocial resilience and protective mechanisms. In J. Rolf, A.S. Masten, D. Cicchetti, K.H. Nuechterlein, & S. Weintraub (Eds.), *Risk and protective factors in the development of psychopathology* (pp. 181–214). New York: Cambridge University Press.

Rutter, M. (2000). Resilience reconsidered: Conceptual considerations, empirical findings, and policy implications. In J.P. Shonkoff & S.J. Meisels (Eds.), *Handbook of early intervention* (2nd ed., pp. 651–681). New York: Cambridge University Press.

Rutter, M., & Garmezy, N. (1983). Developmental psychopathology. In E.M. Hetherington (Ed.), *Manual of child psychology, IV: Social and personality development* (pp. 775–912). New York: John Wiley & Sons.

Rutter, M., & Madge, N. (1976). *Cycles of deprivation.* London: Heinemann.

Ryan, R.M. (1985). Thematic Apperception Test. In D.J. Keyser & R.C. Swetland (Eds.), *Test critiques* (Vol. 2, pp. 799–814). Kansas City, MO: Test Corporation of America.

Sadauskaite-Kuehne, V., Ludvigsson, J., Pagaiga, Z., Jasinskiene, E., & Samuelsson, U. (2004). Longer breastfeeding is an independent protective factor against development of type 1 diabetes mellitus in childhood. *Diabetes Metabolic Research Review, 10*(2), 150–157.

Saddler, T.W. (1995). *Langman's medical embryology.* Baltimore: Williams & Wilkins.

Sameroff, A.J., & Chandler, M.J. (1975). Reproductive risk and the continuum of caretaking casuality. In F.D. Horowitz (Ed.), *Review of child development research* (Vol. 4, pp. 157–243). Chicago: University of Chicago Press.

Sameroff, A.J., Gutman, L.M., & Peck, S.C. (2003). Adaptation among youth facing multiple risk. In S. Luthar (Ed.), *Resilience and vulnerability: Adaptation in the context of childhood adversities* (pp. 364–391). New York: Cambridge University Press.

Sameroff, A.J., Seifer, R., Zax, M., & Barocas, R. (1987). Early indicators of developmental risk: The Rochester longitudinal study. *Schizophrenia Bulletin, 13,* 383–393.

Samuda, R.J., Kong, S.L. Cummins, J., Pascual-Leone, J., & Lewis, J. (1991). *Assessment and placement of minority students.* New York: C. J. Hogrefe/Intercultural Social Science Publications.

Sanders-Laufer, D., DeBruin, W., & Edelson, P.J. (1991). Pneumocystis carinii infections in HIV-infected children. *Pediatric Clinics of North America, 38,* 69–88.

Saraswathi, T.S. (1999). Adult–child continuity in India: Is adolescence a myth or an emerging reality? In T.S. Saraswathi (Ed.), *Culture, socialization, and human development: Theory, research, and application in India* (pp. 119–133). New Delhi: Sage.

Saravia-Shore, M., & Garcia, E. (1995). Diverse teaching strategies for diverse learners. In Association for Supervision and Curriculum Development (Ed.), *Educating everybody's children* (pp. 47–74). Alexandria, VA: Association for Supervision and Curriculum Development.

Sattes, B. (1985). *Parent involvement: A review of the literature* (Report No. 21). Charleston, WV: Appalachia Educational Laboratory.

Sattler, J.M. (2001). *Assessment of children: Cognitive applications* (4th ed.). San Diego: Author.

Sattler, J.M. (2002). *Assessment of children: Behavioral and clinical applications* (4th ed.). San Diego: Author.

Sattler, J.M., & Hoge, R.D. (2006). *Assessment of children: Behavioral, social, and clinical foundations* (5th ed.). La Mesa, CA: Authors.

Sbordone, R.J., & Long, C.J. (1996) *Ecological validity of neuropsychological testing.* Delray Beach, FL: GR Press/St. Lucie Press.

Scheibel, A. (2000, May 6). *A journey through the development of the human brain.* From a speech given at the Spring 2000 Symposium on Brain Research: Implications for Teaching and Learning, Berkeley, California.

Schill, M.T., Kratochwill, T.R., & Gardner, W.I. (1996). Conducting a functional analysis of behavior. In M.J. Breen & C.R. Fiedler (Eds.), *Behavioral approach to assessment of youth with emotional/behavioral disorders* (pp. 83–179). Austin, TX: PRO-ED.

Schore, A. (2003). *Affect regulation and disorder of the self.* New York: W.W. Norton and Company.

Schorr, L. (1988). *Within our reach: Breaking the cycle of disadvantage.* New York: Doubleday.

Schwean, V.L., & Saklofske, D.H. (1999). *Handbook of psychosocial characteristics of exceptional children.* New York: Kluwer Academic/Plenum.

Scott, G.F. (1994). *Developmental biology.* Sunderland, MA: Sinauer Associates.

Scott, J., & Leonhardt, D. (2005). Shadowy lines that still divide. In B. Keller (Ed.), *Correspondents of the New York Times: Class matters* (pp. 1–26). New York: Times Books Henry Holt and Company.

Shapiro, E.S. (2004). *Academic skills problems* (3rd ed.). New York: Guilford Press.

Sharkey, K.J., & Ritzler, B.A. (1985). Comparing diagnostic validity of the TAT and a new picture projection test. *Journal of Personality Assessment, 49,* 406–412.

Shaw, G.M., Schaffer, D., Velie, E.M., Morland, K., & Harris, J.A. (1995). Periconceptional vitamin use, dietary folate, and the occurrence of neural tube defects. *Epidemiology, 6*(3), 219–226.

Shaywitz, S. (2003). *Overcoming dyslexia.* New York: Alfred A. Knopf.

Sheras, P.L., Abidin, R.R., & Konold, T.R. (1998). *Stress index for parents of adolescents.* Lutz, FL: Psychological Assessment Resources.

Shils, M., Olson, J., Shike, M., & Ross. A.C. (1999). *Nutrition in health and disease.* Baltimore: Williams & Wilkins.

Shingles, B., & Lopez-Reyna, N. (2002). *Cultural sensitivity in the implementation of discipline policies and practices* (ERIC Document Reproduction Services No. ED435950).

Shinn, M.R. (1989). *Curriculum-based measurement: Assessing special children.* New York: Guilford Press.

Shinn, M.R. (1998). *Advanced applications of curriculum-based measurement.* New York: Guilford Press.

Shiono, P., & Behrman, R.E. (1995, Spring). *Low birth weight: Analysis and recommendations.* Retrieved July 17, 2006, from http://www.futureofchildren.org/information2826/information_show.htm?doc_id=79875

Shonkoff, J.P., & Phillips, D.A. (2000). *From neurons to neighborhoods: The science of early child development.* Washington, DC: National Academies Press.

Shore, R. (1997). *Rethinking the brain: New insights into early development.* New York: Families and Work Institute.

Shure, M.B., & Spivac, G. (1982). Interpersonal problem solving in young children: A cognitive approach to prevention. *American Journal of Community Psychology, 10*(3), 341–355.

Siegel, L.S. (1999). Issues in the definition and diagnosis of learning disabilities: A perspective on Guckenberger v. Boston University. *Journal of Learning Disabilities, 32,* 304–319.

Siegler, R.S. (1998). *Children's thinking* (3rd ed.). Upper Saddle River, NJ: Prentice Hall.

Simonds, R.J., & Rogers, M.F. (1992). Epidemiology of HIV infection in children and other populations. In A.C. Crocker, H.J. Cohen, & T.A. Kastner (Eds.), *HIV infection and developmental disabilities: A resource for service providers* (pp. 3–13). Baltimore: Paul H. Brookes Publishing Co.

Simpson, R.L. (1996). *Working with parents and families of exceptional children and youth* (3rd ed.). Austin, TX: PRO-ED.

Sizer, T.R. (2004). Preamble: A reminder for Americans. In D. Meier & G. Wood (Eds.), *Many children left behind* (pp. xvii–xxii). Boston: Beacon Press.

Slavin, R.E. (1988). Cooperative learning and student achievement. *Educational leadership, 45*(2), 31–33.

Slavin, R.E. (1990). Research in cooperative learning: Concerns and controversy. *Educational Leadership, 42,* 52–54.

Slavin, R.E., Karweit, N.L., & Wasik, B.A. (1992, December). Preventing early school failure. *Educational Leadership, 50*(4), 10–18.

Smith, L.A., Hatcher-Ross, J.L., Wertheimer, R., & Kahn, R.S. (2005, March-April). Rethinking race/ethnicity, income, and childhood asthma: Racial/ethnic disparities concentrated among the very poor. *Public Health Report, 120*(2), 109–116.

Sooman, A., & Macintyre, S. (1995). Health and perceptions of the local environment in socially contrasting neighborhoods in Glasgow. *Health and Place, 1,* 15–26.

Spiegel, H.M.L, & Bonwit, A.M. (Ed.) (2002). HIV infection in children. In M.L. Batshaw (Ed.), *Children with disabilities.* (5th ed., pp. 123–140). Baltimore: Paul H. Brookes Publishing Co.

Sprague, J.R., & Golly, A. (2004). *Best behavior: Building positive behavior supports in schools.* Longmont, CO: Sopris West.

Sprague, J.R., Sugai, G., Horner, R.H., & Walker, H.M. (1999). Using office discipline referral data to evaluate school-wide discipline and violence prevention interventions. *Oregon School Study Council Bulletin, 42*(2). Eugene: University of Oregon.

Sprague, J.R., Sugai, G., & Walker, H. (1998). Antisocial behavior in schools. In T.S. Watson & F.M. Gresham (Eds.), *Handbook of child behavior therapy* (pp. 451–474). New York: Kluwer Academic/Plenum.

Sprague, J.R., & Walker, H.M. (2005). *Safe and healthy schools.* New York: Guilford Press.

Stanger, C. (1996). Behavioral assessment: An overview. In M.J. Breen & C.R. Fiedler (Eds.), *Behavioral approach to assessment of youth with emotional/behavioral disorders* (pp. 3–17). Austin, TX: PRO-ED.

Stearn, L.N., & Nuñez, R. (1999). *Homeless in America: A children's story: Part one.* New York: The Institute for Children and Poverty.

Steege, M.W., & Brown-Chidsey, R. (2005). Functional behavioral assessment: The cornerstone of effective problem solving. In R. Brown-Chidsey (Ed.), *Assessment for intervention: A problem-solving approach* (pp. 131–154). New York: Guilford Press.

Stephens, R.D. (1995). *Safe schools: A handbook for violence prevention.* Bloomington, IN: National Education Service.

Stewart, J. (1986). *Bridges, not walls: A book about interpersonal communication skills.* New York: Random House.

Stover, D. (1993, May). School boards caught up in debate over tracking. *School Board News, 13*(9), 1–8.

Straus, M. (1992). *Children as witness to marital violence: A risk factor.* Columbus, OH: Ross Laboratories.

Sugai, G., & Horner, R.H. (2002). The evolution of discipline practices: School-wide positive behavior supports. *Child and Family Behavior Therapy, 24,* 23–50.

Sugai, G., Horner, R.H., Dunlap, G., Hieneman, M., Lewis, T.J., Nelson, C.M., et al. (2000). Applying positive behavioral support and functional behavioral assessment in schools. *Journal of Positive Behavior Interventions, 2,* 131–143.

Sugai, G., & Lewis, T.J. (Eds.). (1999). Developing positive behavioral support for students with challenging behaviors. *Miniseries Monograph of the International Conference for Children with Behavior Disorders.* Reston, VA: Council for Children with Behavior Disorders.

Sunderland, M. (2006). *The science of parenting.* New York: DK Publishing.

Suzuki, L.A., Ponterotto, J.G., & Meller, P.J. (2001a). *Handbook of multicultural assessment* (2nd ed.). San Francisco: Jossey-Bass.

Suzuki, L.A., Ponterotto, J.G., & Meller, P.J. (2001b). Multicultural assessment: Trends and directions revisited. In L.A. Suzuki, J.G. Ponterotto, & P.J. Meller (Eds.), *Handbook of multicultural assessment* (2nd ed., pp. 569–574). San Francisco: Jossey-Bass.

Sylwester, R. (1995). *A celebration of neurons: An educator's guide to the human brain.* Alexandria, VA: Association for Supervision and Curriculum Development.

Tagiuri, R. (1968). The concept of organizational climate. In R. Tagiuri & G.H. Litwin (Eds.), *Organizational climate: Exploration of a concept* (pp. 10–32). Cambridge, MA: Harvard University Press.

Tartasky, D. (1999, October). Asthma in the inner city: A growing public health problem. *Holistic Nursing Practice, 14*(1), 37–46.

Tarter, R.E., Kiriski, L., Vanyukov, M., Cornelius, J., Payer, K., Shoul, G.D., & Giancola, P.R. (2002). Predicting adolescent violence impact of family, history, substance use, psychiatric history, and social adjustment. *American Journal of Psychiatry, 159,* 1541–1547.

Taylor, B.M., Pearson, P.D. Peterson, D.S., & Rodriguez, M.C. (2003, September). Reading growth in high-poverty classrooms: The influences of teacher practices that encourage cognitive engagement in literacy learning. *The Elementary School Journal, 104*(1), 3–28.

Taylor, R.B., & Hale, M. (1986). Testing alternative models of fear of crime. *Journal of Criminal Law and Criminology, 77,* 151–189.

Taylor, W.R., & Newacheck, P.W. (1992). Impact of childhood asthma on health. *Pediatrics, 90,* 657–662.

Teeter Ellison, P.A., & Semrud-Clikeman, M. (2007). *Child neuropsychology.* New York: Springer.

Tharp, R.G. (1992). Cultural compatibility and diversity: Implications for the urban classroom. *Teaching Thinking and Problem Solving, 14*(6), 1–4.

Thomas, G.V., & Jolley, R.P. (1998). Drawing conclusions: A re-examination of empirical and conceptual bases for psychological evaluations of children from their drawings. *British Journal of Clinical Psychology, 37*, 127–139.

Thomas, T.N. (1992). Psychoeducational adjustment of English-speaking Caribbean and Central American immigrant children in the United States. *School Psychology Review, 21*(4), 566–576.

Thomas, T.N., & Schare, M.L. (2000). A cross-cultural analysis of alcoholism and social alienation in Panama and the United States. In F. Columbus (Ed.), *Advances in psychology research* (Vol. 1, pp. 163–179). Huntington, NY: Nova Science Publisher.

Thomas, W.P., & Collier, V.P. (2002). *A national study of school effectiveness for language minority students' long-term academic achievement.* Retrieved December 10, 2006, from http://www.crede.uscu.edu/research/llaa1.html

Thurston, L.P., & Navarrete, L.A. (2003). Rural, poverty-level mothers: A comparative study of those with and without children who have special needs. *Rural Special Education Quarterly, 22*(2), 15–22.

Tjossem, T. (1976). *Intervention strategies for high-risk infants and young children.* Baltimore: University Park Press.

Torgesen, J.K. (2004, Fall). Avoiding the devastating downward spiral. *American Educator,* 6–45.

Tozer, S. (2000). Class. In D. Gabbart (Ed.), *Knowledge and power in the global economy: Politics and the rhetoric of school reform* (pp. 149–159). Mahwah, NJ: Lawrence Erlbaum Associates.

Trachtenbarg, D.E. (1996). Getting the lead out: When is treatment necessary? *Postgraduate Medicine, 99*, 201–202, 207–218.

Tucker, C.M., & Herman, K.C. (2002). Using culturally sensitive theories and research to meet the academic needs of low-income African-American children. *American Psychologist, 57*(10), 762–773.

U.S. Bureau of the Census. (2005). *Statistical abstract of the United States: The national data book.* Washington, DC: U.S. Government Printing Office.

U.S. Census Bureau. (2004). *Data for 2004: Child Trends' calculations of U.S. Census Bureau, School Enrollment—Social and economic characteristics of students: October 2004: Detailed tables: Table 1.* Retrieved May 11, 2007, from http://www.census.gov/population/www/socdemo/school/cps2004.html

U.S. Department of Agriculture Economic Research Service. (2005, March). *Rural children at a glance. Economic Information Bulletin Number 1.* Retrieved April 13, 2007, from www.ers.usda.gov/publications/EIBI/eib.pdf

U.S. Department of Education. (2001). *The longitudinal evaluation of school change and performance in Title I schools: Final report.* Washington, DC: Planning and Evaluation Service, U.S. Department of Education.

U.S. Department of Education. (2002). *No Child Left Behind: A desktop reference.* Washington, DC: U.S. Department of Education, Office of Elementary and Secondary Education.

U.S. Department of Health and Human Services. (2000, January). *Healthy People 2010.* (Conference Edition in Two Volumes). Washington, DC: Author.

U.S. Environmental Protection Agency. (2006). *Lead in paint, dust, and soil.* Retrieved July 27, 2006, from http://www.epa.gov/lead/

Valentine, C. (1968). *Culture and poverty.* Chicago: University of Chicago Press.

Vane, J.R. (1981). The Thematic Apperception Test: A review. *Clinical Psychology Review, 1*, 319–336.

Verderber, R., & Verderber, K. (1989). *Interact: Using interpersonal communication skills.* Belmont, CA: Wadsworth.

Verstegen, D.A. (1998). A new ethic for children. *Journal for a just and caring education, 4*, 393–417.

Vygotsky, L.S. (1962). *Thought and language.* Cambridge, MA: The MIT Press.

Vygotsky, L.S. (1978). *Mind in society: Development of higher mental processes.* Cambridge, MA: Harvard University Press. (Original works published 1930, 1933, and 1935.)

Wacquant, L., & Wilson, W.J. (1989). The costs of racial and class exclusion in the inner city. *Annals of the Academy of Political and Social Science, 501,* 8–25.

Wadsworth, M.E., & Achenbach, T.M. (2005). Explaining the link between socioeconomic status and psychopathology: Testing two mechanisms of the social causation hypothesis. *Journal of Consulting and Clinical Psychology, 73*(6), 1146–1153.

Wagner, M., Kutash, K., Duchnowski, A.J., Epstein, M.H., & Sumi, W.C. (2005, Summer). The children and youth we serve: A national picture of the characteristics of students with emotional disturbances receiving special education. *Journal of Emotional and Behavioral Disorders, 13*(2), 79–96.

Wakschlag, L.S., Pickett, K.E., Kasza, K.E., & Loeber, R. (2006, April). Is prenatal smoking associated with a developmental pattern of conduct problems in young boys? *Journal of the American Academy of Child Adolescent Psychiatry, 45*(4), 461–467.

Walker, H.M., Irvin, L.K., & Sprague, J.R. (1997). Violence prevention and school safety: Issues, problems, approaches, and recommended solutions. *Oregon School Study Council Bulletin, 41*(1).

Walton, J.R., Nuttall, R.L., & Vazquez-Nuttall, E. (1997). The impact of war on the mental health of children: A Salvadoran study. *Child Abuse and Neglect, 21,* 737–749.

Warman, K.L., Silver, E.J., & Stein, R.E.K. (2001, August). Asthma symptoms, morbidity, and anti-inflammatory use in inner-city children. *Pediatrics, 108*(2), 277–282.

Wasik, B., & Slavin, R.E. (1993). Preventing early reading failure with one to one tutoring: A review of five programs. *Reading Research Quarterly, 28*(2), 179–200.

Wasserman, J.D. (2003). Nonverbal assessment of personality and psychopathology. In R.S. McCallum (Ed.), *Handbook of nonverbal assessment* (pp. 283–313). New York: Kluwer Academic/Plenum.

Watkins, J.M., & Watkins, D.A. (1984). *Social policy in the rural setting.* New York: Springer.

Watson, T.S., Gresham, F.M., & Skinner, C.H. (2001). Introduction to the mini-series: Issues and procedures for implementing functional behavior assessment in schools. *School Psychology Review, 30*(2), 153–155.

Weber, M. (1968). *Economy and society.* New York: Bedminster Press

Webster, A. (1990). *Introduction to the sociology of development* (2nd ed.). London: McMillan Press.

Wechsler, D. (2004). *Wechsler Intelligence Scale for Children—Fourth Edition* (WISC-IV Spanish). San Antonio, TX: Harcourt Assessment.

Weinstein, R.S., Gregory, A., & Strambler, M.J. (2004). Intractable self-fulfilling prophecies: Fifty years after Brown v. Board of Education. *American Psychologist, 59,* 511–520.

Weiss, A., & Fantuzzo, J.W. (2001). Multivariate impact of health and caretaking risk factors on the school adjustment of first graders. *Journal of Community Psychology, 29,* 141–160.

Weissberg, R.P., & Greenberg, M.T. (1998). School and community competence-enhancement and prevention programs. In W. Damon (Series Ed.) & I.E. Sigel & K.A. Renninger (Vol. Eds.), *Handbook of child psychology: Child psychology in practice* (Vol. 4, 5th ed., pp. 877–954). New York: John Wiley & Sons.

Weisz, J.R., & Weiss, B. (1991). Studying the "referability" of child clinical problems. *Journal of Consulting and Clinical Psychology, 59,* 266–273.

Wentzel, K.R. (1991). Relations between social competence and academic achievement in early adolescence. *Child Development, 62,* 1066–1078.

Werner, E.E., & Smith, R.S. (1980). An epidemiologic perspective on some antecedents and consequences of childhood mental health problems and learning disabilities. *Annual Progress in Child Psychiatry and Child Development, 1,* 33–147.

Werner, E.E., & Smith, R.S. (1982). *Vulnerable but invincible: A study of resilient children.* New York: McGraw-Hill.

Werner, E.E., & Smith, R.S. (1992). *Overcoming the odds: High risk children from birth to adulthood.* Ithaca, NY: Cornell University Press.

Wheeler, S.F. (1993). Substance abuse during pregnancy. *Primary Care Clinics in Office Practice, 20,* 191–207.

White, K.R. (1982). The relationship between socioeconomic status and academic achievement. *Psychological Bulletin, 91,* 461–481.

Whitebook, M. (2003). *Early education quality: Higher teacher qualification for better learning environments. A review of the literature.* Berkeley, CA: Center for the Study of Child Care Employment, Institute of Industrial Relations.

Williams, S., Anderson, J., McGee, R., & Silva, P.A. (1990). Risk factors for behavioral and emotional disorder in preadolescent children. *Journal of the American Academy of Child and Adolescent Psychiatry, 29,* 413–419.

Williams, S., MacMillan, H., & Jamieson, E. (2006). The potential benefits of remaining in school on the long-term mental health functioning of physically and sexually abused children: Beyond the academic domain. *American Journal of Orthopsychiatry, 76*(1), 18–22.

Wilson, W.J. (1987). *The truly disadvantaged.* Chicago: The University of Chicago Press.

Wilson, W.J. (2003). Race, class, and urban poverty: A rejoinder. *Ethnic and Racial Studies, 26*(6), 1096–1114.

Winter, S. (1986). Peers as paired reading tutors. *British Journal of Special Education, 13*(3), 103–106.

Wirt, R.D., Lachar, D., Seat, P.D., & Broen, W.E. Jr. (2001). *Personality Inventory for Children–Second Edition.* Los Angeles: Western Psychological Services.

Witt, J.C. (1990). Complaining, precopernican thought, and the univariate linear mind: Questions for school-based behavioral consultation research. *School Psychology Review, 19,* 367–377.

Witt, J.C., Daly, E.J. III, & Noell, G.H. (2000). Functional assessments: A step-by-step guide to solving academic and behavioral problems. Longmont, CO: Sopris West.

Wolfe, P. (2001). *Brain matters: Translating research into classroom practice.* Alexandria, VA: Association for Supervision and Curriculum Development.

Wood, G. (2004). A view from the field: NCLB's effects on classrooms and schools. In D. Meier & G. Wood (Eds.), *Many children left behind* (pp. 33–50). Boston: Beacon Press.

Wright, J. (2001). The *savvy teacher's guide: Reading interventions that works.* Retrieved December 10, 2006, from http://www.interventioncentral.org

Wright, M.O., & Masten, A.S. (2006). Resilience processes in development. In S. Goldstein & R.B. Brooks (Eds.), *Resilience in children* (pp. 17–37). New York: Springer Science.

Wright, R.O., Shannon, M.W., Wright, R.J., & Hu, H. (1999). Association between iron deficiency and low-level lead poisoning in an urban primary care clinic. *American Journal of Public Health, 89,* 1049–1053.

Wunsch, M.J., Conlon, C.J., & Scheidt, P.C. (2002). Substance abuse: A preventable threat to development. In M.L. Batshaw (Ed.), *Children with disabilities* (5th ed., pp. 107–124). Baltimore: Paul H. Brookes Publishing Co.

Wyman, P.A. (2003). Emerging perspectives on context specificity of children's adaptation and resilience: Evidence from a decade of research with urban children in adversity. In S.S. Luthar (Ed.), *Resilience and vulnerability: Adaptation in the context of childhood adversities* (pp. 293–317). New York: Cambridge University Press.

Yale School Development Program Staff. (2004). Essential understandings of the Yale

School Development Program. In E.T. Joyner, J.P. Comer, & M. Ben-Avie (Eds.), *Transforming school leadership and management to support student learning and development* (pp. 15–23). Thousand Oaks, CA: Corwin Press.

Zemelman, S., Daniels, H., & Hyde, A. (1998). *Best practice: New standards for teaching and learning in America's schools* (2nd ed.). Portsmouth, NH: Heinemann.

Zhang, D., & Katsiyannis, A. (2002, May). Minority representation in special education. *Remedial & Special Education, 23*(3), 180–187.

Zill, N., & Schenborn, C. (1990). *The health of our nation's children: Developmental, learning, and emotional problems–1988 advance data.* Hyattsville, MD: National Center for Health Statistics.

Appendix

Teacher Interview Form for Academic Problems

Student: _____   Teacher: _____
Date of Birth: _____   Date: _____
Grade: _____   School: _____
Interviewer: _____

General

Why was this student referred? _____

What type of academic problem(s) does this student have?

_____

Reading

Primary type of reading series used   Secondary type of reading used
☐ Basal reader   ☐ Basal reader
☐ Literature based   ☐ Literature based
☐ Trade books   ☐ Trade books
     ☐ None

Reading series title (if applicable) _____
Grade level of series currently used by student _____
Title of book in series currently used by student _____
How many groups do you teach? _____
Which group is this student assigned to? _____
At this point in the school year, where is the average student in your class reading?
     Level and book _____
     Place in book (beginning, midde, end, specific page) _____
     Time allotted/day for reading _____

How is time divided? (Independent seatwork? Small group? Cooperative group? Large group?) _____

How is placement in reading program determined? _____

How are changes made in the program? _____

Does this student participate in remedial reading programs? How much?

Typical daily instructional procedures _____

Contingencies for completion? _____

Types of interventions already attempted:
Simple (e.g., reminders, cues, self-monitoring, motivation, feedback, instructions):

Moderate (e.g., increasing time of existing instruction, extra tutoring sessions):

Intensive (e.g., changed curriculum, changed instructional modality, changed instructional grouping, added intensive one-to-one):

Frequency and duration of interventions used:

Extent to which interventions were successful:

Daily scores (if available) for past 2 weeks _____

Group standardized test results (if available) _____

Oral Reading

How does student read orally compared with others in his or her reading group?
_____ Much worse   _____ Somewhat worse   _____ About the same
_____ Somewhat better   _____ Much better
In the class?
_____ Much worse   _____ Somewhat worse   _____ About the same
_____ Somewhat better   _____ Much better

Word Attack

Does the student attempt unknown words?

_____

Word Knowledge/Sight Vocabulary

How does the student's word knowledge (vocabulary) compare with others in his or her reading group?

_____ Much worse   _____ Somewhat worse   _____ About the same
_____ Somewhat better   _____ Much better

In the class?

_____ Much worse   _____ Somewhat worse   _____ About the same
_____ Somewhat better   _____ Much better

How does the student's sight-word vocabulary compare with others in his or her reading group?

_____ Much worse   _____ Somewhat worse   _____ About the same
_____ Somewhat better   _____ Much better

In the class?

_____ Much worse   _____ Somewhat worse   _____ About the same
_____ Somewhat better   _____ Much better

Comprehension

How well does the student seem to understand what he or she reads compared with others in his or her reading group?

_____ Much worse   _____ Somewhat worse   _____ About the same
_____ Somewhat better   _____ Much better

In the class?

_____ Much worse   _____ Somewhat worse   _____ About the same
_____ Somewhat better   _____ Much better

Areas of comprehension where student has success (+)/difficulty (−):

_____ Main ideas
_____ Prediction
_____ Recollection of facts
_____ Identifying plot
_____ Identifying main characters
_____ Synthesizing the story
_____ Other (describe):

_____

_____

Behavior During Reading

Rate the following areas from 1 to 5 (1 = very unsatisfactory, 3 = satisfactory, 5 = superior).

Reading Group

a. Oral reading ability (as evidenced in reading group)   _____
b. Volunteers answers   _____
c. When called upon, gives correct answer   _____
d. Attends to other students when they read aloud   _____
e. Knows the appropriate place in book   _____

Independent Seatwork

a. Stays on task   _____
b. Completes assigned work in required time   _____
c. Work is accurate   _____
d. Works quietly   _____
e. Remains in seat when required   _____

Homework (if any)

a. Handed in on time   _____
b. Is complete   _____
c. Is accurate   _____

Mathematics

Curriculum series _____

What are the specific problems in math? _____

Time allotted/day for math _____

How is time divided? (Independent seatwork? Small group? Large group? Cooperative group?)

_____

Are your students grouped in math? _____

If so, how many groups do you have, and in which group is this student placed? _____

_____

For an **average** performing student in your class, at what point in the planned course format would you consider this student at mastery? _____

_____

For an **average** performing student in your class, at what point in the planned course format would you consider this student instructional? _____

For an **average** performing student in your class, at what point in the planned course format would you consider this student frustrational? _____

For the **targeted** student in your class, at what point in the planned course format would you consider this student at mastery? _____

For the **targeted** student in your class, at what point in the planned course format would you consider this student instructional? _____

For the **targeted** student in your class, at what point in the planned course format would you consider this student frustrational? _____

How is mastery assessed? _____
Describe any difficulties this student has in applying math skills in these areas:
Numeration: _____
Estimation: _____
Time: _____
Money: _____
Measurement: _____
Geometry: _____
Graphic display: _____
Interpretation of graph: _____
Word problems: _____
Other: _____
How are changes made in the student's math program? _____

Does this student participate in remedial math programs? _____
Typical daily instructional procedures _____

Contingencies for accuracy? _____
Contingencies for completion? _____
Types of interventions already attempted:
   Simple (e.g., reminders, cues, self-monitoring, motivation, feedback, instruction):

_____

   Moderate (e.g., increasing time of existing instruction, extra tutoring sessions):

_____

Intensive (e.g., changed curriculum, changed instructional modality, changed instructional grouping, added intensive one-to-one):

_____

_____

Frequency and duration of intervention used: _____

Extent to which interventions were successful: _____

Daily scores (if available) for past 2 weeks _____

Group standardized test results (if available) _____

Behavior During Math

Rate the following areas from 1 to 5 (1 = very unsatisfactory, 3 = satisfactory, 5 = superior)

Math Group (large)

a. Volunteers answers   _____

b. When called upon, gives correct answer   _____

c. Attends to other students when they give answers   _____

d. Knows the appropriate place in math book   _____

Math Group (small)

a. Volunteers answers   _____

b. When called upon, gives correct answer   _____

c. Attends to other students when they give answers   _____

d. Knows the appropriate place in math book   _____

Math Group (cooperative)

a. Volunteers answers   _____

b. Contributes to group objectives   _____

c. Attends to other students when they give answers   _____

d. Facilitates others in group to participate   _____

e. Shows appropriate social skills in group   _____

Independent Seatwork

a. Stays on task   _____

b. Completes assigned work in required time   _____

c. Work is accurate   _____

d. Works from initial directions   _____

e. Works quietly   _____

f. Remains in seat when required   _____

Homework (if any)

a. Handed in on time   _____
b. Is complete   _____
c. Is accurate   _____

Spelling

Type of material used for spelling instruction:
☐ Published spelling series
    Title of series _____
☐ Basal reading series
    Title of series _____
☐ Teacher-made materials _____
☐ Other _____
Level of instruction (if applicable) _____
At this point in the school year, where is the average student in your class spelling?
    Level, place in book _____
Time allotted/day for spelling _____
How is time divided? (Independent seatwork? Small group? Cooperative group?)
_____

How is placement in the spelling program determined? _____
How are changes made in the program? _____
Typical daily instructional procedures _____
_____

Types of interventions already attempted:
    Simple (e.g., reminders, cues, self-monitoring, motivation, feedback, instructions):
_____

    Moderate (e.g., increasing time of existing instruction, extra tutoring sessions):
_____

    Intensive (e.g., changed curriculum, changed instructional modality, changed instructional grouping, added intensive one-to-one):
_____

Frequency and duration of intervention used: _____
_____

Extent to which interventions were successful: _____
_____

Contingencies for accuracy? _____
_____

Contingencies for completion? _____
_____

Writing

Please describe the type of writing assignment you give? _____

_____

Compared with others in your class, does the student have difficulty (please provide brief descriptions):
☐ Expressing thoughts _____
☐ Story length _____
☐ Story depth _____
☐ Creativity _____
Mechanics:
☐ Capitalization
☐ Punctuation
☐ Grammar
☐ Handwriting
☐ Spelling
Comments:

_____

_____

Behavior

Are there social-behavioral adjustment problems interfering with this student's academic progress? (be specific) _____

_____

Check any item that describes this student's behavior:
_____ Distracted, short attention span, unable to concentrate
_____ Hyperactive, constant, aimless movement
_____ Impulsive aggressive behaviors, lack of self-control
_____ Fluctuating levels of performance
_____ Frequent negative self-statements
_____ Unconsciously repeating verbal motor acts
_____ Lethargic, sluggish, too quiet
_____ Difficulty sharing or working with others

From E.S. Shapiro (2004). *Academic skills problems: Direct assessment and intervention* (3rd ed.) New York: Guilford Press; reprinted by permission of the publisher.

Index

Page numbers followed by "*f*" indicate figures; those followed by "*t*" indicate tables.